Making Peace
With Your
Adult Children

Making Peace With Your Adult Children

Shauna L. Smith, M.S.W.

Plenum Press • New York and London

Library of Congress Cataloging-in-Publication Data

Smith, Shauna L.
    Making peace with your adult children / Shauna L. Smith.
        p.   cm.
    Includes bibliographical references (p.   ) and index.
    ISBN 0-306-43767-8
    1. Aging parents--Attitudes. 2. Adult children--Attitudes.
  3. Parent and child. 4. Intergenerational relations.   I. Title.
  HQ755.85.S57 1991
  306.874--dc20   91-7157
                                                             CIP

ISBN 0-306-43767-8

© 1991 Shauna L. Smith
Plenum Press is a division of Plenum Publishing Corporation
233 Spring Street, New York, N.Y. 10013

Printed in the United States of America

In the hope that we will one day understand each other and live in peace.

In the hope that we will one day understand each other and live in peace.

Contents

Acknowledgments

There are many people without whom I could never have written this book.

First, I want to thank my husband and my children for helping me create the kind of family I yearned for when I was a child living in a home that was extremely painful and confusing. The love and support we have created together has given me the strength to heal, grow, and risk.

My husband, Ray Bacigalupi, has allowed me to continually interrupt him with questions about a sentence, a quote, a paragraph, or a chapter. He has been filling in for me in countless areas. He has listened to me panic over the impossibility of explaining a concept I barely understood myself. He has repaired and restored the computer for me uncomplainingly several times. And many of the ideas written here have evolved from our work together as therapists and as a family.

My daughter, Kira, seventeen, has helped throughout with her fresh insights and clear understanding of things that are beyond her years and my ability and with her quiet, steadfast, loving support.

I want to thank my daughter, Chanti, fourteen, for her support too, and for her wonderful ability to just be herself. Also for her willingness to say cheerfully, when I mentioned neglecting her: "I'm not neglected. I'm just free to do what I want."

My original motivation for writing this book was to explain to my mother, Lea Bargad, what I needed from her. She has been willing and eager to know what this is and to work on repairing our relationship. I thank her for her stability, strength, and endurance.

I want to thank my dad, Samuel Levy, for his gentleness, his humor, and his ability to see things in unique and special ways, which have been the foundation of my creativity.

Jean Rosenfeld, my friend and colleague, has devoted many hours giving me much-needed feedback on my manuscript, and has, several times, to my complete astonishment, made sense and organization out of totally disjointed concepts. Her encouragement has helped pull me out of despair and kept me on track.

Laura Davis has believed in this book from the beginning and has been very helpful in identifying parts of my manuscript that needed to be restructured or refined. Her understanding of client issues and literary struggles has been a great support to me.

Thanks to my editor, Linda Greenspan Regan, for believing in the importance of this book, for her helpful corrections, and for insisting that I stay sensitive to my audience. Thanks to Naomi Brier, Candice Simmons, Herman Makler, Susan Van Duyne, and Charles Carmony at Plenum Publishing Corporation.

I also want to thank Robert Smith, Sharon Levinsky, Kathryn Gronke, Claire Bradley, Joey Jasso, and Jacqi Davis for their encouragement, feedback, and support.

Finally, thanks especially to my clients and the many parents and adult children who have shared their thoughts and their hearts with me.

Introduction

This book begins with the past, but it is actually about the future: the future of children, and therefore the future of our world. It is about understanding and reconciliation.

Patterns of blame and resentment have prevented us from reaching each other and from finding the common human threads that connect us all. There are so many pressures and uncertainties in the world: The home should be a haven, where we do not need to be afraid or to pretend.

Unfortunately, few of us have grown up in or created families that offered such a place. Most parents did not know how to create it. Parenting was an incredibly difficult job for most of our parents and for most of us. Few of us were able to be the kinds of parents we hoped we'd be. We were often painfully aware of our lack of knowledge and experience as we tried to meet the needs of the unique individuals who were entrusted to our care. There are so many pitfalls and blind spots involved in raising children. It is unlikely that any of us created a family in which we did not inadvertently hurt our children in some ways.

No matter how old we are, or how successful we appear, most of us still have an inner yearning for a family in which we feel loved, understood, and cherished. We want to feel that our parents care about us and are proud of who we are. We want them to understand how hard we have been struggling and how difficult it has been when we have failed. We want to be able to be open with our parents and to resolve things together peacefully and effectively.

Instead, we frequently find distance, misunderstandings, and unhealthy patterns which are passed down through the generations. Many parents who honestly want to communicate their love for their adult children are unable to do so. Parents who are trying as hard as they can are not reaching their adult children. Instead, they are blocking the possibility of any communication. They do not mean to. And yet they do.

As you read this book, you will begin to understand why this happens so often, and you will find specific skills to use to reverse this pattern in your family. It is my hope that this book will serve as a bridge and a guide to help parents enhance their relationships with their adult children, even those adult children who are angry and hurt.

This book begins by your taking a personal inventory and assessment of your own childhood and then assessing the quality of your adult children's early years. You will then learn how to come to terms with your past and your children's past; how to improve your communication with your adult children; and how to work through conflicts in your current relationships. This book then focuses on letting go of expectations which cannot be met; helps you to deal with losses; and shows you how to draw on your innate abilities and interests in a way that will benefit you, your immediate family, and future generations.

The initial purpose of this book is to open up communication between you and your adult children so that you can know each other on a deeper and more honest level. The ultimate purpose is to enhance your relationships, empowering you to work together to break the cycle of ineffective patterns in the coming generations.

You may be uncertain as to whether or not you should read this book. To help you assess whether this book is for you, see if you fit into one or more of the following categories:

- You are a parent who realizes that you have hurt your children at times and you want to improve your current relationships.
- You are a parent who knew or suspected that your children were being treated harmfully by your partner, other family members, or people outside your family, and you are willing to deal with this now.
- You are a parent who thinks that some of your actions may have been harmful or even abusive. You want to deal with the past and repair your relationships with your children.
- You are a parent who knows that your adult children are exploring their past. They have indicated that they want to work on their relationship with you and you are willing to do so.
- You are an adult child who wants to improve your relationship with your parents and you are previewing this book before you purchase it or recommend it to them.
- You want to reduce the amount of pretense, fear, misunderstandings, or power struggles in your relationships; and to increase the amount of honesty, trust, clarity, and cooperation in your relationships.
- You care about your grandchildren and future generations, and you want to help stop the cycle of hurt and pain that has been passed down generationally.
- You counsel individuals or families or are interested in this subject for other personal or professional reasons.

This book presents one way to approach the world, your children, and yourself. I welcome your feedback about how this process is working for you, although I regret that I am unable to answer individual letters. Please send your responses to me, P. O. Box 188275, Sacramento, CA 95818.

The term *adult children* has been used to refer to people ages eighteen and older, but this age limit is a guide only and depends on the individuals involved. Even if your children are not yet adults, you and they can benefit from this book if they are able to grasp these concepts.

All names used in this book, except for my family's, have been changed. The conversations, scenes, letters, and examples are altered or composites to ensure privacy and confidentiality, unless otherwise noted. The pronouns *he* and *she* have been used interchangeably throughout this book.

User-Friendly Instructions

Making Peace with Your Adult Children is a how-to book, based on my experiences with adult children and their parents in therapy as well as my experiences with my own family. Much of my work involves helping parents and adult children make peace with each other.

This book gives you the option of opening doors you may have felt were closed long ago. It offers you the opportunity to move beyond the problem areas in your relationships.

I would like this book to be user-friendly, a workbook to underline or highlight in, to make notes or drawings on, to have pages bent back or even torn out if you wish. Feel free to copy worksheets you need more of or sections you want to share with your family or friends.

Some parts of this book may not apply to you or to your relationships. Work on the parts that you feel are appropriate for your particular circumstances. Please take this book in the way it is intended: as a guide, a map, a framework for attaining peace within yourself and with your adult children.

There will be many writing exercises in this book, and their purpose is to move you further along on a path that will ultimately lead to increased feelings of self-worth, belonging, and purposefulness. I know that some people do not find writing exercises useful, or may be willing to do some kinds but not others. People are different and you can experiment until you discover the way you work best.

I suggest that you do at least some of the exercises, if you can, because you will probably want to share them with your adult children when you are ready. The more you have written down the less you will have to explain to them. It is also often easier to share written thoughts and feelings because you can say what you want to without interruption. If you cannot do the writing, you can still make use of this book by exploring these issues and by verbally sharing the responses you would have written with your children. Writing is recommended, but not required.

Do the exercises you decide to do on whatever level you feel is best. There will be explanations as well as *Caution* signs posted when exercises or sections are going to be difficult or confrontational. That way you can do a small amount at a time and find additional support if you need it.

There is a lot of work to do, before you even begin to approach your children, which may seem tedious and even irrelevant in places. The truth is that you will probably need a great deal of preparation before actually talking with your children, especially if you have not dealt with many personal issues previously. Even if you have, there may be some areas you have not covered. One of the biggest problems in the past in being parents has been our lack of preparation. All we've had to go by were our role models, role models who probably didn't have any preparation themselves. To prepare for any skill you must go through a training period and then through learning experiences. If you don't catch on right away, you go through more training and experience. This training process is expected in almost every endeavor but parenting.

This book attempts to help compensate for the gap in our training as parents. It won't do it all, but it can serve as a beginning. I've included lists of resources for your further use in several chapters, in the form of books, groups, and people. What is most important is to continue on this journey without getting discouraged or sidetracked. You will not need to memorize ideas or put a lot of effort into altering your behaviors. If you remain open to learning, your perceptions and approach will gradually shift by themselves as you work with and integrate the various concepts that are presented. These internal changes will give you your best chance of improving your relationships with your adult children.

If you are a parent with adult children reading this now, I want to acknowledge you for your courage in taking on a task which is difficult but profoundly rewarding. Your willingness to read this book shows in itself that you love your children and want to repair your relationships with them.

If you have bought this book on your own, it is a good idea to read through it entirely before you approach your adult children as some parts in the last chapters may alter your approach. This will give you the greatest likelihood of opening up meaningful communication. If you are willing to go through this work I know how much you must want a positive response.

If one of your adult children has given you this book or suggested you buy it, please be secure in knowing that he has given this to you because he wants to repair your relationship and because he still loves you on a deep level and needs you to love him in a way he can understand. This book is full of ways you can show him that you care.

If you are an adult child who is buying this book to give to your parents, you may feel apprehensive because you don't know how your parents will respond or if they will respond at all. Risking like this is difficult, and I can guess how much you want your effort to turn out well for all concerned. It would be a good idea to write a letter or a brief note to your parents in the space provided, telling them how much you need them to read this book and to respond. A personal message from you will greatly increase the chances of their reading it and taking it to heart. If you cannot write one at this time, that is okay. I hope that this book will speak for you until you can speak for yourself.

You may have parents *and* adult children you want to make peace with. You have a challenging but profound and exciting journey ahead of you. Begin the communication process with whomever you think would be easiest for you, and work in small, concrete steps.

If an adult child is inaccessible to you, because of death, illness, or unwillingness to work with you on this book or communicate with you, you will need to work through your feelings of grief. There are ways to complete your past that are indirect and I will address these later as well as provide lists of resources that can help you decide what to do next. Eventually, you will be able to move on freely, without guilt or hesitation, knowing that you have done all you can.

At this time, with the best intentions, we are going to slowly learn how to communicate with those we love.

If you are giving this book to your parents, you can use the space below to start the communication process. Let them know how much you want them to read this book and why.

Dear _____,

_____

_____

_____

_____

_____

_____

_____

_____

_____

_____

_____

If you are a parent who has been given this book by your adult child, write down any positive or negative responses you have to receiving it.

_____

_____

_____

_____

_____

_____

_____

_____

_____

_____

_____

If you are a parent who will be using this book, please write down the specific results you would like to attain, in order to clarify and focus on your personal goals.

_____

_____

_____

_____

_____

_____

_____

_____

PART ONE
The Way It Was

CHAPTER ONE

Why Become Involved?

The events of childhood do not pass, but repeat themselves like
the seasons of the year.

ELEANOR FARJEON, quoted in *A Mother's Journal*

Many parents of adult children feel that being a parent of small
children was very difficult for them. They often weren't ready
for children, didn't know how to be parents, were up against
incredible odds just to survive themselves, and did the best
they knew how. Now that their children are grown and are still
needing things from them, the parents wonder if their burdens
will ever end. They're tired and worn down, and feel they've
done a better job with their children than their parents did with
them—and most likely they have. When they were children
they likely didn't complain about their parents or even think
there were problems. That was how life was then and they
accepted it. Even if they sensed that problems existed they
didn't dare speak out or, if they did, it usually didn't help. Until
recently, communication was not a priority and people didn't
generally take time to listen, share, and work things out together. We are still struggling with how to do this today.

Many parents feel that it is unfair that they are being asked
to adjust to their children's ideas now. When they were children, they had to adjust to their parents' ways, and that was
difficult enough. They have been caught between societal and
generational changes which unfairly place a great deal of the
burden on them. Nonetheless, the dilemma and the uncom-

fortableness between the generations remain, and it would be in everyone's best interest to resolve the problem areas between parent and child.

Whatever your present stage of life, one of the most important things you have done in your lifetime is to bring your children into the world. Whether you did a good job or a poor job is not relevant at this time. The fact is, your children are now in a position to shape the future of the world. The concept they gained of themselves from you continues to influence their self-image, their decisions, and the way they run their daily lives. Parents willing to improve their relationships with their adult children will have a positive influence on the generations to come.

As you go through this book, you will find several benefits in becoming involved in the process of reconciliation:

- Your feelings about yourself will be enhanced as you go back in time and reconnect with the small person you were. You will find the child you were, who was naturally spontaneous, loving, joyous, creative, and curious. You will be able to identify and understand the traumas or patterns you were subjected to that may have kept that child from fully developing. Through the exercises in this book you will be able to increase your understanding and appreciation of the child within you. You are likely to get in touch with the fear and sorrow you experienced as a child, but you will also touch deeper levels of love and laughter.

- You will be able to move out of the stagnation and repetition of past patterns and be better able to get on with your life. The confusion and tensions that arise from unresolved interactions will no longer drain your energy.

- You are likely to find improved physical and emotional well-being. Unclear or unhealthy relationships create negative thought patterns which affect your body, as well as your feelings about yourself. The link between physical illness and stress and depression is well documented.

- You will grow individually as you learn about yourself and about relationships. You will be able to better identify your current needs and you will learn how to get those needs met.
- If you can break down the walls between you and your adult children, you will become closer to them. Your children still need you, even though they don't need you in the ways they used to or even in the ways that you or they think they do. The specific ways will be explored in this book. You will become clearer about how you can be supportive of them, and how you cannot. And you will learn how you can meet your adult children's needs without forfeiting your own.
- You will know that you have done everything you can to help your adult children resolve their own childhood issues so that they can move on in their own lives and improve their relationships.
- You will be able to have a positive effect upon the next generation. We all affect the future, and we cannot help that. The cycle of suffering goes on and on like an animal on a wheel. If you are willing to be part of the strong, growing movement of people determined to repair the past you will affect a whole series of generations of children who cannot survive without the work of every generation.

Becoming involved in this process now is important because we cannot know how long we or our loved ones will live. Adult children who have not made peace with their parents before their deaths often carry an enormous burden of regret, guilt, and pain. Parents who have lost their children without reconciling are even more devastated. Do what you can to prevent this from happening to you or your children. Reconciliation will give you and your children a chance to grow individually and together, before it's too late.

The letters below are from adult children, asking their parents to become involved in this process with them. In these letters, the children share with their parents the pain they have felt, the hurts they have sustained, and their need to be validated and loved by their parents. The letters with which their parents have responded follow, and you will be able to see how the parents uncover and disclose their true selves.

These are not representative exchanges. These letters are between parents and adult children who have each been working on themselves individually and have come a long way in this process. The letters from the adult children have been carefully written to be open and non-accusatory. The parents have followed the specific methods that are offered here in responding to their adult children.

It is important to follow the general organization offered in this book because, without a guide, parents and children usually end up in futile battles. When adult children confront their parents they typically begin in an angry and offensive manner. Parents, caught off guard and defensive, usually deny that they have ever done anything hurtful, or they make excuses for whatever wrongdoings they've admitted. They tend to minimize their children's feelings; blame their children; accuse them of trying to hurt them; or don't respond at all. They become so overwhelmed with their own pain they cannot listen to their children. These kind of actions effectively cut off all communication, with both parties going away feeling worse about themselves, each other, or both. Again, I hope you will get involved in this process, so this useless cycle can be broken.

Please read the letters below and write your thoughts about the letters in the space following. You can then make a personal list, if you wish to, of the advantages you see in becoming involved in this process.

Dear Mom,

I don't know how to get across to you how much of a struggle I go through sometimes just to stay alive. I don't want you to know so that it will hurt you, just so that you understand that the things that happened to me have had a serious effect on me. It is hard to deal with the thought that surfaces sometimes that no matter what I do it isn't good enough and that I don't deserve to be alive. I know you are not to blame for all this, because you did the best you could and had your own pain, but if it were not for some of the things you said and did I wouldn't feel this way, because children figure out who they are from what their parents mirror for them, and the mirror you held up to me was very negative, regardless of what you intended.

I just want you to understand what the nightmares and the terrors I had and the destructive and angry behaviors I showed as a child were all about. It wasn't that there was something wrong with me or that I was trying to hurt you. I was not crazy or bad. Those were the only ways I knew how to survive. And I realize now that if I had kept all my feelings inside it would have been worse for me.

I know that my life looks good on the surface, and it is. I have worked very hard and I have wonderful things in my life now and I am grateful for them. But like all children, however old, I still need my parents' acceptance and understanding. I need you to know and acknowledge that I, the child I, am lovable and worthwhile, and I need you to understand that the problems I had were not because of the person I was inside.

If I didn't need this, I wouldn't be approaching you now. If I weren't sure that this is the only way our relationship can exist on a real basis, I wouldn't be approaching you now. If I didn't believe that you did the best you could, and that you were badly hurt too, I couldn't approach you now. If I didn't want to grow and understand you as I am asking you to understand me, I wouldn't be approaching you now. This is so hard for me to say. Please help me to heal our relationship and myself.

Love,

Your daughter

Dear Daughter,

I was shocked when I received your letter. I really never knew before the extent of your hurt. I don't think you really shared it before, you were so angry at me, and accusing. You're right about a lot of what you say. I haven't understood you, although in my own way I tried. I always thought that your actions were designed to punish me for being so controlling when you were small, but I realize now that they were the only way you knew how to express yourself. I guess they helped you to survive. I guess we were both just trying to survive.

I don't think you learned how bad you were as much from what I said, although I guess thinking about it now I said some pretty terrible things, a lot of them the same things that were said to me, but mostly because you picked up my feelings about myself. You know I don't feel like I'm worth much either, no matter how much I do. Until we began talking I never realized how badly I was treated myself. I was always ordered to be still, was beaten if I didn't obey and lived in total poverty. I was terrified and had so many traumas, no wonder I couldn't be a better parent for you. And no one ever talked to me about anything. I guess I was in a way so traumatized myself I couldn't deal with things well in the present.

I'm sorry for the hurt I've caused you, and maybe more for misunderstanding you all the times you approached me and tried to make me understand. Let's continue to talk like this because I want us to get to know each other and I don't want my grandchildren and their children to have to carry the hurts you and I have had to bear. If there is a way to stop all this, I'm willing to try.

Love,

Mom

Dear Dad,

I don't know how to begin this. When I was seven years old you came into my life and I really wanted you there. I'd never met my real father and my only memory of my first stepfather was when he kicked me across the kitchen floor when I was five. I can remember your being alive and fun to be around. I wanted you to be my dad but most of all I wanted you to love me. Apparently I wanted you to love me in a way that you were not capable of. As time passed I remember being jealous of the attention you sometimes gave to other boys and I remember you sitting in front of the television every night until you would fall asleep and I remember you drinking a lot. I remember that you promised to take me places and never did and that you used to make passes at my girlfriends. I am angry about all of this but most of all I am sad because of the love I lost and the difficulty I still have trusting and sharing loving feelings with others.

I realize you were only following patterns you learned and I am not trying to make you feel badly. I also know that I am an adult now and that I need to take responsibility for myself. I just wish we could have had a better relationship. I wish I could somehow break down the barrier I have between us and heal the wounds so that we could be closer now that I am an adult. I wish you could understand how much I needed you and probably more important and harder for me to say is how much I still need you.

Love,

Your son

Dear Son,

I really don't have any idea how to answer your letter. You never told me any of the things you are writing about. You seem to have it all together, a nice car, enough money, a good job, and you usually act friendly enough, although I know we don't talk about much.

I'm not the kind of person that thinks much about things, and I don't have much to say now. I guess what is making me write this is that you say you still need me now.

Well, I guess if I messed up as bad as you say, I better try to make it up to you. To tell you the truth, I didn't even think you cared. You seemed so stuck to your mom when you were a kid, and then you just went off on your own. I think that's part of the problem, maybe we were both trying to get Mom's attention. Who knows.

I'm sorry about what happened between us. I feel real bad now that I realize how it affected you. But you know, I grew up in a different time and I'm not saying that excuses anything, but I really didn't know how to be a father. Coming into a family with four kids at twenty-eight wasn't easy for me. Hell, I was younger than you are now. And there were a lot of other problems. I guess we can talk about them sometime if you want.

Anyway, no point bitchin' about the past. You let me know what I can do, okay, and I'll give it my best shot. I am sorry.

Love,

Dad

EXERCISES

Take a moment to write down your responses to the letters from adult children and the answers they received from their parents:

_____

_____

_____

_____

_____

_____

Write down your personal reasons for becoming involved in this process and the benefits you hope to gain for yourself and for those you care about:

_____

_____

_____

CHAPTER TWO

Context: An Historical Perspective

Only on the basis of an understanding of our behavior can we hope to control it in such a way as to ensure the survival of the human race.

J. WILLIAM FULBRIGHT

At a workshop I attended recently, one of the speakers made the statement: "You can't understand anything without understanding its history." It made sense to me, both globally and individually. Here we will briefly trace societal history to understand the context for many of our familial struggles and in later chapters we will explore our own personal history in order to better understand how our past affects our present.

For many generations parenting methods were based on a repressive authoritarian model. Until the middle of the twentieth century, children were considered the property of their parents and were required to work to meet the needs of their family. Corporal punishment was the norm and the concept of child exploitation did not exist. Children were often treated in ways that demolished their thoughts, feelings, and self-esteem. Parents, teachers, religious leaders, and other adults in authority expected children to fit into the narrow mold created for them. Additionally, children were told that whatever was done to them was done for their own good. Parents treated their children the way their parents had treated them. Child abuse laws did not go into effect until 1964.

Children were considered inferior and destructive until very recently. The common belief held that children needed to be taught to respect their elders through submission and fear, as if respect could be taught rather than earned. The use of threats, punishment, deprivation, indoctrination, and intimidation to control children were standard parenting policy. Children were not supposed to be treated as people with minds of their own. Dependent on their parents and conditioned to believe them, children learned that being treated in a demeaning manner was acceptable. Often, even though parents had their children's best interests at heart, they were so locked into the authoritarian structure that they did not know how to treat their children differently. There were very few families in which there were joint efforts among all family members to identify, understand, and negotiate each person's individual needs.

Additionally, alcoholism was rampant and its intergenerational impact was not yet recognized or understood. The concept of child neglect had not been formed. Emotional illness and spousal abuse were concealed. The sexual abuse of children was extensive. (It is now widely believed that Freud's theories of the Oedipal and Electra complexes were based on his inability to believe that so many of his patients had been sexually abused as children.)

If you didn't grow up under these conditions yourself, your parents or your grandparents did, and we have all been personally affected. Certainly love existed between family members, and everyone was not alcoholic, emotionally disturbed, or physically or sexually abusive. There were compassionate people who functioned in healthier ways than the society they lived in. But it is important to recognize, if your parents or you yourself were harmful as a parent, that society condoned and even encouraged exceedingly severe treatment of children. Many people were unable to see beyond the common view. This was not because they were bad or cruel; they were repeating the methods they had learned. That was the way it was done.

In the 1960s people challenged the old repressive systems. They thought they could correct things by rebelling, but unfortunately what they created was an antiauthoritarian or permissive model, rather than a cooperative or partnership model, where people could work together and negotiate fairly. This era allowed us to begin exploring new methods of dealing with issues, as well as opening up parenting options and growth models. It broke down many abusive traditions, gave children more rights, and freed us from some overly repressive Victorian mores.

However, the 1960s also led us into a period of permissiveness which didn't work very well with children. Permissive parents were trying to compensate for the repressiveness of their parents. But many parents ended up being neglectful, in effect abrogating the parenting role, by giving their children freedoms they did not need and failing to give them the guidance they did. Some parents encouraged their children to act rebelliously as they themselves had been unable to do, and their children proceeded to behave intolerably. Still other parents became overinvolved in their children's lives, and gave them whatever they themselves had not received as children, creating children who either distanced themselves from their families as soon as possible or became emotionally bound to their parents for life. The commonality in all of these families was that the children were not listened to or understood on a genuine level. In actuality, the parents' inability to separate their own lives from their children's lives kept them from meeting their children's real needs—even in families where, to all appearances, the children's needs were being met.

During this period, many family members broke their ties with each other, sometimes creating relief but also causing isolation. Interactions between generations were greatly reduced, and the generations lost the chance to give each other support, to learn from each other, and to work things out together. When changing economic conditions, consciousness, and values pressured both parents into finding jobs outside the home, stable childcare became a considerable problem. Families became further disrupted as divorce laws became relaxed and single-parent households and stepfamilies became common. Blended families created a substitute extended family but brought chaos and competitiveness between family units. Children were caught between divided homes and divided loyalties. Many children were poorly supervised during the day and overcontrolled at night. These changes have helped many people to leave oppressive and unhappy relationships and has given us new options and choices, but the children, as in the old systems, often end up damaged.

Recently there seem to be movements toward more stringent rules and a return to the tightening of the reins on children. This is a regression to the old authoritarian model which did not work well in the first place. We need to work on a new model based on cooperation and partnership, in which everyone's individual needs are addressed. Despite the fact that businesses and families that have shifted to partnership models have been highly successful and effective, much of our society continues to follow a competitive rather than a cooperative model. In this competitive model, composed of winners and losers, for every one person who wins, countless others lose. The continual experience of losing damages people's feelings of self-worth and adds to their frustration. People either conform and do what they're told or rebel and try to beat the system. We still live in an environment that perpetuates the growth of patterns which create poor self-esteem and emotional impoverishment. Though alcoholism, addictions, child sexual abuse, physical abuse, and neglect are now defined, solutions are still only partial. When a parent is charged with a crime, the child often becomes a pawn in the legal system. Often the outwardly wealthy feel inwardly bankrupt. As the father of a severely depressed young child said to me, "We have everything that money can buy, but this is not a happy home."

On the positive side, we are searching for ways to get through the confusion and to learn how to treat ourselves, our children, and each other in better ways. There is an increasing growth in our consciousness. We are beginning to realize which patterns are destructive and we want to stop them. We're weary of the emptiness and we want it to get better now. To do so, we need to understand the reasons for the pain we have received and the pain we have caused. We need to make amends, to understand others and ourselves, and to move on to a more cooperative, moral, and spiritual way of living.

There is a strong and growing movement toward self-healing and connectedness. The vast number of self-help books on the shelves, our longing for global peace, and the yearning for spirituality in many aspects of our lives are proof of this phenomenon. There are many groups for people who are going through incredible struggles and transitions. Many of these groups are self-facilitated or run by leaders who volunteer their time. People who valued materialism and appearances above all else are realizing that possessions alone aren't satisfying.

There is a new hero evolving who is different from the old hero who could "slay dragons" or become wealthy or "successful." The new hero is someone brave enough to overcome his fear of being close and vulnerable to another person; someone who understands himself and will acknowledge his flaws; someone who is able to communicate and is willing to work cooperatively with others. We need to become the heroes of today, because our very survival depends on our ability to communicate and work cooperatively together. The survival of all of us depends on the work of each of us.

It is crucial to understand how both societal history and your personal history have influenced you before trying to communicate with your children. I am basing this statement not only on theory but on twenty years of experience working with families. Parents who are heavily guarded against their own pain and confusion and deny the pain or traumas they experienced as children, find it almost impossible to break down the walls between themselves and their adult children. Many people, particularly in the older generation, are aware of how difficult their parents' lives were. This knowledge makes it difficult for them to explore how they were treated as children. However, when they eventually do tap into some of their early history and understand how these experiences affected them and subsequently affected their adult children, the parent and adult child can begin to communicate. When they share honestly and openly about how their childhoods actually were for them, they often find that their experiences and feelings are very similar. Pride and pretense fall away and feelings of connection and caring surface.

Again, this book is structured so that you will be doing personal work to examine your own history before you approach your adult children. You will focus on the experiences you had when you were a child, and on how things were in your own children's lives. Though these exercises are difficult, they will deepen your understanding of the effects of history on the present. They will help you connect to the inner parts of yourself and your children, and will give you concrete work to share with your children when you approach them. The writing can be done briefly, in notes, or in whichever form you are most comfortable. If you are unable to do the writing, you can do the exercises in your mind and share them verbally later.

EXERCISES

1. List some ways you were treated by your parents that you felt were harmful or ineffective to you or your siblings while you were growing up.

_____

_____

_____

2. In what ways did you act similarly with your children when you became a parent?

_____

_____

_____

_____

3. What are some basic beliefs about parenting that you have never challenged in the past?

_____

_____

_____

_____

_____

4. What beliefs about parenting are you open to questioning, as you continue to sort out the past?

_____

_____

_____

_____

_____

The following song written by Anthony Newley sheds some light on intergenerational patterns. It continues to motivate me to work to improve the relationships between parents and children.

Teach the Children*

A wise man who was asked about his parents once replied,
Of all the undertakings God invented
The parenthood career is most important—then he sighed,
How sad that only amateurs attempt it.
We must soon realize that the happiness of man
Depends upon his dear old dad and mother
Who seldom understand the love and care a child demands
How could they? They don't understand each other.

Teach the children of the world
Teach them now before it gets too late
Teach them how to be the parents of tomorrow
Or they'll become the parents of today
And pass on all our hate and madness
To a whole new generation
And so it goes ad infinitum, ad nauseam, amen.

What pleasure we derive upon this overcrowded earth
In making and remaking our own image
When any fool can tell us where the gift of life's concerned
We take for granted what should be a privilege.
The children of the world are doomed before they reach school
By families who are unprepared and careless
As long as procreation is a paradise for fools
The world will be the victim of its parents.

Teach the children of the world
Teach them now before it gets too late
Teach them how to be the parents of tomorrow
Or they'll become the parents of today
And pass on all our hate and madness
To a whole new generation
And so it goes ad infinitum, ad nauseam, amen.

*Reprinted by permission of Anthony Newley.

CHAPTER THREE

The Advantages and Price of Denial

Those who cannot remember the past are condemned to repeat it.

GEORGE SANTAYANA, *The Life of Reason*

Before we can repair our relationships, we need to explore a concept crucial to self-awareness and eventual reconciliation with our adult children: the concept of denial. Denial is a defense mechanism we use to pretend that what is true is not really true. We create a false reality which protects us from facing things about ourselves and our pasts that we feel we cannot deal with. It also prevents us from becoming self-aware and fulfilled.

Why do we deny the truth about what is happening or happened, even though it means cutting off from ourselves and others? Here are some of the most common reasons.

INABILITY TO HANDLE THE TRUTH AT THE TIME

Denial is actually a very primitive defense mechanism people learn when they are very small. If things are happening around children which are frightening and hurtful, they often cannot handle the pain, and so they deny much of their reality and their feelings. Many children also deny to themselves that their parents, whom they depend upon, are not there to protect or care for them physically or emotionally. Without denial, they would have to face the fact that they are actually on their own—children trying to parent themselves.

An example of denial is the way in which children learn to respond to parents who are continually upset. The children find that noise, motion, and added stressors are intolerable to their parents. The children then learn to keep quiet and repress their feelings. If they keep these feelings locked up over a long period of time, they forget that these feelings ever existed. Denial comes naturally at that point.

PERCEIVED INABILITY TO HANDLE THE TRUTH

People are likely to use the methods of dealing with trauma that they learned when they were small. They often use these methods without carefully assessing the present context and judging if the mechanism is still appropriate. People sometimes automatically continue denying their feelings or what really happened to them in the past because they don't realize that they now have options they didn't have in past situations. People have a way of rationalizing that they made it this far in their lives and that's good enough. Many people have never really thought about assessing the costs they've paid along the way and end up constricting parts of themselves that they no longer need to cut off.

SHAME AND GUILT

Parents who have denied the abusiveness of their own pasts frequently look for someone in their present to blame for their pain, and unfortunately, their children often become their targets. Their children then feel that they are bad or guilty in some way. When they grow up they repeat the pattern of denial and blame and shame their own children. To break the denial at this point means they have to face the shamed feelings they have from childhood as well as shame and guilt for the way they treated their children. So, usually not consciously, many parents try to keep from looking at the pain they have felt or have inflicted on others.

PRIDE

Everyone wants to be a good parent, but perhaps even more everyone wants to have been a good parent. The truth is that most people have tried their best, even if their best was or is hurtful to themselves and others. They simply didn't know any better or couldn't take the actions necessary to make positive changes. I want to stress this over and over, because this book is not about blame; it's about resolution. Blaming is tiresome, ineffective, and deadening and simply cannot continue if we are to ever make peace with one another.

Many people hold onto pride because they assume that the opposite of pride is shame. To lose one's pride therefore feels like losing one's self-respect and no one wants to lose their self-respect. Unfortunately, as we know in the Greek tragedies, excessive pride (hubris) inevitably leads to the downfall of man. I would like to think that the opposite of pride is not shame but humility, as used in the best and most noble sense of the word. Humility is an admission that there is still a lot to learn, that ignorance is neither bliss nor sin, and that mistakes are not failures. Pride, though it is one of the emotions most likely to destroy relationships, is perceived by people as something to keep at all costs. Denial effectively preserves pride, though its price may be the eternal alienation of a child—a heavy price to pay.

LOYALTY

Most children have very strong loyalty bonds with their parents. Sometimes this bond is strongest if the parents have been very hurtful. Because the children have never gotten their needs met, they keep trying to be good children, fantasizing that if they are good enough their needs will get met someday. Children often identify with their parents' pain and try desperately to help their parents, which means protecting their parents regardless of the cost to themselves. Sometimes children identify with abusive parents, and in this way they don't feel as powerless. These children delude themselves into believing that the abusive parents are just and rational and in so doing often become abusive themselves. Children are constantly told that their parents and other adults in authority always have their best interests at heart, when the truth is that many adults are too self-absorbed and too used to repeating their own patterns to see children clearly as individuals.

It is crucial to get beyond the denial that misplaced loyalty creates. To deny that your parents did anything wrong will mean that you will not be able to break down the walls between you and your children. To deny that you were hurt by your parents is to suppress your fears, pain, and anger and unconsciously pass them on to the next generation. The power of loyalty is frightening. A teenager, who came into therapy after she had been hospitalized because of her mother's beating, immediately shut out anyone who said anything against her mom.

DEPRESSION/HOPELESSNESS

One of the consequences of breaking through denial, if it is keeping back an extremely painful time, is that people are likely to experience the feelings they were too little to allow themselves to feel earlier. This can be confusing, frightening, and overwhelming. If they had been able to experience their feelings a long time ago, they might have felt a deep hopelessness and pain, possibly accompanied by suicidal thoughts. If they go back now and remember, those same feelings may surface as if they were really happening now. *It is crucial to realize that these feelings belong to the past and not to the present.* Becoming completely immersed and overwhelmed by these feelings will not help you or your family. If past experiences have been especially traumatic, be sure to go slowly, and get the support you need to deal with your past effectively. *If negative feelings overwhelm you in this process be sure to seek professional help.* The professional can walk you through your past and help keep you from being overwhelmed by negative feelings.

GOING AWAY

Sometimes denial is so important to the survial of a child that the child "goes away" emotionally and mentally and does not consciously experience or remember that a traumatic event or events occurred. Sometimes this leads to multiple personalities and more often to odd memory blanks. People who have been sexually abused as children often split off and have no memories of the abuse even during the time period it is happening. At the time and later they believed that they had a good relationship with the molesting parent, as if the incest had never happened. These memories only surface later, sometimes even many years later, if certain things trigger them. Some examples of common triggers are: Their parent is reported by someone else, they become involved in a sexual relationship, or they have children and odd feelings surface. Sometimes they go into therapy and when their therapist asks them, "Have you ever been inappropriately touched?" they say "I don't know," and then wonder, "Why did I say that?" Then the memories start to leak out in flashbacks, nightmares, or feelings they can't place.

These are many good reasons to have unconsciously created denial. When the instinctive decision to be in denial was made, it was most likely the wisest decision you could have made, considering how limited your power was. There are two important things to consider seriously in deciding whether or not to break through denial and assess your past. First, it is likely that you have resources now that you did not have when you were a child, so it will not be as threatening to break down denial now as it was then. Second, there is a substantial cost to you and to your relationships if you remain in denial.

You have many resources within you now that you did not have as a child. Children are all different, but generally they have very little power in the family, especially in their early years. There is a common misconception that two- or four-year-olds are trying to control the family as if they were born with some evil intention. But this control is just a child trying to satisfy her needs. What does a child need? Besides the basics of food, clothing, and shelter, children need to be accepted, loved, and given attention. They need honesty and understanding, stimulation and quietness. They need to develop a sense of their own personal power as well as trust for the peole around them. Mostly children need to develop self-esteem, which they can attain if their parents feel good about themselves and their children.

Children have very few resources to get what they need. They can cry, yell, scream, and throw tantrums. They can refuse to do what the parent wants if it's not what they want. They can kick and throw things or they can conform and hope they will be noticed and cared for. As a last alternative, they can give up, become frozen, and pretend that things are different than they really are.

As adults we have resources we lacked as children and we have the power to leave situations which are destructive to us. We are able to think deeply about situations and relationships, make assessments, use judgment, speak and be heard. We can better understand what is going on around us and why things happen as they do. No longer children, we do not have to tolerate someone yelling at us or being slapped or belted. As adults we have learned how to handle a variety of situations and circumstances such as working, sharing, making a home, reading, and communicating far better than we could as children. We are no longer dependent on our parents to survive. Adults no longer need to protect themselves in the same way they did as children. Denial is one form of protection we hold onto but it is actually a remnant from the past which is probably not needed and not useful.

The cost of denial is enormous, because it limits and distorts our perceptions of the world. Often people in denial react to current circumstances in extremes of rage, depression, or withdrawal, not realizing that their reactions are so strong because they are linked to the unfinished feelings of the past. They often reenact their past dramas inadvertently, and end up with dismal results that, not surprisingly, duplicate their pasts. People in denial often have vague feelings of being lost, incomplete, or unfulfilled. They may find themselves trapped in patterns that keep them constricted and numb. Often they find that their relationships do not work out or are unsatisfying, or they find they are misunderstood too often. They may sense they are hiding behind work or a smile, trying to please others or to prove that they are all right. But underneath there is the nagging sense that they don't feel good about themselves.

Addiction or compulsivity are common ways people in denial focus their energy. Addictions to substances such as alcohol, prescription or nonprescription drugs, and cigarettes can create slow but steady deterioration of the body. Physical health is likely to be affected in other ways as well, as many illnesses are linked to poor emotional health. Ulcers, back pain, headaches, skin problems, heart disease, and many other illnesses are often related to the stress, anxiety, and depression which denial and pretense bring.

Breaking through denial gives people a chance to be whole, enjoy better emotional and physical health, and have more honest and complete relationships. Not that everything will be perfect or peaceful all the time, but the emptiness will be smaller, the energy higher, and the chance to participate in life in a natural, spontaneous way will greatly increase. Many people who break through denial report that they feel fully alive for the first time.

You may still think that denial serves a good purpose and you would just as soon not tamper with the past. You may believe that the past should remain buried, not thought about, and not discussed. You are right to a point. A certain amount of denial is not only good but is crucial for all of us. We could not go on living day to day without keeping some memory below consciousness. We cannot be thinking about our pain on a continuous basis. Actually, that would be another form of denial, since life is a balance of pain and pleasure for most of us, not one or the other.

But too much denial has a very high cost. I hope you will take a closer look at your past to the degree that you feel capable, and that with the strength of an adult you will deal with the hurts the child inside you has experienced.

A JOURNEY TO THE TRUTH

The story below shows the struggle of one young woman who is deciding whether or not to delve more deeply into her past. Perhaps her story will help you make a decision to go on, if you haven't already decided to do so.

The story begins in the Desert of Lies and is about a young maiden, the daughter of the Lord and Lady of Secrets, who cannot remember the pain and suffering of her childhood but is still haunted by it. She meets a knight who professes his love for her and asks her to be his bride. Although she also loves this knight, she realizes he cannot heal her wounds, and decides that before she can marry she must be free of her haunting childhood. This is how she tells it:

> The maiden decided to go on a journey. She planned to venture forth into the Forest of Truth. She knew that there she would find the truth of her past which would bring her to the

path of truth and beauty. She packed for her journey, not realizing the dangers and horrors this journey would bring.

At last the day came for the maiden to embark on her crusade for answers in the Forest of Truth. When she was only several footsteps inside the boundaries of the forest the poor maiden became fully aware of her oversight. She shivered with the cold truth of what her journey would really mean. Quickly, she turned and ran to leave the horrible Forest of Truth but upon reaching the boundary she stopped. She looked out of the forest and into her home, the Desert of Lies. The sun shone there brightly, but no flowers ever bloomed. In the forest, though, she realized there was darkness but also an abundance of life: growing, thriving plants, flowers, trees, and beautiful clear lakes, and animals bounding over the grassy hills.

The maiden shed a tear and shook her head as her confusion slowly lifted, like a cloud. She sighed deeply and walked back into the Forest of Truth. She decided not to live behind a mask of happiness, but to break through her fears and finally get to a true peace of mind and move her life toward real happiness.

I hope you can use this book as a guide on your journey. You may find you have some difficult memories to deal with, but you will be able to handle them if you go slowly and reach out for support if you need it.

EXERCISES

1. List below some memories of events that you think happened to you which you have not previously dealt with fully.

---

2. What resources do you have now, as an adult, to deal with these issues that you did not have as a child?

_____

_____

_____

_____

_____

3. Besides increasing your understanding of your adult children, what benefits might you personally gain from deeply exploring your past?

_____

_____

_____

_____

_____

_____

CHAPTER FOUR

The Effects of Harmful Childhood Experiences

If you wish to understand others look into your own heart.

SCHILLER, *Votive Tablets*

Most people have been the victims of varying degrees of trauma at some time in their lives. The dictionary defines trauma, in part, as "an emotional shock that creates substantial and lasting damage to the psychological development of the individual." People may also experience minor traumas over a continuous period of time, which can damage their development as well. Sometimes it is difficult to know if you have been the victim of traumatic events since memory can be lost or partial around specific events. It is also common to discount your own pain by comparing it to "worse cases," and not taking your own struggles seriously. One way you can know that painful things have happened to you is to go backwards and find the cause from the effect, as in the smoking gun analogy: If a gun is smoking, it must have been fired, even if you didn't see anyone fire it. Similarly, if you have the symptoms of trauma, you must have had traumatic experiences, even if you do not remember them, can't quite identify them, or felt they were only minor discomforts.

Here we will explore different reactions children have had to early, hurtful childhood experiences. They are given in a general order of time of appearance rather than severity, as severity is difficult to assess. Generally, severity is not only of kind, it is also of intensity and duration. For example, nightmares are common in children, but their severity, recurrence rate, and duration will demonstrate how much trauma the child has experienced, as well as the emotional frailty of the child.

You may feel hesitant as you approach the exercise below which lists symptoms children have as a result of traumatic or painful experiences. This exercise asks you to identify those symptoms you think apply to your parents, those that apply to you and other primary caretakers of your children, and those that apply to your children. If you decide to just glance through it, even acknowledging that your parents, you, and your children have had some of these symptoms can be helpful to your relationship. You can then understand that these are responses to early experiences and that neither you nor they are bad, defective, stupid, or unlovable. You can respect your parents', your own, and your children's struggle with circumstances that were at times difficult and painful and you can work with your children to repair the wounds that you have both experienced.

To understand fully the depth and degree of struggle you have been through I would suggest you try to do the next few exercises thoroughly. I want to encourage you to go on, knowing that it is difficult. You may not have focused on these areas of your life or listened closely to your children's struggles before. Denial may have served you well. Also, it is harder to focus on specifics than to talk in general terms. While you cannot change your past, you can help prevent it from repeating and from taking any further toll on you, your children, and your grandchildren.

Patterns, repeating themselves intergenerationally, are often so strong that they prevent people from learning new techniques in adulthood that would be far more effective in gaining the cooperation they want as parents and in helping their children gain higher self-esteem and to lead more satisfying and productive lives.

If you are upset with the similarities between your symptoms and your children's and begin to blame yourself, you will become immobilized and not go on to the healing part of this process which is essential to breaking the pattern. It is not in your interest to spend a lot of time regretting the past or berating yourself for mistakes you feel you've made. Go through these exercises with the goal of learning and growing and that is the result that you will create.

Caution: The exercises below may connect you to painful feelings. Do as much as you can, and make sure you have the kind of support you need at hand or be willing to reach out and find some. A guide to resources is in Chapter Eleven, "When It's Too Hard to Do It Alone."

EXERCISES

Read the following list of symptoms children display when they have undergone traumatic or painful experiences. You can either go across, checking them for your parents (P), for yourself (M = me), for your spouse or other primary caretakers (PC) of your children, as some of their pain has probably been passed on to your children, and then for your children (C1, C2, C3). Or you can start with your parents and go down each list. Place an asterisk next to any symptoms that were repeated through two or more generations.

SYMPTOMS FREQUENTLY BEGINNING IN CHILDHOOD OR ADOLESCENCE

	P	M	PC	C1	C2	C3
Terrors	—	—	—	—	—	—
Nightmares	—	—	—	—	—	—
Regression to bedwetting/soiling	—	—	—	—	—	—
Withdrawal from people/activities	—	—	—	—	—	—

	P	M	PC	C1	C2	C3
Being scapegoated (picked on)	—	—	—	—	—	—
Feeling shameful, bad, rotten, stupid	—	—	—	—	—	—
Eating problems	—	—	—	—	—	—
Nervous habits: nail biting, hair pulling	—	—	—	—	—	—
Poor self-esteem	—	—	—	—	—	—
Lying	—	—	—	—	—	—
Overcompliance	—	—	—	—	—	—
Excessive shyness	—	—	—	—	—	—
Hiding	—	—	—	—	—	—
Cowering	—	—	—	—	—	—
Self-mutilation (engaging in self-destructive behaviors)	—	—	—	—	—	—
Weight problems	—	—	—	—	—	—
Anorexia (starving oneself)	—	—	—	—	—	—
Bulimia (binging and vomiting)	—	—	—	—	—	—
Somatic problems (such as ulcers, headaches)	—	—	—	—	—	—
Suicidal thoughts or statements	—	—	—	—	—	—
Behavioral problems	—	—	—	—	—	—
Antisocial activity (stealing, violence, gangs)	—	—	—	—	—	—
Unhealthy relationships	—	—	—	—	—	—
Lack of relationships	—	—	—	—	—	—
Obsessive worrying	—	—	—	—	—	—
Inability to feel emotions	—	—	—	—	—	—
Inability to feel sensations	—	—	—	—	—	—
A sense of being unreal	—	—	—	—	—	—
Allowing people to invade one's boundaries	—	—	—	—	—	—

SYMPTOMS MORE NOTICEABLE IN ADOLESCENCE
AND THROUGH ADULTHOOD

	P	M	PC	C1	C2	C3
Depression	—	—	—	—	—	—
Anxiety	—	—	—	—	—	—
Excessive use of alcohol	—	—	—	—	—	—
Excessive use of drugs (prescription or nonprescription)	—	—	—	—	—	—
Lack of trust	—	—	—	—	—	—
Hypervigilance (constantly watching for danger)	—	—	—	—	—	—
Inability to sense danger	—	—	—	—	—	—
Seeking out danger	—	—	—	—	—	—
Little impulse control	—	—	—	—	—	—
Avoidance of touch	—	—	—	—	—	—
Avoidance of mirrors	—	—	—	—	—	—
Perfectionism	—	—	—	—	—	—
Overcontrol	—	—	—	—	—	—
Inability to complete things	—	—	—	—	—	—
Mental illness	—	—	—	—	—	—
Loss of energy or motivation	—	—	—	—	—	—
Panic attacks (panic in response to imagined disaster)	—	—	—	—	—	—
Phobias (excessive fear of something specific)	—	—	—	—	—	—
Promiscuity	—	—	—	—	—	—
Obsessional thinking (continual focusing on insignificant thoughts)	—	—	—	—	—	—
Compulsivity (controlling insignificant events)	—	—	—	—	—	—

	P	M	PC	C1	C2	C3
Consuming guilt	—	—	—	—	—	—
Feeling that thoughts, feelings, perceptions are invalid	—	—	—	—	—	—
Feeling hopeless	—	—	—	—	—	—
Multiple personalities	—	—	—	—	—	—
Irresponsibility	—	—	—	—	—	—
Super-responsibility	—	—	—	—	—	—
Sleep disorders	—	—	—	—	—	—
Mood swings	—	—	—	—	—	—
Suicide attempts (many of which are hidden)	—	—	—	—	—	—

PRIMARY RELATIONSHIP PROBLEMS

	P	M	PC	C1	C2	C3
Isolation	—	—	—	—	—	—
Impoverished relationships	—	—	—	—	—	—
Abusive relationships	—	—	—	—	—	—
Addictive relationships	—	—	—	—	—	—
Sexual disorders (such as lack of sexual feelings, impotence, premature ejaculation, excessive need for sexuality, promiscuity)	—	—	—	—	—	—
Repeatedly being victimized	—	—	—	—	—	—

Sometimes it will be obvious that people have been trau-matized because of the continuous negative words resounding in their minds. These internal voices may be the only apparent symp-toms of trauma in people who have effectively hidden their needs and problems because they perceived their parents to be too frag-ile, threatening, or overwhelmed to listen to their pain. Sometimes these people are perfectionistic high achievers who appear problem-free. They get approval for their efforts, and try to maintain a facade of happiness.

The following is a list of beliefs and attitudes that one woman compiled. It shows what she learned about herself and the world, as a child exposed to early traumatic experiences. These feelings are real for her, despite the fact that she is outwardly quite successful in her life. Do not dismiss these statements as one person's overreaction. Many of us have developed comparable beliefs and attitudes, even though we usually don't talk about them. Think carefully about which people in your family had similar beliefs about themselves and the world as you fill in the blanks below. Put an asterisk next to the beliefs and attitudes that are being carried intergenerationally.

	P	M	PC	C1	C2	C3
I can't expect anything good from anyone.	___	___	___	___	___	___
I have to work hard for anything I get.	___	___	___	___	___	___
I have no sense of humor.	___	___	___	___	___	___
My body is ugly.	___	___	___	___	___	___
I have to be perfect to be okay.	___	___	___	___	___	___
I have to hide my real self or others will find out how awful I am.	___	___	___	___	___	___
No one would love me if they really knew me.	___	___	___	___	___	___
I'm a bad parent.	___	___	___	___	___	___
I'm not adequate sexually.	___	___	___	___	___	___
I'm not artistic.	___	___	___	___	___	___
My opinions don't count.	___	___	___	___	___	___
If I disagree with anyone, I'm wrong.	___	___	___	___	___	___
I'm crazy.	___	___	___	___	___	___
I have to stick it out no matter what.	___	___	___	___	___	___

	P	M	PC	C1	C2	C3
If I were good enough I'd be happy.	—	—	—	—	—	—
If there is a God, he doesn't care about me.	—	—	—	—	—	—
I am bound to have a life of pain.	—	—	—	—	—	—
Other people are not to be trusted.	—	—	—	—	—	—
People only stay with me because they find me useful.	—	—	—	—	—	—
At best I'm unlovable; at worst I'm a detriment to society.	—	—	—	—	—	—
I'm unfeeling.	—	—	—	—	—	—
If someone seems to love me, I must have fooled them.	—	—	—	—	—	—
I'm incompetent in areas everyone else is competent in.	—	—	—	—	—	—
If I hurt, it doesn't matter.	—	—	—	—	—	—
Feelings don't really count.	—	—	—	—	—	—
Everyone would be better off if I were dead.	—	—	—	—	—	—
The kids would be better off with someone else.	—	—	—	—	—	—
My kids only love me because they don't know any better.	—	—	—	—	—	—
I have no musical talent or taste.	—	—	—	—	—	—
I need someone else to protect me. I can't do it myself.	—	—	—	—	—	—
I'll be depressed and miserable all my life.	—	—	—	—	—	—
I deserve to be miserable.	—	—	—	—	—	—
I did terrible things when I was young.	—	—	—	—	—	—
If I make a mistake, I deserve the worst.	—	—	—	—	—	—

	P	M	PC	C1	C2	C3
If I tell someone I want something from them, it's an unreasonable burden on them.	___	___	___	___	___	___
Maybe if I give enough to others, they'll love me and I'll deserve to take up space on earth.	___	___	___	___	___	___
Everything else comes before me.	___	___	___	___	___	___
My judgment is very questionable.	___	___	___	___	___	___
I should be more active, exercise more.	___	___	___	___	___	___
If I relax, I'm wasting time.	___	___	___	___	___	___
I'm not worth spending money on.	___	___	___	___	___	___
Playing is a waste of time.	___	___	___	___	___	___
I don't deserve to have fun.	___	___	___	___	___	___
Conflict must be avoided at all costs.	___	___	___	___	___	___
If I do something someone doesn't like, I'm bad.	___	___	___	___	___	___
I'm bad anyway.	___	___	___	___	___	___
I should be able to do everything well all the time.	___	___	___	___	___	___
Happiness is only an illusion.	___	___	___	___	___	___
There's no one I can trust, including myself.	___	___	___	___	___	___
If I allow myself to be vulnerable, I'll be abused.	___	___	___	___	___	___
I'll never be good enough, so why try?	___	___	___	___	___	___
I should provide what other people want no matter what the cost.	___	___	___	___	___	___
If something goes wrong, it's my fault.	___	___	___	___	___	___
I'm too picky.	___	___	___	___	___	___
My expectations are unreasonable.	___	___	___	___	___	___

	P	M	PC	C1	C2	C3
I'm a hopeless case.	—	—	—	—	—	—
I should be able to fix anything.	—	—	—	—	—	—
I'm not coordinated.	—	—	—	—	—	—
No one cares if I'm hurting.	—	—	—	—	—	—
Everyone is tired of dealing with my problems.	—	—	—	—	—	—
Life is a serious business.	—	—	—	—	—	—
If I tried harder and were better I could make the world better for others.	—	—	—	—	—	—
There's no chance of happiness for me in family relationships.	—	—	—	—	—	—
Only when I die will the pain stop.	—	—	—	—	—	—

This may have been a disturbing exercise, if several of the above apply to your parents, to you, to other caretakers of your children, or to your own children. Most people do not consciously think about their pain and to do so can be frightening and overwhelming. Again, it is important to confront the past and deal with it so that it doesn't continue to repeat itself.

If you did not check any of the above effects as applying to your family, there are two possible reasons for this:

The first is that everything was in fact handled in a positive, healthy, growth-oriented way in your family. I see so few families like this that my tendency is to doubt their existence, but I know they are possible. If you believe this is true for you, make sure by:

1. Going through the exercises in the next chapter and seeing if the patterns there apply to your life.
2. Visualizing yourself as a child and taking a moment to look into the child's eyes. Do you see health and happiness there without signs of fear or pain, loneliness or confusion?

3. Checking with your children to see if they see things as you do. If one of your children gave you this book, you may be missing some important information and it would be a good idea to ask them to clarify the reasons they wanted you to read it.

The second possibility is that you missed a lot of what went on in your family, either because it seemed so natural and normal (it was all you'd ever known) or because it was too much for you to handle on a conscious level. It's frightening to consider, but it is not unusual for people to block out completely and lose major portions of their lives because they are unable to face the truth at the time. If you think the second possibility applies to you, keep reading to find out more about yourself and your childhood.

If you are like most parents, you will have at least some of the above areas checked, and you will have a lot to share with your adult children when you are ready to talk with them. For now, here are some questions for you to think about and respond to before you go deeper into your background and identify some of the patterns used in your family.

EXERCISES

1. How have you explained your feelings, attitudes, and behaviors to yourself for most of your life?

_____

_____

_____

2. How have you explained your children's feelings, attitudes, and behaviors?

_____

_____

3. If you did not connect your own or your children's feelings and behaviors to events in your life before, what is your response to

considering that they may have been generated by early traumatic events or painful situations that happened to you?

_____

_____

4. What are your feelings toward the child you were who struggled through a childhood that perhaps should have been less
   hurtful, safer, and more joyous?

_____

_____

5. What are your feelings toward your children, who had to struggle through their own difficulties?

_____

_____

6. Which feelings from childhood do you still have, that have either stayed just below the surface, have come up when there
   has been stress or crisis, or that you carry with you on most
   days?

_____

_____

7. Which feelings do you think your children still carry?

_____

_____

_____

If in going through these exercises you have found many
similarities between your own and your children's symptoms
of trauma, see this as a way to create a bond of closeness be-

tween you, not to create anguish for yourself. Guilt and blame are useless emotions that will hurt you needlessly and further alienate you from those you need and love. You may feel confused if you checked several items for yourself but you do not have any memories of traumatic experiences. You also may feel bewildered if you have checked several items for your children but are not aware of any traumas that they experienced. Sometimes parents do not know about the traumatic events that have happened to their children. As you open up your relationship with your children, they are likely to share more details of their past and you may learn things that you do not know as yet. It is also not unusual for people to be unaware of the many ineffective actions that can create the symptoms listed above. The following chapters may help clarify which patterns in your family may have created these symptoms. It may also stimulate your memory, and then things will make more sense to you.

CHAPTER FIVE

Harmful Patterns and Traumatic Situations

When you betray somebody else, you also betray yourself.
Isaac Bashevis Singer, Interview, *N.Y. Times Magazine*

Here you will have a chance to look at your own life and see if any harmful patterns your parents were subjected to and you grew up with have inadvertently been repeated with your children. As children we learn from our families how we should be, not only through words but by example, and, unless there has been a powerful intervention in our lives, we tend to repeat much of what we've learned. Without intervention these patterns will likely be repeated with our grandchildren, regardless of whether or not they were useful to our parents, ourselves, or our children. It's not that we don't want it to be different when we realize that things are not working well. Most of us in fact are determined to do a good job parenting, and do as well as we can. But we often take on the roles our parents had when we get married or become parents. We marry people who allow that role to be repeated. This would not be a problem if our parents had been in a cooperative relationship with each other and had been able to listen, share their feelings, understand us, and taught us skills in communication. Nor would it be a problem if our parents had modeled giving, receiving, and fair conflict resolution. But most of us have not been that fortunate. This chapter is for those parents who wish they had been able to do things differently when their children were home, are willing to look at the patterns that caused intergenerational pain, and are willing to deal with their children in a more positive way in the present.

It is difficult to predict the damage that a particular action or pattern will have on children. Sometimes the atmosphere pervading the home is more devastating than a particular action or event. Even a seemingly normal home where the parents are overly rigid can create a frozen and uncommunicative atmosphere that can harm a child. In families where the child's needs are continually overpowered by the parents, the child is often severely emotionally impaired. In a home where there is an open and cooperative atmosphere, occasional mistreatment, while not recommended, may not be as much of a problem. Intensity and duration sometimes determine the impact of trauma, rather than the kind of behavior. The age of the child at the onset of a traumatic event and the emotional strength of the child make a difference in the impairment which follows. The damage incurred partially depends upon the way the person who has been harmed is responded to after the trauma and on whether or not the destructive actions were halted. In a family that is open and healthy, traumas can be spoken about, ended, worked through, and integrated, and the effects will not be as critical as when the child's feelings are ignored or denied. Unfortunately, until recently most people didn't understand how to deal with trauma, and healthy families were and still are a rarity. Consequently, most children who were the victims of mistreatment and abuse did not have anyone to help them through those traumas.

The amount of damage people have sustained from their childhoods depends on a number of factors besides those directly related to their parents. These include their own personality and fragility, other people's influence, traumas and circumstances outside the home, and the times in which they lived. Children have been physically and sexually abused by professionals such as physicians, religious leaders, teachers, and therapists, as well as by caretakers, relatives, neighbors, scout leaders, acquaintances, and strangers. They have been tormented by their peers and their siblings. Their parents may not even know about the events that have transpired.

However, the single most powerful force that affects children is the environment within the home. Most home environments have been based on the dominance-submission model which created fear and resentment on a daily basis. This pattern has repeated generationally, regardless of whether the people involved were aware of this or desired it.

Some of the patterns of behavior listed below are now considered abusive, even though they were considered normal behavior in the past. Any of the actions listed fit into the category of abuse if the consequences for the child were severe. The dictionary defines abuse as "the wrongful or unreasonable treatment by deed or word of another person." In the case of children, it includes physical, emotional, or sexual mistreatment as well as neglect. Abuse is a strong word and seems to imply purposeful commission of cruel, unthinkable acts. In my opinion, abuse, like any other harmful action, is committed out of ignorance, helplessness, or a compulsion to repeat patterns. Almost all people who abuse others have been abused themselves. If you are a person who was abused or was abusive, it is crucial for you to understand this and to deal with these patterns so that you can help stop abuse in the succeeding generations.

Note: Sometimes we see the opposite of a strong pattern, which actually is the other side of the same problem, for example when someone who grew up in an authoritarian home creates an extremely permissive home. In these cases, many of the dynamics are the same, except reversed. In the instance of a permissive parent who came from an authoritarian family, the children often end up being abusive to the parents, unsuspectingly programmed by the family dynamics to play out the authoritarian pattern.

The following is a comprehensive list of harmful actions which cause the effects listed in the last chapter. Each situation needs to be assessed on an individual basis to understand the toll various patterns have extracted from each individual. Again, *Caution: If many of the items on this list apply to your parents, yourself, or your children, you are likely to experience uncomfortable feelings including anger, tears, guilt, shame, pain, and, certainly, confusion. As with the previous exercises, plan to get support right away if you need it.*

The following chapters will give you methods to help you work on and resolve these feelings. Facing your past in an honest way is an incredibly courageous act for anyone to undertake. I doubt that anything else in this book will be much harder.

EXERCISES

Instructions: Again, use the code below as you check through the following list of harmful actions to see who in your family has been subjected to them. You can either go across, checking them for your parents (P), yourself (M = me), your spouse or other primary caretakers (PC) of your children, and then for your children (C). Or you can start with your parents and go down the list. If an action was repeated through the generations, place an asterisk by that item.

PHYSICAL MISTREATMENT

	P	M	PC	C1	C2	C3
Spanked, slapped, pinched, shaken	—	—	—	—	—	—
Pushed, thrown, kicked, or punched	—	—	—	—	—	—
Burned, bitten, or choked	—	—	—	—	—	—
Hit with belt, wooden spoon, or other objects	—	—	—	—	—	—
Tickled by person unwilling to stop	—	—	—	—	—	—

	P	M	PC	C1	C2	C3
Forced to eat	—	—	—	—	—	—
Forced to have enemas	—	—	—	—	—	—
Held down or forced to remain immobile	—	—	—	—	—	—
Being threatened by any of the above	—	—	—	—	—	—
Watching any of the above	—	—	—	—	—	—
Other _____	—	—	—	—	—	—

EMOTIONAL MISTREATMENT

	P	M	PC	C1	C2	C3
Name-calling (rotten, bad, stupid, slut, lazy, ugly, fat, selfish, etc.)	—	—	—	—	—	—
Unpredictable mood shifts	—	—	—	—	—	—
Violent outbursts	—	—	—	—	—	—
Long periods of silence	—	—	—	—	—	—
Taking away valued things	—	—	—	—	—	—
Threatening to take away valued things	—	—	—	—	—	—
Invalidating or discounting thoughts, perceptions, or feelings	—	—	—	—	—	—
Invading thoughts, disallowing privacy	—	—	—	—	—	—
Overprotectiveness	—	—	—	—	—	—
Perfectionism, overcontrol, or unrealistic expectations	—	—	—	—	—	—
Obsessiveness over food, defecation, cleanliness, neatness, health	—	—	—	—	—	—
Religious fanaticism	—	—	—	—	—	—
Extensive criticism, disrespect, humiliation	—	—	—	—	—	—
Breaking promises made to the child	—	—	—	—	—	—

	P	M	PC	C1	C2	C3
Parentifying the child (putting child in an adult role)	—	—	—	—	—	—
Extensive use of the child as confidant	—	—	—	—	—	—
Living through the child	—	—	—	—	—	—
Watching any of the above	—	—	—	—	—	—
Other _____	—	—	—	—	—	—

PHYSICAL OR EMOTIONAL LOSS OR NEGLECT

	P	M	PC	C1	C2	C3
Insufficient holding and touching	—	—	—	—	—	—
Lack of proper feeding, shelter, clothing, basic care	—	—	—	—	—	—
Being busy, ill, gone, or emotionally unavailable	—	—	—	—	—	—
Allowing negative behaviors to go on without stopping them	—	—	—	—	—	—
Overpreoccupation with other things	—	—	—	—	—	—
Empty or poor communication	—	—	—	—	—	—
Frequent moves	—	—	—	—	—	—
Death of someone close	—	—	—	—	—	—
Loss of someone close	—	—	—	—	—	—
Watching any of the above	—	—	—	—	—	—
Other _____	—	—	—	—	—	—

ADDICTIONS

	P	M	PC	C1	C2	C3
Alcohol	—	—	—	—	—	—
Drugs, prescription or nonprescription	—	—	—	—	—	—
Hypochondria or phobic behaviors	—	—	—	—	—	—

	P	M	PC	C1	C2	C3
Eating disorders: obesity, anorexia, bulimia	—	—	—	—	—	—
Exercise	—	—	—	—	—	—
Religion	—	—	—	—	—	—
Work	—	—	—	—	—	—
Spending	—	—	—	—	—	—
Gambling	—	—	—	—	—	—
Other _____	—	—	—	—	—	—

SEXUAL ABUSE

	P	M	PC	C1	C2	C3
Overstimulation, including exposure to pornography, excessive nudity, or provocative encounters	—	—	—	—	—	—
Inappropriate touching of the child	—	—	—	—	—	—
Having the child touch the adult inappropriately	—	—	—	—	—	—
Masturbation of, with or in presence of child	—	—	—	—	—	—
Oral or anal sex, or intercourse with child	—	—	—	—	—	—
Using objects sexually on child	—	—	—	—	—	—
Knowing or suspecting sexual contact and doing nothing	—	—	—	—	—	—
Age-inappropriate bathing, sleeping, touching	—	—	—	—	—	—
Negative messages about sexuality or bodies	—	—	—	—	—	—
Silence about sexuality or bodies	—	—	—	—	—	—
Watching any of the above	—	—	—	—	—	—
Other _____	—	—	—	—	—	—

MISCELLANEOUS POTENTIALLY HARMFUL SITUATIONS

	P	M	PC	C1	C2	C3
Spousal hitting, pushing, shoving, beating	—	—	—	—	—	—
Tense or fearful family atmosphere	—	—	—	—	—	—
Keeping secrets	—	—	—	—	—	—
Lying	—	—	—	—	—	—
Exposure to criminal activities	—	—	—	—	—	—
Mental or emotional illness of a family member	—	—	—	—	—	—
Physical incapacity of a person in the family	—	—	—	—	—	—
Alliances in the family, creating split loyalties	—	—	—	—	—	—
Affairs outside of the marriage	—	—	—	—	—	—
Bitter separation or divorce	—	—	—	—	—	—
Multiple or serial relationships or marriages	—	—	—	—	—	—
Marital relationship which endures because of fear or obligation	—	—	—	—	—	—
Problems denied or ignored	—	—	—	—	—	—
Someone in the family scapegoated (blamed for all the problems)	—	—	—	—	—	—
Children used as a primary relationship	—	—	—	—	—	—
Children taught fear because of their parents' fears	—	—	—	—	—	—
Enmeshed family systems (people emotionally invading each other's boundaries)	—	—	—	—	—	—
Disengaged family systems (people emotionally distant from one another)	—	—	—	—	—	—
Other _____	—	—	—	—	—	—

Answer the following questions to the best of your ability. Choose *one* of the items that affected you greatly and use it as representative of what you experienced and learned as a child. You may decide to repeat this exercise with several items to get a clearer picture of what it was like for you as a child.

Item chosen: _____

1. Who are the people involved?

_____

_____

2. What were the circumstances?

_____

_____

3. What were your thoughts about the events at the time?

_____

_____

4. How did you feel?

_____

_____

5. What did you learn from these events, about the world, adults, and yourself?

_____

_____

_____

6. What decisions did you make about how to handle relationships and family at that time?

_____

_____

_____

7. How have those decisions affected your life?

_____

_____

_____

For one or more of the items that affected your children:

Item chosen: _____

1. Who are the people involved?

_____

_____

_____

2. What were the circumstances?

_____

_____

_____

3. What were your thoughts about the events?

_____

_____

_____

4. How did you feel?

_____

_____

_____

5. How do you think your child felt?

_____

_____

_____

6. What do you think your child learned about the world, adults, and herself?

_____

_____

_____

7. What decisions about how to be in relationships do you think your child made at that time?

_____

_____

_____

8. How do you think those decisions have affected your child's life?

_____

_____

_____

Please remember: the specific action that you or your child was exposed to and the number of times it occurred may or may not be important. What is important is how it affected you or your children. Each person is different and an action that may appear mild and may be mild to someone else can dramatically violate someone who is sensitive to it. The barometer of the hurtfulness of an action is the consequences to the receiver.

A one-minute public service bulletin on television for mental health showed models of five fetuses, just before birth, which were lined up consecutively in order of destructibility. One was made of iron, one of aluminum, one of clay, one of wood, and one of glass. Then, a hammer came down on each one. The iron infant was not dented, the metal one was, the clay one sustained cracks, the wood infant was splintered, and the glass infant shattered.

Even if you or one of your children were not affected by a particular action, that does not mean that another person was not or should not have been. Even if the rest of your family when you were growing up was not affected, that does not mean that it did not affect you.

What is important now is to learn how to deal with what happened to us as children. But first, we will explore some important concepts such as anger, control, anxiety, responsibility, and blame.

CHAPTER SIX

Imperfect People in an Imperfect World

I simply can't build up my hopes on a foundation consisting of confusion, misery and death . . . I can feel the sufferings of millions and yet, if I look up into the heavens I think that it will all come right, that this cruelty too will end, and that peace and tranquility will return again. . . . I still believe that people are really good at heart.

ANNE FRANK, 1944

In an ideal world people would not be hurtful to each other and we would all work together to create the happiness we each yearn for. While this is the kind of world we are striving for, we still have a long way to go. We are imperfect, and we need to deal with ourselves and with each other with that in mind.

It is my belief that we all have the potential to behave well or badly in varying degrees. Whether our more positive or negative traits surface depends largely on our environment, our life experiences, and the patterns we have learned as children. We all have both sides, and we all are capable of being destructive at times.

People are likely to repeat the abuse they have experienced if they have not dealt with it. Most people who dehumanize others have been dehumanized themselves. People who act superior to others have been treated as inferior to others. People who have been abusive have been abused themselves. Many people who have unresolved rage and pain as a result of having been abused are explosives waiting to go off at those who are powerless. The targets of abuse have traditionally been minorities, nationalities, women, those who are different, and especially children. We must struggle to understand what causes harmful behavior so that we can change the conditions that create abuse.

Blaming people for their actions is a useless activity that simply perpetuates abuse. Blaming themselves or others seems to be an attempt by people to make sense out of what has happened to them. It gives them the illusion of control. Life seems easier if it is black and white and we do not have to deal with the gray areas. If people are either bad or good, decisions can be made easily. You avoid, lock up, or kill bad people, and you befriend good people. Of course you must keep up a pretense of goodness at all costs: otherwise, you are bad. This can be very problematic, because at times we all do "bad" or destructive things. None of us is perfect. Unfortunately, many people who set themselves up as perfect have been egomaniacs whose black-and-white thinking led to genocide. We must learn to live with the grays in our lives, with seeming contradiction and with paradox, because they are inherent parts of our world.

People also blame others because they have been steeped in a tradition of sin and punishment. People are terrified of being blamed (and punished and shamed) for what has occurred, and so they quickly look for someone else to blame. It is another historical pattern that each generation learns from the one before. And the blaming continues, another outmoded concept that divides us from each other.

Of course we want to stop abusive behavior immediately when it is occurring. But if these behaviors are not understood and dealt with they will resurface as soon as another opportunity arises. We need to all work together to figure out how we can avoid activating harmful actions, and how we can increase the amount of compassion and creativity in the world.

Anger is often the precipitating cause of abusive behavior. It can be an extremely powerful and destructive force if it is unleashed irresponsibly. To those around an angry person, anger seems as if it is his primary emotion. But, from one perspective, in actuality anger is a front for other, deeper emotions which if expressed may leave the person feeling exposed, vulnerable, and defenseless. The angry person is unconsciously defending against experiencing and expressing feelings such as fear, humiliation, pain, loneliness, helplessness, and confusion.

How people take out their anger on others is worth exploring because it is often the first step in generating actions that lead to a cycle of abuse. Anger in the raw is often used destructively, on ourselves or on others, and perpetuates the abusive cycle. It is best to use anger as a signal that something needs to change and as an indicator of unresolved old issues which need to be dealt with, rather than an emotion to be casually unleashed. Anger gives us a great amount of energy, and this energy can be partially released under safe, controlled circumstances in which no one will be harmed. People can pound pillows, exercise, throw darts, draw their anger, or write hate letters they do not send. It is a good idea to keep enough of the energy anger generates to *solve* the identified problem, rather than to intensify the conflict. It takes a great deal of energy to deal with or leave a harmful situation, and to create change, either in our own circumstances or societally.

The three examples that follow show three families where there is abuse by parents who are reenacting their own unfinished childhood dramas. The first involves anger, the second control, and the third terror. We will then consider whether these people are "to blame" for their actions.

EXAMPLE 1

Mary, twenty-three years old, went into a rage at her four-year-old daughter, Janis, for not doing what she had been told to do. Mary pushed Janis so hard that the child fell and broke her arm.

Anger was the very real emotion Mary experienced, although it was not her deepest feeling at the time. Several deeper emotions were underneath her anger: helplessness at not knowing how to communicate with her daughter; humiliation because she thought she was so incompetent she couldn't even control a four-year-old; and exhaustion because she was alone, still a child herself in many ways, working to support herself and two young children. In Mary's family during her childhood, as in many other families, anger was sufficient reason to attack someone weaker than oneself. When her mother or father were angry at Mary (felt out of control, incompetent, hurt), they hit her with a belt until she did what she was told. When Mary grew up and had her own children, she didn't realize that there were alternative ways to respond to conflicts besides discharging rage.

Mary probably would not have resorted to violence, breaking her daughter's arm, if she had been able to resolve some of her own childhood issues around her parents. As a mother, Mary was blindly following patterns she had learned from her parents' treatment of her. If she had understood that her anger was a symptom of underlying feelings, and had known that there are other ways to deal with anger besides being violent, the situation would have ended differently. She might have identified the deeper emotions inside her and dealt with them. She might have called a hot-line for stressed parents. She might have used her anger as energy to find a support system, to call the district attorney's office to get child support payments from her ex-husband, and to get counseling to deal with her own frustration and pain. She might have diverted some of her anger into nondestructive action by challenging her daughter to a race around the block, thereby changing her daughter's mood and her own. She might have stopped and listened to her daughter, who was confused and unable to follow the orders her mother had given in a desperate and aggressive manner.

EXAMPLE 2

Staying under tight control is another common device people use to cover up their feelings. Jim was brought up in a repressive household, where control by adult males was unquestioned. When he married, he made sure that the children as well as his wife were obedient and silent. The home had to be spotless and the meals served in a particular way at a particular time. Unfortunately, two of his children were passive and fearful, like his wife; one was domineering, following his example; and another was involved in criminal activities.

For Jim control was needed to maintain stability and power. It allowed him to keep people at a distance, to feel powerful, and to avoid getting connected to his deeper feelings. Underneath his carefully constructed outward control was rage at his parents for their domination of him, with the underlying feelings of fear, humiliation, and deep loneliness. Jim needed to learn to express rather than suppress his deepest feelings.

Jim would not have established such a repressive household if he had been able to deal with his inner turmoil and had learned to relate to people in an equal and open way. If he had been able to find a safe place to express his anger at his parents, or had confronted his parents, or accessed his inner emotions of hurt and sadness as well as laughter and passion, his entire family would have been different. If he had not been controlled himself by the need to keep control, he could have been more flexible and open to negotiation. Had he learned skills in communicating and in participating, he would not have had to go through a major portion of his life feeling isolated and removed. He would have realized that real power comes from being secure on the inside, not from controlling people and objects on the outside.

EXAMPLE 3

Carolyn's mother died when Carolyn was seven, and she was shuttled from one relative to another, never feeling that she belonged anywhere. When Carolyn became a mother herself she lived in mortal terror of something dreadful happening to her children, causing her to suffer another loss. Carolyn monitored everything her children did, from their food to their friends, thereby reversing her own experience of neglect. However, this resulted in the neglect of herself instead, as well as the neglect of her children's real needs. She almost drove herself crazy trying to beat the odds of life and death. Her youngest son lived with her throughout his adulthood, filling her vast need for someone to be with her. At age thirty-nine he still had not become an independent person. Carolyn never dealt with her childhood terrors.

Carolyn needed to work out her grief over the loss of her mother, as well as other losses she had experienced being moved from place to place. She needed to deal with her irrational childhood belief that she was responsible for her mother's death, and with her feeling that there was something wrong and bad about her. Her feelings of shame about not growing up in a family, and her anger and grief at not belonging anywhere needed to be acknowledged and discussed. Her constant, underlying terror could have then been relegated to the past instead of remaining entangled in her own and her children's present.

Each of us has the potential to be either stagnant and destructive, or growing and creative. If the underlying emotional problems we bring with us are not addressed, we are likely to repeat the abusive patterns we have experienced. Once we become aware of our behavior patterns, and the part we play in perpetuating abusive cycles, we have a choice about how we will act in the future. If we all work together toward the goal of awareness and understanding, we can affect not only ourselves but the larger society around us.

Are we responsible for our harmful actions? If we have been brought up in households where we do not learn alternative behaviors, can we do things differently than we do? Is Mary responsible for harming her children? Is Jim? Is Carolyn?

The term responsibility isn't really a problem as long as by responsible we mean being the source of an action or accountable for an action. It is when responsibility and blame are used interchangeably that problems arise.

Many people equate being responsible with being to blame, but the Grolier International Dictionary has eight definitions for "responsible" and none of them include blame. These meanings are:

- Legally or ethically accountable for the care or welfare of another.
- Involving personal accountability or ability to act without guidance or superior authority.
- Being the source or cause of something.
- Capable of making moral or rational decisions on one's own, and therefore answerable for one's behavior.
- Able to be trusted or depended upon; reliable.
- Based upon or characterized by good judgment or sound thinking.
- Having the means to pay debts or fulfill obligations.
- Required to render account; answerable.

Let's take the example of Mary breaking Janis' arm. Under the law, Mary was not justified by insanity or any other extraordinary circumstances. In that case she is held responsible, being the source of the action and therefore accountable, and she may be incarcerated as a result. But is Mary to blame for her actions? Given other choices and interventions, would she have been able to do something different, like punch a wall, cry, talk to Janis, take time out, call a friend, or stop and think about what was underneath her anger?

Was Jim to blame for being repressive and controlling? Given how much emotion he kept stored inside and how limited his field of vision was, could he have acted differently, without a powerful intervention that never happened?

Considering Carolyn's traumatic life experiences, could she have had a healthier relationship with her children? Given the enormity of her fear, could she even have used the knowledge that we must let go of those we love or we distort them and destroy their spirit?

These are important questions to address, because if we focus on blame we have a difficult time understanding and feeling compassionate toward strangers, friends, parents, families, our children, and ourselves. People's external presentation of themselves often has little to do with how they feel inside, and while their actions may be extremely harmful, and the consequences to their children serious or even debilitating, they need to be understood, not blamed.

If someone grows up in a home where he wears filters that remove the color from his vision, the world appears gray to him. He reacts to the world as if it were gray—and the world reacts back to him similarly in response. How can he be blamed for not seeing the full spectrum of color if it has been denied him?

It isn't that people are not responsible for their actions. They are clearly the source of the action and are accountable for that action. But given the child they were at birth, the circumstances they lived in, the knowledge they had, the limitations of their perspective and the behavior they modeled after, how could they have acted differently? They acted out their own pain and anger and they need to be understood and shown nonharmful ways to act.

The main point of this chapter is: You are not the enemy and your children are not the enemy. Neither are your parents. Neither are the other people who have hurt you. If there has to be an enemy, let it be the patterns and ignorance that have caused so much pain and confusion to so many of us.

Caution: The questions in the following exercises may bring up angry and painful feelings.

EXERCISES

1. Think of a time you were the target of someone else's anger. What were the circumstances? What do you think the person was feeling underneath the anger?

_____

_____

_____

_____

2. How could they have dealt with the circumstances differently if they had been aware of the underlying reasons for their anger?

_____

_____

_____

_____

3. Think of a time when you were angry. What were the circumstances? What did you feel below the anger?

_____

_____

_____

_____

4. How could you have dealt with the circumstances differently if you had been aware of the underlying reasons behind your anger?

_____

_____

_____

_____

5. Write about a time you have felt the need to keep those around you under control. What were your feelings underneath?

_____

_____

_____

_____

6. How could you have acted differently if you had not been limited by the need to control?

_____

_____

_____

_____

7. Think of a time when you were terrified of losing someone or something you felt was vital to your existence.

_____

_____

_____

8. What did you learn about safety and security that still affects you now? Can you see how much better you could deal with things if you were not trapped by old patterns?

_____

_____

_____

9. Do you believe that people are to blame for their inappropriate and harmful actions? Why, or why not?

_____

_____

_____

10. Have you committed acts that you regret and that you hold yourself responsible for? Do you feel that you are to blame for them?

_____

_____

_____

_____

11. Is there any real value in blaming people? If so, what specific value?

_____

_____

_____

_____

12. Does assigning blame to yourself help to deal with these issues or would you be better off understanding why you acted as you did, and being open to new options?

_____

_____

_____

PART TWO
Personal Healing and Growth

CHAPTER SEVEN

Patterns and Perspectives

I have no doubt that behind every crime a personal tragedy lies. If we were to investigate such events and their backgrounds more closely, we might be able to do more to prevent crimes than we do now with our indignation and moralizing.

ALICE MILLER, *For Your Own Good*

You may have had only minor difficulties while growing up, or you may have lived in a virtual quagmire of problems. Many people have gone through much more pain than they are aware of, and facing this fact is extremely difficult for them.

Let's take a break from the intensity of our own work and look at some theories that explain how patterns come about in the first place. Here we will explain some basic counseling concepts that can help put these problems in perspective and can begin to show you how to shift patterns so that they do not become a permanent part of your life. One thing is certain: Problems are universal; no one gets by unscathed. My intention is to help you to utilize the past not to create a future that is problem-free, but to create a future in which problems can be handled with a minimum of stress, anxiety, and depression.

If your childhood was extremely difficult, it is important to do the work of sorting and healing gradually, in small steps. It is as if there is a deep swamp between where you are now and where you want to be. Going directly into the swamp and across to the other side may be faster, but you might not make it across and the recuperation time might take longer than the time it would have taken to get across slowly. Also, the pain can be extremely intense. My recommendation is to go into the swamp step by step, working things out and gradually lowering the level of the swamp as, section by section, the old garbage is drawn out of the water. That way you can go through at ankle depth instead of having to hold your breath while you go across and risk becoming exhausted or drowning. This is especially true if you are doing this work on your own.

There are many theoretical models for understanding the dynamics that create personal and relationship problems. Three that seem particularly useful in defining this area are summarized below, including examples of how they apply to families. These summaries are very brief and general. They only explain a small part of the theories they refer to. Reading some of the excellent books listed at the end of this chapter or other books in these areas will give you an in-depth understanding of the theories and how they work. The cases are deliberately simplified and abstracted to clarify the points being made. Family dynamics are too complex to be outlined adequately in a few short paragraphs.

SCRIPT THEORY FROM TRANSACTIONAL ANALYSIS

Transactional Analysis is based on what is called a life script—a combination of messages people have received from their parents directly and indirectly—and the messages their parents have implicitly modeled for them. This script tends to be passed down from generation to generation, unless there is awareness of it and some kind of intervention. Scripts can control the way you feel about yourself, the things you believe and the behavior patterns you follow. They are extremely powerful and can control every area of your life. For example, if the father in a family is alcoholic, one or more of his children will probably follow an addictive behavior pattern. They may become addicted to alcohol, but even if they do not drink, the same addictive pattern will be present in their interaction with something else, for example addiction to money, work, sex, or drugs. These are not as obvious at first, but the addiction is very real. Behavior, attitude, and pattern are modeled for the child over and over by the parents, in words and by example, and modeling is the most powerful form of influence. Most of us have modeled ourselves after one or both of our parents, in many areas, often in ways we swore we would never repeat. Very strong interventions in our lives are necessary to break this hypnotic pull.

Here is an example of the power of scripts and modeling. Read through this scenario and see what you think is going on in this family.

Sharon was brought into therapy by her husband in a last-ditch effort to save their marriage. She had left the relationship six months earlier, giving him the logical reason that she had been a slave for the *twenty years* of their marriage and was tired of it. This perception of her marriage appeared to be pretty close to the truth, as even her husband agreed, and returning to school had awakened·her to her untapped potential. It was clear that she drastically needed to change her role in the family. However, she had never asked for anything before in her marriage, so she couldn't rationally blame her husband for not sharing in household chores without taking some responsibility herself for not speaking up. In the present, her husband was taking care of the children after work and weekends, doing all the housework and cooking and was willing to do whatever she wanted or needed to make their marriage work. He felt a strong bond with his wife and he was totally committed to the family. Sharon felt as though she also wanted to try again, but as soon as she went near the house she became terrified. She felt that it would be impossible to return and work on the marriage. She said that her feelings had died and that she didn't think they could be restored. It wasn't until she revealed that her mother had killed herself *after twenty years of marriage* that the missing pieces began to fit together.

If you didn't know her past history, you might easily conjecture that Sharon had left her family for any or all of the following reasons:

1. She had become a liberated woman and wanted to be on her own.
2. She was sick of being used.
3. She was having an affair and wasn't telling anyone.
4. She was irresponsible and unfeeling.

Once you have more of the puzzle pieces, however, you can see the scripted messages from her childhood. Clearly, Sharon is at least partly caught in a repetitive cycle that was leading to her repeating her mother's suicidal pattern. Her leaving was her attempt to save herself.

Without understanding her script, it is likely that friends and acquaintances might have advised her to leave home and start a new life. This might have helped, but more likely she would have broken up her family and still remained in a severe depression that she didn't understand.

What was more useful for Sharon was for her to:

1. Try to understand what drove her mother to suicide, and to make sure that she did not have the same painful circumstances in her current life.
2. Allow herself to grieve over her mother's death and relegate her pain to the past.
3. Express her anger at her dad for the ways in which he failed her mother.
4. Continue to work with her husband and find out how his pattern as well as hers had allowed the marriage to deteriorate.

THE "MOBILE" THEORY OF THE FAMILY

Another therapeutic concept can be understood by visualizing a mobile and conceptualizing how all of the pieces are dependent on each other. In *The Dance of Anger* author Harriet

Lerner writes about underfunctioning and overfunctioning in a relationship. For example, if one person in the family takes on most of the responsibility in the relationship, another member often becomes passive-dependent; if one person is passive-dependent, another often becomes responsible to balance the "mobile." If one person is very rational, another may become overemotional; if one is very intense, another may withdraw. If we are not whole or have not integrated the many aspects of ourselves, we find people or create people who can balance our deficiencies.

The mobile becomes dependent on all of the people being there to play their parts, and they are all dependent on their counterparts to continue their roles. An additional problem is that people begin to identify who they are with the role they are placed in, severely limiting their self-concept. If all of the people had all the necessary emotional parts, in varying degrees, inside them, they could leave and return to the family without falling apart or having the structure fall apart. If people have parts missing, a child born into the family may be expected to fill the role that is missing for the family and will become powerfully hooked into the family's dynamics.

Here is an example to illustrate the Mobile Theory:

Tracy grew up in a home where her parents were determined to have their family work well. Both of her parents had come from chaotic households and both had lost one of their parents in their early teens: one as a result of alcohol-related illness and another in an accident. This couple was determined not to repeat their past, but they unwittingly set the stage for it to reappear in their children's generation. They never touched alcohol, but acted addictively; they were very religious, strict, and self-controlled. They were also terrified of conflict and agreed with each other on almost everything. Though successful in the world's eyes they had very little awareness of their true selves, which were hidden in fear.

As a child, Tracy had felt unwanted and unaccepted. Her parents had strong, ambivalent, underlying feelings toward her. Tracy had been a spontaneous and uncontrolled child, and her parents were fearful of losing the control they had worked so hard to attain. Unconsciously, they had been fascinated by and envious of her independence and openly emotional outbursts. Tracy had little success in her attempts to stay in control, partly because she was subjected to a "double bind," that is, she had been told to be in control but simultaneously given covert messages to be out of control. In her teens she went totally out of control and began taking drugs, drinking to excess, acting out sexually, and attempting suicide. Her parents, her friends, and her teachers were unable to understand why. She came from the perfect home. She knew why. "There's something terribly wrong with me," she sobbed. "I'm such a disappointment to myself and my parents. Everyone else has self-control. I don't know what, but there's something terribly wrong with me."

Again, it is easy to make generalizations about Tracy, such as "she's a difficult child" or "she's a hysteric." Currently, it is in vogue to say that she was simply caught by the influence of the youth culture. While some of this may apply, more of Tracy's symptoms derive from the dynamics in her family. In actuality:

1. Tracy was unable to live up to the unrealistic, rigid expectations of her parents.
2. She was trying to respond to the overt message of being in control and the covert message of being emotional and she was feeling crazy because she couldn't do both.
3. She had become the outlet for the missing emotions in the family and was expressing her parents' pain and confusion from their own childhoods that they had denied existed.

The best thing for Tracy to do was not necessarily to shape up and gain control over her life; in fact, in her current state she was simply unable to do that. Finding new friends was probably a good idea, but that in itself wouldn't have helped her deal with the deep confusion and poor self-esteem she had. What finally did help were the following:

1. She began to understand and not be a captive to the mixed messages she had been given about restricting/expressing her feelings.
2. She entered individual and then family therapy.
3. She talked with her parents about what she learned from them and what they had been taught in their own childhoods. These discussions broke down the wall of isolation between them so that they could understand their family patterns and balance their roles more evenly.

GESTALT THERAPY: UNFINISHED BUSINESS

One of the concepts of Gestalt theory is that the human mind is structured so that it wants to complete unfinished events, and that it persists in trying to do so until an event feels completed. Therefore, whatever feels incomplete for you will become the focus of your attention.

Visualize a large screen composed of foreground and background. Completed events can be viewed as closed circles and incomplete events can be viewed as partial circles. Whatever feels unfinished will be in the foreground of this screen. For example, if right now you are thirsty, hungry, or uncomfortable, your focus may be partially on your hunger, thirst, or discomfort, and your attention will not be fully on the words you are reading. You could conceptualize your thirst as an incomplete circle which would be in the foreground of this screen. If you get a drink and are no longer thirsty, you will then be able to close this circle and it will recede into the background and not interfere with your attention any longer.

In Gestalt this concept is extended to any unfinished problems you may have from childhood; psychologically there is a need to complete unfinished business. Instead of simply receding into the background, unfinished problems stay in the foreground, influencing your present actions, choices, and feelings, even if you are not aware of them. Any time a situation which is similar to an incomplete situation from the past comes up it will have all the impact of the past situation. Your struggle to complete the present becomes extremely difficult. There is also the tendency to try to recreate the same situation so that you can finally complete it in the present. Here is where we get the compulsion to repeat past patterns.

Here is an example of "unfinished business:"

Gary was a thirty-six-year-old man who had been in a relationship with a woman for eleven years, and although he was willing to live with her he was not willing to marry her, stating that he was a "confirmed bachelor." Gary maintained that getting married interfered with independence. Eventually this relationship broke up and he found himself in a new relationship which after three years began to sound like the first. His girlfriend wanted a commitment and she wanted to get married. He was not interested. This time, however, he really didn't want to lose the relationship and his girlfriend told him that marriage was a bottom line: because she had teenagers and they lived in a conservative community she needed to be married or she was not willing to stay in the relationship. They came in for couple counseling to explore this issue. What Gary described when he pictured being married was a feeling of being trapped and suffocated, as well as feeling that he was going to be annihilated. Tracing back to his past, his relationship with his stepfather surfaced—his stepfather had been very supportive of him before he married Gary's mother, but after the marriage he underwent a radical shift. He went from being active, playful, and fun-loving to being passive and drinking excessively. He gained an enormous amount of weight, and ignored Gary most of the time thereafter.

It is possible that Gary was afraid to get married because:

1. He hadn't met the right person.
2. He was a typical male chauvinist who abused women.
3. He was in love with his mother, a victim of the Oedipal complex.
4. He was in a power struggle with his girlfriends.

But here, as with Sharon and Tracy, the past has caught up with Gary and made him a victim of its powerful pull. The primary reason Gary was unable to get married was because he was terrified, with good reason, of turning into his stepfather. It was not in Gary's long-term interests to find a woman who would accept him in a noncommitted relationship or to continue having serial relationships, because the past would never have been resolved.

What Gary needed to do and actually did were:

1. He worked through his incompleted feelings around his stepfather and separated himself from this negative role model.
2. He worked on his identity as a male who could receive and give love and respect in a family.
3. He completed the past and moved on to the present.

EXERCISES

1. What are some of the patterns you learned as a child?

_____

_____

_____

_____

_____

_____

2. What role did you play in your family?

_____

_____

_____

_____

3. What traumas and problems did you have as a child that you have not had a chance to work through?

_____

_____

_____

_____

_____

_____

4. How do you think you would be different if you had grown up in a family where your parents were secure in themselves and gave you feelings of security and self-worth?

_____

_____

_____

_____

As you go through the next three chapters you will be doing several exercises which will help you to deal with your past. You will be looking at your relationships with your parents. Then you will be getting in touch with the child you were. Finally, you will have a chance to experience how it would have felt to have been parented in the specific way that will be presented for you.

RECOMMENDED READING

Scripts People Live, Claude Steiner
Games People Play, Eric Berne
The Missing Piece Meets the Big O, Shel Silverstein
The Adult Children of Alcoholics Syndrome, Wayne Kritsberg
The Family, John Bradshaw
The Dance of Anger, Harriet Lerner
Born to Win, Muriel James and D. Jongward
Gestalt Therapy Verbatim, Fritz Perls

CHAPTER EIGHT

Unfinished Business with Your Parents

> If we could read the secret history of our enemies, we should find in each man's life sorrow and suffering enough to disarm all hostility.
>
> HENRY WADSWORTH LONGFELLOW

To repair your relationships with your children, it will be helpful to first repair your relationships with your own parents. The more complete the past is for you, the more open you will be to the present. Completing things involves coming to terms with the past, and it's important to note that completing doesn't mean forgetting. It means integrating the past into the present: remembering, learning to live with the memories, and making the past a part of who you are now.

Here are several things you can do to help begin the completion process.

EXPLORING YOUR PARENTS' HISTORY

Finding out about your own parents' lives and history will greatly help you understand more clearly how your self-image, attitudes, and beliefs were formed. It will also help you to understand how crucial it will be to your adult children for you to share your history as they try to sort out their lives and values.

The following questions can be answered in several ways.

Probably the most effective way is to ask your parents, if they are accessible, to search their memories with you and to find the answers. It will help your relationship with them as you grow to understand them better and will give you a chance to share with them on a deeper level than you have in the past. The questions are specific, so that they can be answered concretely, unlike the rambling memories many of us have that are sometimes idealized or dramatized. *Caution: Your parents may not be willing or able to respond in the way you would like them to.*

If asking your parents is not an option, answer the questions from your memories of stories they have told you, from what you suspect must have happened, given the times they lived in, or from information you can gather from other family members or friends of theirs. You can also create a dialogue with your parents in your mind, as if they were with you, and the answers will likely be fairly accurate. If none of the above ways help, then make up answers that you think are true: They will be closer to the truth than you at first might think.

Here are some questions you can ask yourself, or them. They are ideas for you to take off from. Answer as many as you want or ask your own questions, which may be more relevant to your family.

1. What kind of home did my parents grow up in?

   _____

   _____

   _____

2. What did they think of themselves as people while they were growing up?

   _____

   _____

   _____

3. What traumas did they undergo in their childhoods?

   _____

_____

_____

4. What kind of social, political, and economic environment did they live in?

_____

_____

5. What attitudes were they exposed to about important areas such as the work ethic, money, sexuality, roles, parenting, the reasons for living, beliefs about dying?

_____

_____

6. What was their relationship with their brothers/sisters like?

_____

_____

7. Were they or others in their immediate family put into certain "roles," such as "the responsible one," "the black sheep," or the person who tries to make everyone get along?

_____

_____

8. Were there harmful behavior patterns in the home such as sexual abuse, alcoholism, or severe physical or emotional punishment that they had to endure?

_____

_____

9. How were differences treated in their home growing up?

_____

10. If they were to say that they knew their parents loved them but they can't say how, just how did they know? Did they know, or are they actually in denial?

11. Why did your parents marry each other, if they did? Convenience, money, security, attraction, love (not the same as attraction), planned marriage, pregnancy, to escape their home, familiarity (repeat of the circumstances of their childhood: for example, coming from an alcoholic home and marrying an alcoholic), timing?

12. How prepared were they to marry and raise a family? Had they resolved their childhood issues? Did they have any skills? Did they know how to resolve conflicts or understand and value differences? Had they grown up themselves?

13. What about their sense of personal achievement? Did they focus mainly on survival or did they find out what they wanted to do in their lives and follow through?

14. What traumas did they undergo as adults? What deprivations or losses?

_____

_____

15. What dreams did your parents have that they gave up?

_____

_____

16. What overwhelmed them when they were in their twenties and thirties trying to raise you and your brothers and sisters?

_____

_____

17. What were the historical events that took place during the time you were a child that affected them and their attitudes?

_____

_____

18. What patterns did they repeat from their childhoods in trying to parent you?

_____

_____

19. If they were hurtful to you, how did they learn to be that way? What events created their ability to hurt others?

_____

_____

20. Imagine your parents are able to start over. What do you think their lives would have been like if they had had the resources that are available now?

_____

_____

_____

Stop for a few moments and consider the following: What are your feelings now that you have tried to answer parts or all of these questions? What did you think and feel toward your parents before you answered these questions? Are there any changes within you in terms of further understanding and compassion? If not, can you conceive of some time in the future when this may come about? Note your discoveries in the space below.

_____

_____

_____

_____

One woman discovered the following about her mother. It helped to see her mother as a child who had been hurt, a child trying to deal with her own traumas and survival. Here is what she wrote:

My mother grew up in Poland right after World War I and was subjected to army raids when she was small. She has vivid memories of hiding under the bed afraid to breathe. Her father had left for England when she was eight months old and she didn't see him again until she was eight, when she and her mother escaped from Poland to England in a wagon filled with hay. She learned to live in fear and isolation. Her mother continually compared her to a cousin who was supposedly much prettier.

She learned early that money is scarce, sexuality is forbidden, life is about struggle, and children are a burden. Emotional abuse was a way of life and differences were put down or mocked. Her mother resented her and her father used her as a friend and confidant when they were reunited.

She married my father because he pursued her tenaciously

and she didn't want to be single. She had resolved nothing and had neither the skills nor the understanding you need to be even a moderately good parent. Her mother had rejected her, and she felt worthless and unlovable. The depression further augmented her fear, and financial problems were never-ending. Her entire life was about trying to survive. She never pursued her ability to draw and write, but worked with numbers instead, and while she was reasonably successful she never followed her heart. She became extremely compulsive about food, cleanliness, and neatness, and was anxious and controlling most of the time.

I feel a lot of sorrow for my mother, as she never lived in a loving home or had the opportunity to fulfill herself. If she had grown up in a loving family, my fantasy is that she would have been involved in the arts, married someone stable instead of my father, and been at peace within herself.

The purpose of this search is not to glorify or feel sorry for your parents, but simply to understand them and begin, at some point, to feel compassion for them.

WRITING LETTERS TO YOUR PARENTS
OR PARENT SUBSTITUTES

Caution: You may feel a lot of intense feelings such as anger, frustration, and pain as you go through these exercises and discover things you would just as soon leave alone. Getting your feelings out on paper often helps to release them so that you can move on. It is important to go through these processes to some extent, particularly to release anger that may be hurting you by festering inside or that you may inadvertently be displacing onto others. It will also help you understand what your children may have gone through or may have to go through if they are struggling to deal with these issues too.

You may feel that you want to be understanding and compassionate toward your parents and not delve into negative thoughts and feelings. Especially if your parent is ill or deceased, you may have strong feelings of loyalty that will make it more difficult for you to express your own pain and anger, even though your parents will not know what you are writing. A way to get by this is to realize that ventilating your feelings in a way that can harm no one is often a first step in a process that will lead you to a place of compassion and understanding toward them. If we accept what our parents did, however, before we have identified and experienced our own feelings and struggles, we are neglecting a crucial part of our own healing and we remain disconnected from ourselves. Without facing our true feelings, we end up dragging our emotions, attitudes, and patterns from the past into the present, creating a continuing repetition of events. This will continue to block our attempts to create open, caring relationships with our adult children.

Following are four examples of letters that parents of adult children have written to their own parents that they did not send. Writing these letters gave them a chance to release and clarify their feelings toward their parents. It would be helpful for you to do these also, either in writing or in your imagination.

The purpose of the first letter is to identify and express what happened to you as a child, and how that affected you, without concerning yourself with why these things happened. It is a vehicle for ventilating and experiencing the feelings you had that you probably were not allowed to express, or that you were punished or isolated for expressing. The letter, which can harm no one, can be as furious, plaintive, and uncompassionate as you feel when you access the hurt you felt in the past or that you feel now as you recall past experiences.

If your father beat you with a belt for some infraction, do not for now consider all of the stress he was under, or the circumstances, or his history, or how you guess you probably were rotten and deserved to be beaten. Instead, express how you would feel now if someone two or three or four times your size held you down, told you to pull down your pants, and then inflicted physical pain on you, possibly saying, "If you cry you'll get more of the same." How hard it would be now for you to hold down your rage, fear, tears, and feelings of humiliation. How resentful you would feel that people were unwilling to talk about the problem at hand and trying to solve it rather than suppressing you with their greater physical strength. Imagine how you would have felt as a small child, not listened to or understood, and unable to fight back or to escape.

If your mother was overcontrolled, perfectionistic, and critical, a highly damaging combination to a child, think of how it would feel if while you were exploring you picked up and accidentally dropped one of her pieces of china. Feel the harsh look, the angry words, the heavy hand, all letting you know that you are stupid, careless, clumsy, and bad. The person you depend upon, perhaps worship, shames you for being curious and for being yourself. Think about how it would feel now if you were to pick up something breakable, drop it, and have someone three or four times your size shame you. There are other ways to teach children that work more effectively than hitting or shaming. Of course parents don't want their china broken. But they don't want their child's spirit broken either. (Scenes like this always make me wonder what would be wrong with putting valuables up on a shelf where they won't be in the child's way, instead of trying to put the child on a shelf so the child won't be in the object's way.)

These are real scenarios played out day after day on children. Our responses as children were real: fear, shame, disillusionment, and rage. These are the feelings we bring with us into the next generation, if they are not expressed and completed in the past.

The purpose of this exercise is not to create pain and anger. The purpose is to diffuse the feelings that are already there so they are not turned inward on ourselves or displaced onto other people.

This letter was written without the intention of mailing it.

Dad,

I do not choose to challenge you on why you did what you did to us. It's done and we have suffered. Now I am finally trying to deal with my anger and my anguish in a constructive way instead of taking it out on myself. I used to think you were wonderful, and I worshipped and feared you and thought that everything that was wrong was everyone else's fault. That was before I opened my eyes and really looked at what you did.

You were so terrible to us. While I was growing up I lived with feelings of tremendous guilt because part of me hated you even though you were my father, and I was supposed to love you. You were a tremendous failure in the role of father. You let us down over and over. We deserved support and you never gave us any. You made us believe we were useless because you either humiliated us, ignored us, or whipped us. We used to have to go out into the woods and pick out the largest branch we could find to be beaten with. If it was too small for your specifications we had to go back out and find a larger one, knowing we would get it twice as hard. How could you treat your children like that?

I went from caring and wanting to please you to just not giving a damn. Now the only thing I want is for you to hurt in your heart as I have done. It would be too much to ask that you'd really feel sorry. I don't think you could. Your pride, ego, whatever you want to call it, is your ruler. You will go to your grave always right and wondering what's the matter with everyone else.

A letter stating how you wish it could have been can be a powerful way to shift some of your feelings into an exploration of what you needed. The letter below, also not sent, attempts to do this.

Dear Dad,

I wish so much I could have had a father who could have cared about me as a person, who would have valued my attempts and been excited by my successes. A parent who would have shown me how to love and care, how to work things out, how to treat people with respect. I wish I'd had a father I could be proud of, that I could walk with as I have seen other friends walk with their fathers, their arm in their dads', talking about nothing and everything, feeling as if they belonged somewhere and as if they were worthy of being loved and cherished. It has been such a deep emptiness inside me never to have had that kind of treatment from you. It actually made me desperate for anyone who would treat me even a little kindly, even if I had to pay for the kindness after.

If you write a third letter to your parents, that you do not send, telling them how sorry you are for them, you will get closer to how little they actually got out of life. This will also help you get closer to feeling compassion rather than anger, although, as you can see in the letter below, it may take awhile to work out all of your underlying anger.

Dear Dad,

You have no idea how much you missed out on. Your wife and children were terrified of you. You were isolated and lonely and bitter for your entire life. You never accomplished a thing that was of value to anyone, not even yourself. You used to go to work, come home, sit around and smoke and drink, and take out your frustration on us, and that was all you did day after day, except a couple of times a year you went hunting. You wasted so much. We would have been there for you, if only you could have appreciated us, but you never noticed that. You worked all day and bitched all night. In between, you took out your frustration on us. What a life to have. It's a dreadful waste, when I think about it now. I can't get over the waste. I really do feel badly for you as well as myself. I really pity you for what you will never have.

Finally, writing a fourth letter stating how you wish it could have been for your parents, and therefore for you, can help complete the process.

Dear Dad,

I wish you could have been raised in a different environment, where you could have learned how to listen and how to care. I know you were treated brutally yourself, that your parents never spent time with you, and that your hatred has to do not with us but with your own past. I wish some gentle and understanding person had been there for you, and that you had found some way to express yourself when you were young and vital and able. I wish I could have helped, but I was just a child, and though I am now an adult I am still not able to give you what you needed when you were small. Even if I could, I wouldn't, because now I have my own pain to deal with and my own children and theirs. I have to save my energy for myself and them. I still wish though that you had been touched with some love and care when you were young. You would have been so different in the way you treated us and in the way you cared for yourself.

Another useful exercise is to write letters that you think your parents would have written to their parents if they could have been aware of the things you have become aware of. Most likely their underlying feelings are not that different from yours. This will again illustrate how persistent the patterns of abuse have been and how painful it is to all of us to continue this cycle.

USING THE ARTS TO PROCESS YOUR JOURNEY

A powerful way to express feelings is through art, music, dance, stories, or poetry. The art forms draw on a part of you that is primitive and close to your heart. If you have an affinity for one of these art forms, you may want to use it as a natural way for you to work through your feelings about your family. If you are not accustomed to using any of these media, here is a chance for you to express yourself in a new way. This is not an exercise that will be graded or evaluated. It is not an exercise to prove or disprove your artistic abilities. You can use mediums such as drawing, music, dance, sculpture, collage, combinations of these, or any medium you can think of. If you use art, this exercise sometimes works best if you use the opposite hand from the one you ordinarily use. The purposes of this exercise are to express your feelings, to learn and to grow, not to impress anyone.

EXERCISES

1. Represent by drawing or any other medium your feelings of pain, frustration, and anger toward your parents, for the times and ways they hurt you and the circumstances you had to deal with.
2. Represent what it was like for you as a child growing up in your family.
3. Represent the way you think it was for your parents growing up in their families.
4. Represent your parents' feelings toward their parents and the circumstances they had to deal with. Notice if there are similarities between your representations of your feelings and theirs.
5. Represent the way you wish your childhood had been.
6. Represent the way you wish life had been for your parents, and therefore ultimately for you and your children.

Resolving your feelings about your parents is usually a slow process, and it is difficult to do it alone. The next two chapters will help you to get in contact with the child you were and to heal some of the wounds you experienced as that child. If you find it too difficult to do this work alone, or if you feel you want support through it, don't hesitate to reach out for assistance. Chapter Eleven offers some ways to go about getting professional help.

CHAPTER NINE

Accepting the Child within You

We are all born for love; it is the principle of existence and its only end.

BENJAMIN DISRAELI

It is easy to dismiss the concept of connecting with our inner child as simplistic or dramatic. Like many important concepts, however, hearing and reading about them is very different from experiencing them.

My own picture of the child within is one that conceptualizes the child as the core of a person—the natural self that is born basically innocent and unarmed. As the child's world becomes threatening and painful, the child, needing to defend herself, acquires layers of protection. Defenses begin to grow and barriers are set up to shield the child from hurt. The layers are like onion skins which grow around the child and gradually hide her, often even from herself. Additionally, the child learns roles from her parents or takes on roles in the family which all serve to add still more layers around the natural self. As a result of all this, the child's energy becomes diverted from playfulness and curiosity to guardedness and fear.

If we continue accumulating layers of defenses and roles over the years, we lose our connection with the person we would naturally have been if we had been given the protection, care, support, and nurturing we originally needed. The purpose of reuniting with our inner child is to allow us to experience the feelings we have cut off and to explore options that should have been rightfully ours.

The following exercises show some ways you can access your inner child—with all of its delight, playfulness, and curiosity. For all of the exercises below, you will need to find a quiet place without interruptions and some private time. They can be done alone or with someone supportive to be present who can listen to you and encourage you. *Caution: Some of these exercises are intense and can bring up a variety of complex, primitive feelings. Be sure to reach out for support if you need it.*

1. Go through your old photographs and find some pictures of yourself at different ages. Look at the pictures as if they are of someone else. Find one or two at several ages that you are drawn to, either because of the expression on the child's face or because of something special you see in her. Keep looking at the photographs until you can feel nurturing and protective of the child; until you can see her innocence shine through.

What do you see in the child's eyes? What do you think she is feeling?

_____

_____

What kind of care is the child being given?

_____

_____

As the child gets older, what changes do you see?

_____

_____

What kind of parenting did the child receive that was useful?

_____

_____

_____

What kind of parenting did the child need that she did not get?

_____

_____

What kind of parenting did the child get that was harmful?

_____

_____

What did the child learn that was not helpful?

_____

_____

What could the child learn now that would be helpful for her future?

_____

_____

_____

2. Pretend you are safe and alone, in a dark room. Scenes from your childhood appear on a screen in front of you as if they are being shown from an automatic slide projector. You find yourself able to access memories that are long forgotten.

Mark, who had been physically abusive to his past three wives, was determined to find out why he could not control his violence. When he closed his eyes, he saw vivid slides: of his parents looking hatefully at each other; of his mother's eyes filled with tears; of his father's cat-o'-nine tails coming toward him; of himself at age six, standing between his parents, trying to protect his mother from his father's fists. Through this experience he recognized how much he had turned into the father that he loathed and feared. He realized he did not need to spend his whole life without an identity of his own. It took a lot of other work, but this exercise helped him reconnect with the gentle parts of himself.

3. Visualize yourself in a theater where the story of your life is being presented on screen. This is a good technique to use if you have been in extremely abusive or painful situations, because any time the movie gets too frightening you can change the way you are viewing it. You can change to being a person in the last row of the theater, watching yourself watching the movie. This distances you from the pictures on the screen even more. You can have imaginary controls in your hand which can make the pictures move closer or farther away, make the colors fade or brighten, or you can slow down or speed up the scene. This way the films are less likely to overwhelm you. After viewing this movie, you can change some scenes to ones that would have offered you more protection and nurturing, to experience how you wish it had been and to lessen some of your pain.

One woman who had begun having memories of being molested by her father was able to see what had happened when she projected the scene onto a screen. With the controls in hand, she could make the picture very dim and far away, and have the sounds decrease, so she could explore the memory without falling into so much terror she would not be able to function. In this way she could integrate what had happened to her without breaking down. She used this method to create a new scene afterward in which the police intervened and arrested her father and a safe person was there to hold and comfort her and take her away from the terrifying situation. She brought this scene closer and brighter and this helped diminish the impact of the original abuse. She was able to gradually experience the feelings with the memory at later times, as she needed to in order to integrate the trauma.

4. Another way to make contact with your inner child is to create a picture of the child within you in your mind. One way you can do this is by getting into a relaxed state and creating a picture of yourself at whatever age you wish as you remember or imagine you were. If you choose to, go through the following visualization in your imagination and see what happens for you. It can be helpful to have someone to read it to you slowly or to read it yourself onto a tape and then play it back. It will probably be more intense if you close your eyes as you will be able to get into the imagery more deeply.

You are walking slowly down a wide, spacious beach. You have all the time you need, to do whatever you want to do. You have nowhere else to go and nothing else to do, but to feel the sun's rays warm and gentle on your face and arms. The sand is luxurious beneath your feet, and you can feel a gentle breeze and hear the sounds of water in the background. The anxieties, worries, and frustrations you have been feeling are gradually subsiding and fading into the distance, allowing you to savor the ease of walking, slowly and comfortably.

You come to a narrowing of the beach and it seems as if the beach has become a path leading you forward. Curious about where it leads but somewhat apprehensive about what you may find at the end of it, you cautiously continue. You don't know if it is your imagination or not, but the sun feels even warmer than before, and the sound of the water seems stronger. You feel almost as if you are in a different state of consciousness here on this isolated but exquisite deserted beach.

As you walk farther, you notice that the sand off to the side is on a higher level, like a sand dune. You don't think much about that until you realize that inside the sand dunes are what appear to be caves and you realize that the path is narrowing and getting closer and closer to the dunes. You look ahead and see that the path eventually ends at the opening of one of the caves. This cave is apparently carved out of the dunes which are now almost directly in front of you.

Just a few more steps and you are at the entrance to a large cave which has light warm sand on its surface and a darker, cooler sand in its interior. Hesitant, you consider turning back, but you realize that you are tired and hot and the pull of the cool interior draws you toward the cave where you can rest for a while from your long journey.

Inside the cave the light is dimmer, but not really dark. Your eyes adjust to the light and you breathe a sigh of relief as the coolness relaxes you. In the center of the room is a sculpture of a small child made of sand, and surrounding the sculpture is a museum of things connected with the child. As you walk closer to the sculpture, you become aware that the child is you and that it is your childhood that is in front of you, sculptured in sand. As you look carefully around, you can see the child's family, other important people the child has known, and different events in the child's life. As you explore you begin to see which events in the child's life have supported her and which events have kept her from being able to grow. You begin to understand who the child is and how she has become the person she is now. You stay there, looking around, for as long as you need to in order to integrate what you have seen into your present life.

You turn and begin your return from the depths of the cave. As you walk into the sunlight you realize that you are no longer alone. You feel the presence of the child in the cave and you realize she is with you. She has become a part of you as she was once a long time ago, and you make a deep commitment to her to take care of and protect her. You continue on your long, slow walk on the beach. You know that you will continue to learn how to love the small child who is now in your care. The sun is again warm on your face and hands, and you come back, step by step, to the present, to the time and place you were at before you began your journey.

5. Grieving for the child inside can be an important step in healing as you go through a mourning process for the child you were. If you feel, as many of us do, that your child never had a chance fully to live, you may need to grieve the loss of that part of you. Giving yourself time to mourn for the person you were, who did not get a chance to thrive, will help in the healing process. You might find yourself beginning with denial statements, which tend to minimize the child's pain, like: "Well, it

really wasn't that bad. . . . There were children who were much worse off. . . . My parents did the best they could. . . ." and so on. After getting past that, you will probably begin to feel sadness and compassion for the small child who didn't get the chance to express herself freely or to be parented properly. Then you might feel anger at the child's parents or other adults who weren't there when they were needed so badly, as well as the circumstances that were present at the time. After, there might be a sense of the injustice and unfairness of it all, with indignation that the world has not gotten its priorities straight yet. Lastly, perhaps a resignation or acceptance that what happened cannot be changed and that there is in a sense no one to blame. At this point it is possible to begin to give the child hope for a new life, with ourselves as adults now able to parent the child we were. We need to be the ones to value, protect, and nurture this core part of ourselves.

6. Write a letter to your parents asking them for the things you needed from them that they couldn't give you. Then write a letter back, from them to you, saying what you needed to hear from them. This is a way of consciously creating for yourself the kind of parent that you needed. (This is a conscious process, and is therefore not a form of denial, which is an unconscious process.)

Here is a sample letter from a man whose father would not communicate with him, and the response he made up for himself, pretending it was from his father. It would have felt better to him if his dad had actually written the response, but at least in this way he was able to create in fantasy what he could not have in reality.

Dear Dad,

For so long I have wanted to develop a relationship with you but I have not known how. I needed compassion and caring from you but instead I was time and again misunderstood and left feeling hurt and empty.

Providing food and shelter is a very small part of being a father. When I needed emotional support I received a lecture and when I needed to be heard and understood you would not listen. I was expected to understand and be there for you, even as a small child, but what about me? Instead I got beaten and yelled at. It hurts to know that my own father still has no idea of who I am, my ambitions, my dreams, my weaknesses, and my needs. It could have been easy for you to learn more about me. It just would have taken a little time and understanding.

I have a son now, who I love very much, and what I want more than anything is for him to give me the chance, as he grows up, to just listen to him, not judge or give advice, to just listen. I have to move on from the pain of my childhood, because of the love and closeness I want with my wife and my son. It must be sad to have your son give up on you emotionally and I am sorry for that, but I cannot continue to allow my past and present emotions and frustrations to control me and keep me from being who I wish to become. I hope you find your peace too.

Dear Son,

I have been thinking a lot about what you wrote, and I have to admit that it hurts. Mostly it hurts because I realize the truth in what you say. I don't know anything about you or my other children. I have become an isolated and lonely man, old before my time. All that I can say is that I really didn't know any better. That was what I learned from my parents and that is what I taught you. I remember beating you up when you didn't do what I wanted and being blind to your tears, until you finally stopped crying. I couldn't stand seeing your weakness. I wanted you to become tough, like me. A man's man. Hard but empty inside.

I wish it had been different and that there could have been a relationship between us. Or that I could have at least listened and been there some of the time when you needed me. I didn't understand what it meant to be a father. Your letter is really the closest thing to a clue that I've ever had.

I know you can't forget the past, but I wish you would understand that to the best of my ability I did love you, and I do care now. I am proud and relieved that you are leaving the

violence behind and are going to make your family now different from what it was when you were the child. If there is some
way I can make amends, let me know and I will do whatever I
can.

Your Dad

7. Spend some time taking care of the child inside you as if
you are the child's parent. As the adult you are now, access
your most nurturing parts and hold the child you were, play
with him, take him for walks in the sunshine, or run and laugh
together.

Elaine grew up in a home in which she felt a lot of bitterness and tension on a daily basis. The eldest of eight children,
Elaine had never learned how to simply play because she was
always responsible for the younger children. When the other
children played, her role was to watch them, and watch them
she did. Consequently, she became an observer of life rather
than a participant, so much so that she didn't even realize how
much she was missing.

When Elaine was an adult, she went through the process
of grieving for the child that was inside her that never had a
chance to be a child. After that, however, she decided that she
would give the child a chance to do the things she had watched
others do. In simple ways, she began to parent herself. She
began slowly, by buying some watercolors to create childlike
paintings of flowers and houses and trees, in bright colors or
even the "wrong" colors if she felt like it. She began to take the
time to taste her food and relish in the flavors, something she
had never been able to do because she was so busy taking care
of others. She found a stuffed animal that she would normally
have given to someone else and kept it for her own. She spent a
day at the beach playing in the sand, laughing as she ran from
the waves, exhilarated that she did not have to worry about
anyone's safety but her own. All of these were small but important steps to Elaine, because she had lost that part of herself so
long ago, and, with that part of her, much of her passion and
joy for living.

Choose several things from the list below that you used to love to do as a child, that you could allow yourself to do now. Next choose several things you think you might enjoy doing that you watched others do and wished you could have done. Do this exercise for pleasure, not to prove anything, in whatever time frame works best for you. These activities can be done alone or with a supportive friend.

Make yourself a snack and relish it.

Wear clothing you're comfortable in.

Fix your hair the way you want to.

Laugh aloud.

Do a jigsaw puzzle.

Do a crossword puzzle.

Read fairy tales.

Sing in the shower.

Take a bath with bubbles, toys, or soap paints.

Sit in a hot tub.

Make yourself hot chocolate.

Wrap yourself in an afghan.

Write a story or a poem.

Be with a pet.

Play with a ball.

Play hopscotch.

Jump rope.

Flip cards.

Go roller skating.

Go bowling.

Play pinball machines.

Play chopsticks on the piano.

Play the guitar and sing folk songs.

Trade baseball cards.

Take a walk.

Explore, for no special reason.

Sing a song.

Take a nap.

Go to the country.

Be with a friend.

Buy something special for yourself.

Make a painting.

Sketch or doodle.

Make something out of clay.

Rearrange your room.

Go boating.

Watch something light on TV.

Read a book.

Spend time in the garden.

Go dancing.

Dance in your living room.

Sit in the sun.

Just sit and think.

Watch people.

Begin a project.

Play a board game or cards with friends or children.

Make a snowman or throw snowballs.

Sit by a fire and dream.

Go fishing or clamming.

Go on a hike.

Listen to music.

Run, jog, or skip.

Take a bike ride.
Visit a museum.
Walk barefoot by the water.
Play Frisbee with a friend.
Go horseback riding.
Talk on the phone.
Daydream.
Kick leaves, sand, or pebbles.
Go see a light or emotionally satisfying movie.
Rent a light or emotionally satisfying movie.
Get closer to your religious or spiritual beliefs and values.
Help someone.
Go to the mountains.
Listen to the sounds of nature.
Make up a song.
Bake something and give it away or share it.
Gaze at the moon or the stars.
Talk about your interests to people who are supportive.
Express your love to someone.
Make a card for yourself.
Make a card for someone you love.
Go to the library.
Watch birds.
Go to a fair, carnival, circus, zoo, or amusement park.
Make a new friend.
Read the funnies or humorous books.
Play racketball, tennis, or Ping-Pong.
Play checkers or chess.

Start a stamp, doll, or coin collection.
Do things with children, pretending you're a child.
Collect things at the beach.
Go to garage sales.
Water ski, surf, scuba dive.
Do a project in your own way.
Cry and then comfort yourself.
Give a party (don't do the cooking unless you love to).
Get up early and watch the sun rise.
Walk out in the rain.
Write in a diary.
Learn to do something new.
Visit a friend.
Get a massage.
Get a hug.
Have a picnic in the park.
Read magazines.
Sleep in late.
Buy something at a toy store that you've always wished for.
Buy a dollhouse.
Buy a doll.
Buy a cuddly stuffed animal.
Do scientific experiments.
Go swimming.
Read a children's book.
Make a sand castle.

_____

_____

_____

_____

_____

8. Recall past times in your life when you were cared for. Most likely there was someone, even if it was not a parent, who nurtured you and made you feel special. Go back into your past and scan for times in your life when you felt you were loved or lovable.

Kelly remembered a special birthday at her grandma's when she was about five. She remembered just being with her grandma and her grandma making her special pancakes with syrup and powdered sugar. She recalled her grandma making her a bubble bath and putting on nice music for her to listen to. Afterward, her grandma wrapped her up in a great big soft bath towel and dried her off. Then she gave her a great big powder puff with white powder that she let Kelly use. She remembered being tucked in and sung to sleep in her grandma's big bed, feeling her grandma's voice and love surround her. This memory was a place Kelly could go to and realize that she had not been a bad child and that she was entitled at least sometimes to be treated in a special way. She could take this memory and relive it as often as she wanted to and receive the warmth and good feeling it brought to her.

9. Remember the list of one woman's negative internal voices in Chapter Five? If you listen, you will probably find many similar voices going on in your own mind. Some common messages are: "You are stupid, rotten, ugly, deformed, lazy, or selfish." Our negative feelings about ourselves are often a direct response to these negative messages, which we received, not necessarily verbally, as children. Often we don't pay attention to these voices. We just feel hopeless and depressed and can't tell exactly why.

Cognitive therapy shows one way to deal with these voices. This approach involves responding to the irrational statements we hear with rational statements. When we respond rationally to the negative statements about ourselves, the distortion dissolves and our positive parts become apparent. Our feelings of self-worth improve as we reduce the power of the negative messages. Then the innocent child we were becomes visible.

The following example demonstrates the negative effects of these voices and demonstrates countering them by responding to their irrational judgments with rational statements. Use this method next time you feel overwhelmed by negative thoughts about yourself. It will help you free your inner child from the negativity and hopelessness that follow these messages and also help you deal with the situation at hand effectively.

Jon, age thirty-five, was angry, depressed, and discouraged because he had been laid off from his job in the banking industry after working there for eleven years. He was furious at their treatment of him, but deep down felt that he deserved to be let go and they had only kept him as long as they had because they hadn't noticed his incompetency. The negative messages from his parents (you're not as good as your brother; you don't do anything right; how can you be so stupid; you'll never make it) were getting louder daily as the actual laying off at the bank validated Jon's beliefs about himself. Here is how a typical negative cycle would go for Jon:

An event would happen which objectively was neither negative nor positive in itself. Here the event was getting laid off. In this case, Jon was actually much more interested in international affairs than banking and had mainly chosen banking because he was modeling himself after his father who had been in banking for most of his life. Being laid off actually turned out to be positive for Jon, as it ultimately allowed him to get work in an area that he loved and that suited him.

After an event happened, Jon would automatically make a judgment about the meaning of the event. In this case, loss of a job evoked in Jon fleeting pictures of times in the past when he felt he had failed. These images were followed by negative words from the past. Jon's voices said:

- You can't do anything right.
- You never were any good.
- Your brother would never have gotten fired.
- You're lucky they ever hired you at all.
- You'll never get anyone to take you on—you can't fool everyone.
- You're a failure.
- You've always been a failure.
- You're doomed to always fail.

Notice how black-and-white and toxic the voices are. They are uncompromising and global. Feelings of worthlessness, depression, humiliation, fear, and anxiety are likely to be generated from a barrage like this. These feelings do not surface in response to the present event alone. They are in response to going back in time and reconstructing all of the negative criticisms from childhood, dragging up all the mistakes of the past, and projecting them into the not foreseeable future as if they have actually happened. The problem then becomes how to fight these destructive voices that you can barely consciously hear, that are based on pictures you are barely able to see.

Let's finish this process and see where it leads. Then we'll go through the same cycle again, but this time in a far more effective way. The way Jon responds to the negative voices is to feel anxious and upset. What this creates is stress, a primitive reaction of your body to danger. In primitive times, if attacked by an animal, your body would go into the flight-or-fight response, bringing your blood into your arms so you could fight or into your legs so you could run. Unfortunately, that didn't leave a lot of blood in your brain where you needed it to figure out how to solve the problem at hand.

At the first sign of attack, people are likely to go into the defense mode they learned when they were small by watching the grownups around them. Some ways Jon might react, when he learned he was being let go, might be to act aggressively at work, threaten people, or make a scene. He could withdraw by turning inward and becoming depressed, drinking his troubles away, or leaving that part of the country. The purpose of whatever action he takes at this point, however, is not to solve the problem at hand but simply to relieve the stress. Unfortunately, the original problem still remains and Jon now has new negative feelings about himself to reinforce the old ones from his past.

The trick to dealing with reacting blindly rather than responding rationally hinges on stopping yourself at the point the pictures are flashing and the negative voices are triggered in your head. Right at the beginning, you can stop and realize that the pictures and words are an exaggeration and that these are the same voices that you hear over and over. You can remember that they will lead to a negative stress cycle that will make you feel terrible and will not help you get your needs met or solve the problem at hand. The negative words can be written down and replaced with realistic statements that make sense in the current circumstances. Then you will have the positive energy you need to handle what you need to.

Here is how Jon changed his messages to be realistic and nondestructive to his sense of self:

- "You can't do anything right" was changed to "Sometimes I do things ineffectively, but often what I do turns out quite well."
- "You never were any good" was changed to "I'm not perfect, but I'm human and have goodness in me just as anyone else."
- "Your brother would never have gotten fired" was changed to "I'm not my brother, and I'm not in competition with him. He has his own problems, anyway."
- "You're lucky they ever hired you at all" was changed to "I've done at least an adequate job for eleven years, and they are lucky to have had me there. I was responsible and hardworking and made a lot of money for them at

the bank. I probably would have done an even better job if this had been work of my own inclination and choosing, but since it wasn't I showed a lot of discipline and perseverance in staying and doing the best I could."

- "You'll never get anyone to take you on—you can't fool everyone" was changed to "Some people may not hire me; I'm not perfect. But there are many jobs in which I will be an asset to the company and if I am true to myself about doing what I feel is significant and meaningful to me I won't need to fool anyone about my attitude and intentions."

- "You're a failure" was changed to "I've made mistakes; that's the only way to learn."

- "You've always been a failure" was changed to "I have definitely made mistakes and failed in accomplishing some things, but I have also been successful in many areas."

- "You're doomed to always fail" was changed to "Not true. Some failure is part of living, and that's fine. It's only through failing that you can eliminate things that don't work for you. That's when it's important to go on, and not get permanently discouraged."

As a result of these new statements, Jon went beyond his depression, anger, and anxiety. Instead he felt accepting of the past events and himself, and curious about how he could use this experience in a positive way. He became more in contact with his inner core and used the child's natural wisdom and energy to find out how he could create what he wanted in his life. This took time and effort, but he was eventually successful in finding a career in a field that was in harmony with his values and interests.

10. Art can be one of the most powerful ways to heal yourself and move on. Through art you can process your feelings as they change and you can also create change in your

drawings that will help you progress. You could do a drawing, for example, of being trapped in a cage, if that was how you felt. In your next drawing, you could create an opening in the cage, a person to let you out, you could shrink yourself, enlarge the openings, or do anything you liked to free yourself. You can then use your drawings as a blueprint for attaining your freedom.

Visualize the following progressive drawings which show the progression from the initial realization of how a childhood trauma felt to creating a way out of the trauma for the child:

- One person drew a series she called "Unholy Trinity." In the first drawing, she has drawn the child nailed onto a cross, her father's hand clutching a bottle and her mother sitting and doing nothing. The person continued this process by next drawing her father inside the liquor bottle which she corked up; then creating another drawing with the child off the cross and being cared for by her mother.
- Another person drew a child curled up and trying to cover his ears to not hear his mother's anger and tears. In the next drawing he shows the mother being taken care of so she does not have to continue hurting the child.
- One series showed a child suffocating under her overweight mother. In subsequent drawings, the child becomes larger, stronger, and more confident, and the mother deflates so she can be pushed off the child and the child can breathe freely.
- In another group of progressive drawings, the child is drawn inside a bag hanging down from the ceiling by a rope and her father, a mask over his head, stands next to her with a club. In subsequent drawings her father beats his own rage and pain, instead of his daughter, with his club. He then takes off his mask, showing his humanness. The child cuts her way out to freedom.

Doing progressive drawings can help immeasurably in defining and working through the process of freeing your inner child. *Caution: Your drawings may evoke images that are extremely potent. Keep working with them until you have shifted the images enough to create some safety for the child.*

RECOMMENDED READING

Homecoming, John Bradshaw
Outgrowing the Pain, Eliana Gil
After the Tears, Jane Middleton-Motz
Repeat After Me, Claudia Black

CHAPTER TEN

Nurturing and Effective Parenting

The family is formed not for the survival of the fittest but for the weakest. It is not an economic unit but an emotional one. This is not the place where people ruthlessly compete with each other but where they work for each other. Its business is taking care, and when it works, it is not callous but kind.

ELLEN GOODMAN, in *The Boston Globe*

Here I will present one way to parent which has worked for me and my family. I would like you to try this method as if you were a child in a home where the parents used the methods that are described. In this parenting approach parents share with their children honestly, listen to their children's ideas and feelings, and work with them in a loving and respectful way to resolve conflicts or differences. The exercises which follow will help you determine whether you would feel differently about yourself now had the people in your home used this model. They will also help you consider if your children would have felt and acted differently had they grown up in a home where things were handled using this model.

The purposes of this chapter are:

- To give you the chance to go back in time and see how it would have felt to have had people respond to you in a way that creates high self-esteem and integrity in children.

- To give you concrete skills to use with your adult children when you approach them.

The parenting methods presented here are based on principles that have been expressed by many people, especially Dr. Carl Rogers, who created Person-Centered Therapy; Dr. Thomas Gordon, founder of Effectiveness Training, Inc.; and Dr. Haim G. Ginott, child psychologist and author of *Between Parent and Child*. I have adapted their ideas in ways that have worked for me. Learning to use new methods instead of old patterns takes effort on the part of parents, but the results of these changes are visible in their own growth and in the improved relationships they have with their children and with others.

Throughout this chapter, when examples are provided, be the child, not the parent.

An interaction with my daughter, Kira, who was three years old at the time and is at this writing seventeen, demonstrates use of some of these skills. (Be Kira in this example, not me.) We had taken a winter weekend vacation at a hotel that had a built-in pool with a spa. It was pretty cold, so we were using only the spa. Kira, however, wanted to go into the pool, which was not heated. Like most parents, perhaps, I told her "No. You can't go in, because it's too cold." Kira, not being a very aggressive child, merely left the spa in tears and went back into the room wrapped in a towel and lots of unhappiness. I followed and tried to explain (adults know so much more than kids about these things) that if you get chilled you can get sick and that there was a good reason for not going into the cold water. At which point Kira stated directly (some might say impudently, but she was telling the truth, which we say we want our kids to do) that she wasn't sick, but I was. Sure enough, there I was caught in the act of coughing, sneezing, and looking pretty bad.

I stopped for a moment and remembered all the times my mother had overprotected me and prevented me from skating or playing in the snow because I might get sick and die. I realized then that I was repeating my mother's actions instead of looking at the current situation. I thought that this would be a good time to stop reenacting my childhood drama, and instead to be in the present with my daughter. "Tell me what your idea was if you want to, Kira," I said. "I just want to go in for a minute, and then I'll go right back in the hot water. I won't get cold. You'll see," she said. Well, I agreed, and she went into the pool laughing and happy for a couple of minutes and then back into the spa and she never did get sick. What she learned was to trust her own sense of things and not to be afraid. This was an invaluable lesson and one that many of us never learn. The worst that could have happened was that she would have gotten a cold. Then she could have decided if the swim had been worth the cold. Of course if there had been real danger involved it wouldn't have worked out as easily. But most things can be worked out, if you are willing to listen and be honest with yourself.

There are three main skills that are the keys to being an effective parent when a problem arises. These are: *listening, self-disclosing,* and *resolving conflicts*. When there is no problem people can do what they usually do, like laughing, playing, working, or loving. If family members are not hurting themselves or anyone else, they are simply expressing their unique styles. What a family does is up to the individual members. Unfortunately, in many families, problems never get resolved and tension continually pervades the home. Follow the sections below so you can experience what it would have been like to have been in a family where these principles were applied.

LISTENING

Effective listening is putting your current feelings aside to hear how someone else is feeling at that moment. You have to feel supportive of the person you are with to do this well, and to care about how the person is feeling right then more than you care about how you feel right then. You need at least to feel capable of waiting before you express your own feelings. On a deeper level, it involves referencing the part of you that has felt similar feelings to the person you are listening to, shifting to his situation, and being able to convey clearly to the person that you understand his experience.

For example, if a teenager tried to talk to her dad about how upset she was that her boyfriend had broken up with her, it would work best if her dad refrained from giving her advice or reassuring her that she is a great kid and better off without the jerk. It would be most helpful to her if her dad listened to her instead and gave her the chance to express herself. One of the most important parts of listening is patience and silence.

While his daughter is talking, her dad will have a minute or two to search his own life and to access times he was rejected, perhaps by a friend, on a job, or in some other way, so he can remember how it felt to be in that position. He probably felt hurt, pain, self-doubt, anger, humiliation, or all of these. Accessing his feelings may be difficult for him if he is used to denying his feelings and acting as if feelings don't matter, as many of us do to protect ourselves. But it is possible to penetrate the surface and locate the feelings. What the dad would do next is to let his daughter know, by his words and demeanor (but *not* by talking about his experiences, which draws the focus back to him) what he guesses she must feel. In words, he could say something like, "It hurts to be rejected, doesn't it?" or "You must be furious at him," or anything that shares his understanding of how she feels, so that she does not feel alone. If he is wrong she will correct him and they can continue talking. If he is right, she will breathe a sigh of relief, knowing that she may have lost a boyfriend but she still has her dad.

Read the following example as if you are the child rather than the parent:

You are four years old and your toy which you have been happily enjoying has just gotten stuck under the couch where you can't reach it. Your lips turn down and tears rush to your eyes as you try to get your short arms under the couch but all you end up doing is pushing the toy even farther away. You whimper for a while but no one hears you so you start to howl and when no one comes you begin to get so frustrated you can hardly stand it. It feels like you will never have your toy again. Finally, your father comes into the room. At this point he can be either positive and supportive, saying things like, "Uh-oh, looks like you're having troubles. Something stuck under there?" which will probably make you feel somewhat better. "Someone understands. Maybe he'll help," you think, relieved. Once your father figures out the problem, he can get your toy out, since he has longer arms and the strength to move the couch. Or he'll come in and say, "Cut out that damn noise, you brat," leaving you just as frustrated as before at not getting your toy and now also frustrated at being misunderstood. Now it's in your ball park. If you've been exposed to a lot of aggression, you may react aggressively, both because you are more frustrated now than you were before and because that is the way things are resolved in your family. If you are very afraid of your father, however, you will probably choose a different route. You will cower, or be still, obeying your father's message. What have you learned in this second scenario, which will be repeated thousands of times before you reach adolescence? Here are some probable lessons:

- Bigger, stronger people have more rights than smaller, weaker people.
- My needs and wishes are unimportant.
- I'm in the way.
- I'm something bad (whatever brat means).
- There's no point trying to get help when I need it.
- Problems don't get worked out.
- My daddy doesn't care about me.
- I'd better keep quiet.
- I have to yell louder and louder to get what I need.
- I can't depend on other people.

You would have learned some heavy lessons, and if Dad was alcoholic or more abusive you would have learned even heavier ones.

By contrast, in the first scenario, where the father retrieves the toy, you would have learned:

- My needs are important.
- My dad cares about me.
- People listen to other people when they have problems.
- Problems can be solved.
- I can communicate and be understood.
- My dad is someone I can trust and depend upon. Big, strong people take the time to help smaller, weaker people.
- When I get big I can help smaller people.
- I'm a worthwhile person.
- It's okay for me to share my feelings with others.

This is a very different way to go out into the world. With these lessons learned, you would feel confident and caring, and that the problems you encountered could be dealt with in ways that work.

I can't say enough about how important stopping and listening is in order to find out what is really going on. One child cried and cried at night and his mom ignored him as she had been told, so she wouldn't spoil him. When she learned about listening it occurred to her that the crying might mean something important. She finally took him to a pediatrician who discovered he had a congenital hip problem. This was the reason he could not get comfortable at night.

Teenagers complain over and over again that their parents don't listen. At a presentation for parents and teens at a church, we had everyone close their eyes and we asked the parents how many thought they really listened to their teenagers. About half of the parents raised their hands. When we asked the teens how many felt their parents listened, not a single hand was raised. This was a middle-class, average group of people.

In therapy, people invariably are brought to tears when they are truly listened to and understood. Our inner voices have become private and shielded because we have been ignored, shouted down, or misunderstood, often and consistently. It doesn't have to continue.

There will be more examples of listening as we go on in this book. It will be crucial for you to be able to use this skill when you talk to your adult children.

EXERCISES

Think of a time in your childhood when you had a difficult problem you couldn't take care of by yourself, and there was no one there to help you. Write down the details of this problem and how you felt at the time.

_____

_____

_____

_____

What did you do to survive? What lessons did you learn when you found out that you couldn't count on adults to help you?

_____

_____

_____

_____

Now think of the same problem, but imagine someone being there with you and listening to you—listening with their heart as well as their head. How does it feel to be heard and understood?

_____

_____

_____

_____

Imagine them helping you now, either by showing you how to deal with the problem, helping you handle it, or, if it was too big a problem for you to handle at all, taking care of it for you. How does it feel to be supported in this way?

_____

_____

_____

_____

How might you have been different if people had been there for you in the way you needed?

_____

_____

_____

_____

SELF-DISCLOSING

The second skill which is required for effective communication is self-disclosure, which is a specific kind of openness. It means describing what is real for you and sharing it. This kind of disclosure allows your deeper thoughts and feelings to be visible to another person, which tends to make you vulnerable but also makes you very human and real. Most people respond favorably to self-disclosure, because they can identify with your feelings, especially if your body language, facial expression, and voice match your words.

Figuring out what you are trying to disclose can be difficult, because feelings are not always simple and we often have to deal with ambivalent feelings: yes, we feel glad, but part of us feels scared. It is important to convey the entire message.

Finding out what your feelings really are can take some work. Some people suggest focusing on your bodily state, so that you can identify the tension or sadness or anger within you. Others say to trust your intuition, or your heart. These are excellent ideas, and work well, especially if your reference for feelings is reliable, that is, if you grew up in a family in which you learned how normal feelings work. If you grew up in a dysfunctional family, however, unraveling feelings is usually more complex. Sometimes people who have experienced a lot of pain become so used to it that they consider being in pain a normal state. Then if someone victimizes them they do not even realize that they are being treated badly, because it doesn't feel bad to be hurt; it feels normal and familiar. They have dissociated from their pain, and are not conscious of the hurt. Other people become extremely sensitive to pain and get upset about anything that triggers the old wounds. Sometimes people shift from being dissociated to being hypersensitive, which makes their current feelings even more difficult to sort out.

Our references for people and experiences are based on our pasts. The map we make of the world limits our perception of the world and our original map goes back to early childhood. As we become more knowledgeable about our childhoods and about how we have learned to react, we can reconstruct our maps to match our current worlds. We will then have more appropriate responses to the present. If you have been doing the work in this book, much of your life has come to consciousness, where it needs to be in order to know what your map of the world was. As unfinished business gets completed you can see and feel things in the current day to day more clearly and you can disentangle the past from the present. You can then continue to adjust your map as your life changes. You will be able to work on your present relationships and when you find yourself overreacting you will be able to trace the triggers that have pulled you into the past.

Another complication in self-disclosure is that people often only share their more surface emotions such as anger and resentment. Unfortunately, when they share anger they often receive anger back because anger tends to be taken as an attack. Self-disclosure works a lot better if the feelings underneath anger, such as fear, hurt, confusion, humiliation, disappointment, loneliness, or helplessness are shared rather than anger. These feelings are nonthreatening and deeper. They are likely to elicit compassion and the desire to help.

In order to self-disclose you just need to express what you are feeling at the moment, including your ambivalence or uncertainty if they are present. If it is difficult for you to talk about your feelings, let the other person know that. If you want a specific response (to be listened to, for example) tell that person so he'll know what you want from him. If you are hesitant about talking because you are worried about how the other person will respond, say so. If your feelings are confused and you need the other person to be patient and allow you time to sort them out, tell him that.

These are the times to share your inner feelings with someone else:

- When you are close to someone and you want him to know more about you.
- When you need to talk to someone about your inner thoughts and feelings and there is someone you can trust available.
- When you have positive feelings toward someone and want to let him know that you appreciate or value him.
- When you are connected to someone but you have a barrier that needs to be taken down.
- When someone's actions are directly interfering with your needs being met.

In the following example, the mom begins to self-disclose to her child, but realizes that listening is called for too. Notice how the dialogue below leads to an easy resolution of the problem.

Pretend you are the child in this scene:

You are six years old and you just came in from playing outside. You brought in dirt on your feet and there is now a trail of brown mud behind you on your parent's carpet. You knew you were supposed to take your boots off outside but you just got into a fight with someone and you are upset and having a hard time keeping from crying. Your mom comes in and sees the dirt.

What would your mother actually have done?

_____

_____

_____

_____

Many parents would either hit their child, yell at them, or punish them by taking away privileges. They would shame them and the child would feel bad, selfish, and inconsiderate. And the sad thing is, hitting, yelling, and other punishment techniques don't even work. If they did they wouldn't have to be repeated over and over and over again.

Imagine now that you have walked into the room. Your mother sees you and is horrified at the mess you are making over the carpet. However, she takes a few seconds to breathe while she stops you from walking any farther. She remembers quickly her mother's reaction, yelling at her, face ugly and accusing. Then she self-discloses. "It's really hard to clean mud off the floor when I've been working hard all day. It just feels like too much sometimes," she says. "Sorry," you say. "I forgot." Your mom says, "How come . . . ?" but her words trail off because she realizes how unhappy you look. "Did something happen outside?" she asks, and you begin to cry and tell her about your problem outside with your friends. She listens and lets you know that she understands how mean kids can be sometimes. You let out a sigh of relief, then feel guilty about the floor. "I'm sorry," you repeat again, this time meaning it. "That's okay," she says, "we all make mistakes. Let's just take care of it so it doesn't muck up the whole carpet. Okay?" "Okay," you say, and you work together for a few minutes to correct a mistake that, really, anyone could have made, not only a child.

How would you have felt if you were the child in this circumstance?

_____

_____

_____

_____

How would your children have felt if they were treated in this way?

_____

_____

_____

_____

CONFLICT RESOLUTION

Common Ground: A Friendship Model for Resolving Conflicts

Resolving conflicts can be extremely difficult if people do not agree to some basic guidelines. I've called the model below *Common Ground* because you will be finding a solution which encompasses the common ground that you can all live with. It is the kind of model you probably use naturally with your friends, and so it is also a *friendship model*. This model has six steps for creating acceptable resolutions to many relationship conflicts. Each step does not have to be followed each time you have a conflict and sometimes the entire process can be done verbally. A form outlining these steps is at the end of this chapter. Feel free to copy and use it with your family.

Step 1. Set the tone: Express your intention and determination to make sure that *all* the people involved in the conflict feel good about:

- Themselves and each other
- Their relationship
- Their ability to work things out together
- The solution(s) decided upon

Step 2. Identify and list those things that are important to each individual.

Step 3. Use everyone's *creative energy* to come up with a list of possible solutions. Don't critique solutions initially because criticism inhibits creativity. List your solutions. Write down "Leave it as it is" as one solution.

Step 4. Cross out any solutions that *anyone* feels are unacceptable to him.

Step 5. Choose a solution or combination of solutions from the ones that remain, after discussing them. If you wish to, give yourself another alternative in case the first solution does not work. (First we'll try this, and if this doesn't work, we'll try that.)

Step 6. Imagine how the solution or solutions you have decided upon will work out in reality. Figure out what it will take to follow through on the solutions. Try to straighten out any foreseeable problems in advance. Check with each person to make sure he understands what he is agreeing to and that he is comfortable with this solution. The solution does not have to be perfect: It just needs to be *acceptable* to all those involved. If it is not, someone will end up feeling as if they've lost and not carry out their end, or do so with resentment.

When you actually implement your new agreements, you

may find a problem you did not predict before. That's fine. If you have created a backup solution, you are prepared. If not, go through the process again. Save your original ideas. It's usually easier the second time, and definitely doesn't take nearly as long as arguing about the issues over and over.

Pretend you are the daughter in the following scene, and learn from your dad how to go through this process. See if you can identify the skills used as the scene unfolds.

You are thirteen and you are really into popular music. You also like to listen to it at its loudest volume. Your dad keeps yelling at you to turn the damn thing down and when that doesn't work he says he'll throw it out if you can't be more considerate. You know he probably won't do anything and you figure it's worth the possible consequences to listen to the music the way you want to, so you turn it down temporarily but turn it up again in a few minutes.

Your dad decides to approach you in a different way this time. He knocks, comes into your room, and says gently, "I'm having a problem and I need your help. Would you please spend a few minutes with me now?"

You roll your eyes, expecting a lecture, but you shrug your shoulders and say, "Sure . . . what is it?" You figure you'd better turn off the stereo, so you do.

Your dad sits down with you and says, "Y'know, I guess music is really important to you, but when you play it so loud I can't concentrate on other things I need to do. Also, it hurts my ears and affects my mood. I wonder if there's something we could do that would make this house comfortable for both of us?"

You don't exactly understand what he's driving at, so you say, "I guess."

Then he asks you for some paper and a pen and shows you the idea of conflict resolution that he's learned from his business or his counselor or somewhere. "This is different," your dad says. "It's a way of dealing with things so we both feel good about the results . . . so no one feels like they've lost . . . ." You don't know what you're supposed to say so you just wait.

"Well, the first thing we're supposed to do in this approach is to figure out what things are really important to each of us, so we can figure out ways for both of us to get them."

You start to get the idea that this is going to take awhile. "Dad, this sounds complicated. Is it going to take very long?" you ask.

"Probably," your dad says, "but it'll be worth it if we straighten this out so we both feel good about the solution, don't you think?"

"I guess," you say, unconvinced.

"It'll be okay, honestly," he insists, and he looks so hopeful and sincere you decide to go along with it for awhile.

"Okay, hon, the first thing we're supposed to do is to keep in mind that it's important for us to feel good about ourselves and each other; to have a good relationship, to feel good about working together, and to feel okay about our final solutions. Know what I mean?"

"I'm not sure," you say.

"Well, if these things are what's really important to us, we won't be so concerned with having to be right or getting our way. You'll see. It'll make a difference. I'll write them down—okay?"

"Sure," you say. It's almost starting to make sense to you.

Your dad writes down:

What's important to both of us

> To feel good about ourselves and each other.
> To have a good relationship.
> To know we can work things out together.
> To know that we're both okay with the solutions we agree on.

"The next thing we're supposed to do," your dad says, "is to write down what's important to each of us. We have to figure out what really is important. We might think having a big-screen TV is important, but it may not be *that* important to us. Especially if we don't have a lot of extra money. What may actually be important is to have something interesting to do. There'd be lots of less expensive ways to do that. Right?"

". . . I guess," you say, sort of getting the idea.

"In the problem between us, what is important to me is to feel relaxed at home and not to have my ears hurt. I'll write that down, okay?"

"I guess," you say.

What's important to Dad

> To feel relaxed at home.
> To not have his ears hurt.

"So, what do you think is important to you?" your dad asks when he's finished. "I'm not sure," you say. "I don't know exactly what you mean."

"Well, let's try to find out. How come you like to have the music so loud?"

"Mmmmm . . . I don't know exactly. It jazzes me up, puts me in a good mood, cuts out everything else." You think about it some more. "My music has to be loud so I can feel the beat. Sometimes the words are good too. You ought to listen to them sometime."

"I'd like to," your dad says, "Music was important to me at one time, too. Let's list what's important to you now though and maybe listening together can be one of our solutions."

What's important to me

> To be in a "jazzed" mood.
> To be in my own world.
> To not have to think.
> To feel the beat.

"Is that it?"
"Yes," you say. "Now what?"

"Well, the next step is to think up ideas. Just say anything that comes to mind, and we won't talk about them until later. At the end either of us can wipe out anything that we feel is unacceptable, that is, any solutions where we feel we will be upset if that solution is picked. Get it?"

"Maybe I'll get it as we go," you say. "It sounds confusing."

"Okay, let's try it." your dad says, and you and your dad begin to come up with ideas of how to solve the problem. Here's the list you come up with:

1. Everyone get into the music.
2. Turn it up for just part of the time, so there's quiet time too.
3. Use headphones past a certain decibel.
4. Dad listen to his kind of music on headphones.
5. Get a heavier door on your room.
6. Add a door to the living room.
7. Get a white-noise tape to counteract the sounds.
8. Have a signal that gets results when it's too loud.
9. Dad wear ear plugs.
10. Throw out the stereo.
11. Throw out Dad.
12. Move out.
13. Listen to it loud after school only before Dad gets home.
14. Dad learn to ignore music some of the time.
15. Dad learn to enjoy music.
16. You find other ways to escape, like drawing, talking on phone more.
17. Have more time together so family time becomes more fun.
18. Have friends over more.
19. Learn to enjoy the music at a lower volume.
20. Leave things the way they are: Dad getting upset, yelling, and no change happening.

"Now is when we cross out anything that we can't live with," your dad says. "If the solution isn't going to be okay with you, or me, we can cross it out. Let's go through them together."

Between you, you cross out number 6 because your dad says he can't easily add a door because the doorway is too wide and he didn't think your mom would go for it. Dad listening to his kind of music on earphones, number 4, and wearing earplugs, number 9, go, too. You cross out throw out stereo, number 10, and your dad decides he wants to stay, and crosses out number 11. You both cross out your moving out and you cross out listening only when Dad's not home, number 13. Finding something else, number 16, seems silly to you. Your dad crosses out leave things the way they are, number 20, and you agree things aren't great the way they are.

"Now we're supposed to choose from the ones that are left. They can be combinations of several, or however we want to do it. And we can have a backup plan if the first solutions don't work. It's our decision, together."

After a lot of talking back and forth and figuring pros and cons, you decide on the following actions:

- You agree to listen to your stereo at a reduced volume when your dad is home. "Sometimes I turn it up just to annoy you," you admit to your dad, kind of shame-facedly. "Well, maybe I deserve it sometimes," your dad says. "Maybe if we were closer and did things together and talked sometimes you wouldn't feel resentful toward me."
- Your dad agrees to be more understanding of the importance of the music and be more tolerant of the loud noise . . . to think of the sounds as a reminder that you are there and that you are special to him.
- If your dad needs to concentrate on something particular and the stereo is up too loud, he agrees to come into your room and ask you to please turn it down and to let you know how long it needs to be low.

- You agree to spend time together when you can share some of your music with your dad.
- You decide that you want to get to know each other better and plan to have other times talking to each other or doing things together.

As an alternative solution, if these don't work, your dad offers to look into putting a solid core door on your room. They're not real expensive and that way you'd have more privacy too.

You then go through these solutions in your imagination and think about whether or not these steps will work. Your dad says you're supposed to take out any parts you think won't work after all. You realize that sometimes you want to turn the stereo up high and you add one more solution:

- When you *really* feel like turning it up you will either check with your dad first or if you haven't and it's bothering him he'll let you know and you'll turn it down and keep it down. If this is a continuing problem you'll talk about this again.

You then set up a time to get together to listen to music. Your dad says that if these solutions don't work out it just means you need to try another solution, not that anyone's bad or wrong. It sounds good to you, and you actually look forward to trying all this out.

What are your thoughts about using this process, which is used in varying forms in business and professional workshops all the time?

_____

_____

_____

How did your dad or mom handle conflicts in your family?

_____

How do you think you would have felt as a child if your dad or mom had worked things out with you in this way?

MORE COMPLEX ISSUES

Conflict resolution generally does not work when parents disapprove of a behavior of their child which does not concretely affect his parents. The parents may believe that the child's behavior is having a negative affect on the child and that it would be in the child's best interest for the child to change. However, often the child does not have the same belief.

In some conflicts which arise in this area, parents try to change their child because they have unresolved issues of their own which are being projected onto the child. The parents may be interfering in or trying to control their child's life because of their own difficulty with allowing the child freedom and independence. They may be relating their own self-worth to their child's appearance and behavior, and trying to mold the child in a way that "looks good." The child's behavior may be activating unfinished problems from the parents' own past, and they may be inadvertently trying to resolve their own issues through the child. In these cases, the parents' issues need to be sorted out and handled by the parents individually, without involving the child.

When parents are genuinely concerned about their child's welfare, it is fine to let their child know about their concern in a sensitive and clear way. The parents will need to tell their child why they are concerned and to listen to the child's feelings.

This is different from nagging the child. It is easiest to communicate if the parent and child initially make an agreement to listen to each other's point of view. This is most likely to happen if the parent talks to the child respectfully and does not come across patronizing.

If what the parent is saying makes sense to the child, he may change his behavior because he feels he has learned something valuable. Sometimes he will change because, even though he doesn't fully understand his parent, he respects and values his parent's opinion. Other times he will listen but decide he needs to learn by his own experience, which is a legitimate way to learn, even though it can be costly. Parents cannot always protect their children from pain or harm. Parents who are overprotective actually cause their children harm because they do not give their children the chance to learn how to protect themselves.

Usually when the child is doing something that is clearly self-destructive the behavior is a symptom of something underneath that needs to be addressed. In these instances, it would be negligence not to confront the behavior. It is very important to listen and share for as long as it takes to get to the real problems underneath. Professional help may be necessary. In the case of drug or alcohol addiction, there are some specific steps to take which you can learn in an Al-Anon or Narcanon group. Resources are listed in the next chapter.

As a result of the conversation below, because the mom is willing to listen and self-disclose about her own feelings after she expresses her concern, many family dynamics surface which would not have been dealt with if the child's behavior alone had been addressed. *Be the child in the following scene:*

You are fifteen years old and you have begun wearing provocative clothing and heavy makeup. You have also been cutting school, have been uncommunicative, hanging out with friends your mom doesn't approve of and she suspects that you have been abusing alcohol. Your mom is worried about you. She's been advised by her friends and the school to tighten the reins on you but since, like most adolescents, you simply lied and hid more things, she tries instead to understand how you're feeling.

Your mom starts: "Honey, I'd like to talk to you about some things that I know you're pretty sensitive about. In some ways it's not my business but I care a lot and I'm pretty worried about some of the ways you're acting and the things you are doing. Could we please talk for awhile?"

You figure here comes lecture time again and the last thing you want to do is listen to her talk about how impossible you are. "I'd really rather not," you say, in a tone that is meant to stop this from going any further.

"It's really important to me," your mom says. "I know I usually just lecture you, but that's not what I want to do this time. I just want to let you know that I am concerned and that I want to understand more about what you are going through."

"I'm not going through anything," you say. "How come you're interested in what I think all of a sudden, anyhow? You've got all the answers."

"I think I'm starting to realize that I don't have all the answers and that maybe I've been trying to tell you what to do without knowing anything about what I'm saying. I'm worried about the clothes you're wearing and I'm upset that you're cutting classes. I'm also concerned about your friends and the fact that you're drinking. I think you have a lot of potential and it's hard to see it go to waste."

"I hate it when you judge me," you tell your mom. "That's all you ever do, judge me and my friends."

"You think all I'm doing is judging you and putting you down?"

"You are. You wouldn't want me to go around judging all the things you do. I don't think much of them, you know."

"You don't?"

"No, all your phony friends and your phony world."

"I'm getting the idea of how bad it feels to be labeled and judged," your mom says quietly.

"Good," you say. "Cause that's how I feel all the time. Dad says I look like slime and that I'm a slut and you criticize everything I do. I'm tired of it."

"Sounds like you have a right to be tired of it," says your mom.

"I wish you'd just accept me," you say. "Just think that maybe I'm doing what I need to do for now. Stop making me feel like shit."

"I didn't realize I was hurting you so much," your mom says. "I was just thinking about how much you were hurting yourself."

"What do you mean, hurting myself?"

"Well, not going to school, drinking, the friends you hang out with . . ."

"I feel good with my friends. They accept me. At least they're not phony, like Dad, pretending to be all holy to everyone. At home he's always drinking and tearing me down, calling me a slut and scum . . . and other words no one would even believe he'd use."

Your mom is silent.

"Go ahead, defend him like you always do," you say, disgusted. "I said I didn't want to talk about this, anyway."

"No," your mom says. "You're right. Dad shouldn't be drinking so much or saying those things to you. This really hasn't been a very good home for you for a while, has it?"

"What do you think?" you ask.

"I guess that was a dumb question," your mom says. "Maybe the problem isn't your clothes. Maybe it's that we don't understand each other. I really want to make this different. I should have listened to you a long time ago, but better now than never. I know you don't trust me, but I really care about you and I want us to have a relationship. Please help me. I don't want to keep living a life of lies and pretenses."

You look at your mom, confused. She has tears in her eyes

and looks lost and broken. You realize that this time she's not crying about you: She's crying about herself and her life. "I'm sorry, Mom," you say. "I didn't mean to make you feel bad."

"You didn't," your mom says, "I've been feeling like this for a long time. I just didn't want to face it. Thanks for caring."

QUESTIONS

What are your reactions to this scene?

_____

_____

_____

As the teenager, what did you need from your mom?

_____

_____

_____

What part did you receive?

_____

_____

_____

What do you think this family would be best off doing now?

_____

_____

_____

In the scene above, the mom would not have gotten anywhere if she had tried to use power techniques on her daughter. Her daughter would have rebelled more and withdrawn further, and the underlying issues would not have been dealt with. Underneath the flamboyant facade was a troubled child who had developed poor self-esteem and great confusion about her world. Underneath the father's facade were pain and anger from a repressive childhood. The mother had been trained to follow her husband's desires, and had ended up passive and unhappy, following the doctrine that keeping a united front between parents is more important than using your own mind and voicing your own opinions. She had almost totally submerged her own identity.

If you are going to confront someone on an issue that doesn't affect you directly, be prepared to listen and self-disclose for as long as you need to, on the deeper levels below anger that contain hurt, pain, and confusion to find out if there are serious problems going on.

The most powerful tool we have in helping children grow up to be caring and responsible and able to communicate in a healthy way is the modeling we demonstrate for them. We can have a strong, positive influence on people we love *if* they respect who we are and how we live, and want to know our opinions and seek our advice. It goes back to working on our own issues, learning skills and using them. What we need and want to teach children is to care about themselves and others, and that can best be taught by treating ourselves and them in a caring and respectful way.

EXERCISES

Imagine a home and family that the child within you would have liked to have had. Create a nurturing and supportive atmosphere in which the child is encouraged to grow.

1. What would the atmosphere in this home be like? Would there be a lot of structure or more freedom? Would people be able to ask questions and receive answers? Would there be a sense of sharing and understanding? Would there be laughter? Would people be affectionate with each other?

_____

_____

2. How would people express their thoughts and feelings? Would they be open and honest? Would they express their fears and confusion instead of taking out their anger and frustration on the people around them?

_____

_____

_____

3. How would feelings be treated? Would they be taken seriously? Would people consider how you felt before they made decisions that involved you? Would your feelings be handled respectfully? Would you be allowed to deal with feelings by yourself if you wanted to?

_____

_____

_____

4. How would people share with each other? Would they be open and honest? Would they share at appropriate times? Would they speak respectfully? Would sharing flow naturally? Would people share their love and caring?

_____

_____

_____

5. How would differences between people be handled? Would people appreciate and value differences of opinions, styles, ideas, and feelings? Would people try to understand each other? Would they be willing to learn from each other? Would

the person who was different and in the minority have their differences be considered important too?

_____

_____

_____

_____

6. How would conflicts be resolved? Would people care about what was important to each other? Would conflict-resolution techniques be used? Would everyone work together so that in the end everyone would feel positive about the end results and each other?

_____

_____

_____

_____

RECOMMENDED READING

P.E.T.: Parent Effectiveness Training, Thomas Gordon
Between Parent and Child, Haim Ginott
Liberated Parents, Liberated Children, Adele Faber and Elaine Mazlish
On Becoming a Person, Carl Rogers
A Warm Fuzzy Tale, Claude Steiner
For Your Own Good, Alice Miller

COMMON GROUND: A FRIENDSHIP MODEL FOR
RESOLVING CONFLICTS

Step 1: Set the tone.

What's important to both of us

    To feel positive about ourselves and each other.
    To feel good about our relationship.
    To be able to work things out together.
    To all feel good about the solution(s) we decide upon.

Step 2: Identify individual issues.

What's important to you   What's important to me

Step 3. Create possible solutions.

Step 4. Cross out unacceptable solutions.
Step 5. Choose solutions and back-up solutions.
Step 6. Imagine how the solution will turn out in actuality, and see
if it is acceptable to everyone.

CHAPTER ELEVEN

When It's Too Hard to Do It Alone

The therapist can interpret, advise, provide the emotional acceptance and support that nurtures personal growth, and above all,
he can listen. I do not mean that he can simply hear the other, but
that he will listen actively and purposefully, responding with the
instrument of his trade, that is, with the personal vulnerability of
his own trembling self.

SHELDON B. KOPP,
If You Meet the Buddha on the Road, Kill Him!:
The Pilgrimage of Psychotherapy Patients

If your childhood was particularly hurtful or the hurt went on
for a long time, you may need to find professional support.
Even if you feel that your family life wasn't that bad, you are
likely to heal and grow more quickly if you reach out for help.
You can learn a great deal from other people and apply what
has worked for them to yourself and your relationships. You
can find positive role models in therapy and in growth groups,
and you can get some of the things that you needed that you
did not receive as a child.

Therapy offers you a safe place to go through the process
of healing and growth. You will have someone there with you
as you share the traumas you've endured and the difficulties
you are struggling with. You will have support and assistance
in sorting out what you need to deal with, in identifying and
changing patterns, and creating new options. You can receive

141

encouragement in seeing and developing your strengths. There are many professional, caring therapists who can be helpful to you on your journey. There are many growth groups also, that are free or low-cost, that can support you toward that end. A resource file is included in this chapter.

People have many reasons for not reaching out for help, all of which have some legitimacy to them. It is a good idea to understand the trade-offs either way so that you can come to an informed decision. The following are some common concerns:

SELF-SUFFICIENCY

Many of us have grown up believing that people's worth depends on their ability to be self-sufficient. Self-sufficiency is important, because we want to avoid becoming overly dependent on someone else, which can cripple us, and prevent us from taking the steps we need to take. However, too much emphasis on self-sufficiency can harm us as well. Many people don't begin therapy until they've suffered needlessly for a long time, because they've been taught that it's a sign of weakness to reach out for help.

Many of us learned at a very early age not to bring our problems to our parents, and were ridiculed or ignored if we asked for help. We were supposed to know how to solve problems by ourselves and we were not supposed to make mistakes. In actuality, our parents often did not know how to help us, and put up a tough facade to cover up their own lack of knowledge. It can be difficult to do everything by ourselves, since we often do not have the answers we need readily available to us. If we do not reach out and ask for help, we become stuck with repetitive and limited options.

There is some dependency involved in the therapeutic relationship, but this is only temporary. If you do decide to go into therapy, it is important that you maintain your independence and your ability to make your own decisions. Sometimes therapy can be extremely useful in facilitating breaking out of a dependency relationship that you are in on a personal level. If your family has been very enmeshed, therapy can be a bridge toward your independence.

TRUST

Trust is a basic issue in therapy, for several reasons.

1. Therapists are doing their jobs for a fee, so in a sense there is always a secondary interest on the therapist's part. You are buying what the therapist is selling, and as the relationship becomes close and the therapist seems to be caring and supportive it is not uncommon to wonder if it is all because of the paycheck you are delivering. My answer to my clients, which will be different for each therapist, is that they can pay me for my time and for my expertise but they cannot pay to care. That is something that grows out of the relationship. The fee charged for services helps assure that the time spent in therapy is used for the client's needs, not the therapist's.

2. As in any other field, there are some disreputable people, and it is difficult to know whom to trust. It can be very difficult to risk again after a harmful experience in therapy. Some intensive workshops give people momentary highs but leave them back at square one in a few weeks. At the end of this chapter there are some guidelines for finding a reputable therapist and group. You may have to try several before you find what you are looking for.

3. If you grew up in a family where your trust was broken you probably have a negative view of good faith. "Never give a sucker an even break," may sum up how you believe most people treat others, and you may be determined not to let yourself get caught in that position. It is hard to get past those early experiences which created a strong map of how you believed the world was.

Learning to trust—with awareness—can be a profound

experience which you can get in individual, couple, family therapy, or in a group. Trust seems to be based on the high probability that: People around you will be fairly predictable over time; that they will have your interest in mind as well as their own; that they will communicate honestly and allow you to communicate honestly with them; that they will not pretend to be someone they are not; and that they will be willing to acknowledge it if they make mistakes or hurt you. The advantage of being trusting in appropriate situations is that you do not have to be "hypervigilant," that is, always waiting for someone to take advantage of you, which puts a great deal of stress on your body. Also, not trusting puts great limits on relationships, and keeps them from being as fulfilling as they could be because some barriers always remain. The alternative to trusting is being isolated, which can get very lonely. Finding a therapist you can learn to trust can be a huge step toward repairing your relationships because you will begin to let down your defenses and be more able to connect with those you love.*

COST

Therapy costs from about $50 to over $100 an hour (at this writing) and can greatly strain your financial budget. Fifty sessions at $75 each add up to $3750. This may seem very high to you. Before you write therapy off, however, consider the following:

- Most insurances will either pay for part of your short-term therapy, up to twenty sessions a year; or for long-

---

*Confidentiality helps to create a safe and trusting therapeutic relationship. However, confidentiality is limited by law under some conditions, such as: suspected child abuse, molestation, or neglect, and danger to self or others. Therapists may have to break confidentiality in certain legal situations. Consult an attorney to find out the laws in your state.

term therapy, up to fifty visits per year, often with a deductible at the beginning.

- You may be able to take out a short-term loan.
- The cost of therapy may be deductible from your income taxes as a medical expense.
- Many therapists, if you are unable to pay full price, have sliding scales and will lower their fees, or let you make payments over time.
- You may be able to find a clinic that has no fees or reduced fees.
- Groups are a legitimate alternative to individual or family therapy. There are many self-help groups which are free or low-cost. Groups led by therapists usually cost from $20 to $40 a session.
- The cost of healing major physical illnesses caused by emotional problems is also very high, and at the end of the cure the emotional problems remain.
- You may be spending your money in other ways that may not be as valuable to you in the long run.
- Your emotional, mental, physical, and spiritual health are vital to your being.

TIME

People often feel that they don't have enough time to go into therapy. It is extremely difficult to take time out, just for yourself and for working on your own growth. In actuality, though, time is all we have, moments to use or not to use to create what we want to have in our lives. So many people come into therapy and say, "If only I had dealt with this earlier, when I was a teenager," and feel distressed that it took so long to get started. The quality of your life and your relationships is one of the most important things in the world. Don't underestimate its importance; don't overestimate the time you have.

LOYALTY TO YOUR FAMILY

Many people feel that they are being disloyal to their families if they reveal secrets they have been instructed overtly, covertly, or by example not to discuss. One of the major signs of a dysfunctional family is that people are not open to scrutiny or questions. This pattern often persists long after people have left their families and even after their parents have died. If no one ever talked about Dad's drinking or Mom's temper, it may seem wrong to speak of it even now. You may have received messages that you or those you loved would be harmed bodily if you talked about certain things, or that people would be so upset they would have a heart attack, a stroke, a breakdown, or would kill themselves. There are equally powerful messages being given from superficially healthy families who are living with a facade around them. They convey to their children nonverbally that if they tear down the facade their family has built they will all collapse like a house of cards.

REVEALING YOURSELF

It can be frightening to expose your innermost feelings to a stranger, especially if you have not expressed yourself before or if you have tried and been humiliated, yelled at, invalidated, or ignored. Also, sharing may feel like an impossible task if you don't know how to share your feelings honestly. You may feel shame about some things you have done or some things that were done to you. You may be frightened by some of your thoughts and fantasies and feel that they are unacceptable. If you can gather the courage to reach out regardless, you will be able to explore these thoughts, feelings, and actions in a safe environment. This will allow you to feel safer and more open in your personal relationships.

When I was nine years old, in fourth grade, I was unable to do my homework for several days, and I went up to the teacher, after class, very nervously, and told him that my parents had been fighting every night and I hadn't been able to get my work done. I remember him glowering at me and walking out without even a hint of understanding, leaving me trembling and humiliated. In retrospect, he probably had no idea how to respond to me, or perhaps he didn't even understand the words I was mumbling. However, this incident reinforced the veil of secrecy we were surrounded by and I didn't talk openly about it again for ten years, not to the counselors I was sent to nor to my friends.

CONTROL

Therapy eventually touches issues that will probably make you feel out of control and that can be very frightening. For many people, being out of control has meant being victimized in the past. There is no easy way around this except to go slowly and build trust with the person or people you are sharing with. Sometimes realizing that your need to be in control is controlling you and that you are therefore not actually in control makes a difference. This awareness can break the illusion that you possess more power than you actually do. Trying to keep in constant control is a very tedious job since you are always in a state of tension.

Sometimes people are afraid that they will hurt themselves or others if they lose control. With a competent therapist, you will be able to explore these fears and work through your feelings in a way that is not dangerous.

THE NEGATIVE IMAGE ASSOCIATED WITH GOING TO THERAPY

If you haven't been in therapy before, you may feel that going to a therapist means there's something wrong with you.

Realistically, the old view of therapy has completely changed: It has been estimated that 40 percent of Americans have seen a therapist for help with problems and this percentage is increasing. Therapy used to be something people tried to hide, but now it's become a statement that they care about themselves and their families enough to take the time and effort to deal with their problems. I think since people have become conscious of their physical health and realized how much stress emotional problems put on their bodies they have become more and more willing to work those problems out.

NO ONE WOULD UNDERSTAND

If you have tried to talk to people before and they have misunderstood what you were trying to tell them, gave you advice you didn't want or need, told you how much worse off they were, or discounted your feelings in any of a number of different ways, you may have gotten the message that what happened to you was something no one would understand. If you have never tried to share your inner feelings, you may believe that you won't be able to explain what you feel or what has happened. Most therapists have been trained in listening and understanding, and have learned to pick up cues about feelings and will help you express them in your own way. If your therapist is not able to do this in a way that seems positive to you, you may want to find another therapist.

Going to a group is harder because there are a lot of people but easier because you don't have to talk at all. You can listen to others who will most likely have similar struggles and problems to work through, and with time you may feel comfortable enough to share your feelings as well. Many groups have rules about listening, such as an amount of time allotted to each person, advice and feedback only if they are requested, and confidentiality.

I don't want to pretend that there is no risk involved in

seeking a therapist or group. The first group or therapist you go to may not be the right one for you. I went to four different therapists briefly before I found someone who worked well with me. As a therapist, I don't always work well with each person who comes in to see me, and I doubt any therapist does. There is nothing wrong with admitting that therapy is not working and finding someone who is right for you.

CHOOSING A THERAPIST

The particular method a therapist uses is generally not as significant as the relationship you establish with the therapist. The following list shows some things that may be significant to you. Many of them you have a right to expect. Put the list below in order of importance to you. Some people are comfortable with more structure while others prefer more flexibility. Some people care whether a therapist is male or female while others do not. Find a therapist that suits you, but find out first what is *most* important, in case you can't find all the things you want. Add your own priorities to this list.

- Offers a comfortable, relaxed atmosphere.
- Treats you respectfully.
- Has fees that are within your ability to pay, or a payment plan.
- Has times that you can fit into your schedule.
- Was recommended by someone you trust.
- Is someone who understands what you are trying to communicate.
- Is someone who opens up options without telling you which you have to take.
- Is someone who does not make you feel bad or wrong.
- Gives you honest feedback so that you can learn about yourself.
- Is covered by your insurance plan.

- Has phone access if you are in crisis.
- Is structured and formal.
- Is flexible and informal.
- Communicates warmth and caring.
- Self-discloses at appropriate times.
- Keeps a comfortable distance between you.
- Gives you skills you can use to resolve your own problems.
- Is ethical in the therapeutic relationship.
- Can meet some of your needs for nurturing.
- Is someone you can use as a role model.
- Uses a particular form or method you feel would work best with you.
- Agrees with you about the length of time therapy will take.
- Is a male or female therapist.
- Will be staying in the same location and in the field of therapy for the duration of therapy.
- Specializes in the specific area you want to deal with.
- Is in a particular age range.
- Is in a particular ethnic group.

_____

_____

_____

CHOOSING A GROUP

There are some advantages to groups, because there are many people to interact with, to learn from, and to make contact with. The main disadvantage is that your time is shared with many people and if you tend to be quiet you may not get your needs met. Sometimes groups are a useful adjunct to therapy and may reduce the time it takes. The list below will give you an idea of the broad range of areas that groups are offered in.

Alcoholics Anonymous
Al-Anon and Alateen
Overeaters Anonymous
Narcotics Anonymous
Adult Children of Alcoholics
Co-dependents Anonymous
Families Anonymous
Domestic violence
Parenting
Recently divorced or widowed

Survivor's groups
Assertiveness
Specific physical illness
Single parents
Grandparents' support
Anxiety/phobias
General support
Bereavement
Depression

HOW TO FIND A THERAPIST

The books listed on page 154 are designed to help you find out about the different kinds of therapy and how to figure out where to find help.

Some general ways that are effective are:

•*Friends or aquaintances:* Ask them if they can recommend someone. This is probably your best method, because you will be able to get direct information about the therapist's style and abilities. Also, many therapists do not have room for new clients, but will make exceptions for personal referrals and add a client or two to their caseloads.

•*Self-help groups:* Participate in such a group and find out from other people who they go to: another way of getting onto the personal referral track.

•*Physician referrals:* Many doctors have a list of therapists they work with. They get feedback from their patients about how therapy is working for them, so they can give you some recommendations.

•*Insurance plans:* If you belong to a Health Maintenance Organization or a Preferred Provider Organization they will have a list of therapists who are participating providers and may be able to tell you some details about the therapists' areas of expertise.

Professional organizations: There are likely to be professional organizations in your area that can refer you to a psychiatrist, psychologist, social worker, or family therapist close by. The lines between the different professional schools have become increasingly vague. All of the professionals can be helpful. The major difference is that only psychiatrists can prescribe medication. Sometimes other therapists work jointly with the psychiatrist as a medical consultant. At times other medical doctors may prescribe medication as an adjunct to therapy.

Places of worship: Some religious leaders have had training in counseling and may be able to help. Most have too many other commitments to take people on for long-term therapy. However, they may know of therapists in the area whom they could recommend.

A personal development or relationship class: Many therapists seek out clients through teaching classes. In classes you can see how they present themselves, observe the skills they have, and check out your comfort level in talking with them.

Local organizations: Here is a small sample of places you may be able to call to find a therapist or group.

Mental Health Association
Family Services Agency
Catholic Social Services
Jewish Family Services
Crisis Intervention Clinic
Alcoholics Anonymous, Al-Anon and Alateen
Adult Children of Alcoholics and other Twelve-Step Groups
Survivors' groups for victims of child sexual abuse
Groups for battered women
Rape crisis centers
Directory for help organizations (at the public library)
National Health Information Clearinghouse Hotline (800-336-4797)
The National Institute of Mental Health

•*Colleges sometimes have counseling services:* Caution, some therapists will be student interns and may not have the skill needed to work with you if you have difficult problems. They also may only work for a short time, as they will be leaving after a semester or two.

•*The yellow pages:* In my opinion, not the best place to look, because the biggest ads do not necessarily mean the most qualified therapists. It is a good place to look, however, in case there is someone's name you recognize as having been referred to you previously.

QUESTIONS

1. What reasons would you have to consider going into therapy?

_____

_____

_____

2. What would prevent you from reaching out for a therapist or a group?

_____

_____

_____

3. What advantages might you gain from reaching out?

_____

_____

_____

4. What is your plan at this time?

_____

_____

_____

RESOURCES

Making Therapy Work by Bruckner-Gordon, Gangi and Wallman, Harper & Row, 1988. (This book can help you in your decision, clarify what you can get out of therapy, and show you how to use therapy most effectively.)

The Psychotherapy Maze: A Consumer's Guide to Getting In and Out of Therapy, by Ehrenberg and Ehrenberg. (Describes the different types of therapies offered.)

Mental Health Directory, U.S. Government Printing Office, Washington D.C. (202) 783-3238.

PART THREE

Making Peace

CHAPTER TWELVE

Breaking Down the Walls

> For one human being to love another, that is perhaps the most difficult of all our tasks, the ultimate, the last test and proof, the work for which all other work is but preparation.
>
> RAINER MARIA RILKE

In order to make peace with your adult children you will need to break down several barriers that often get in the way of communication. It may seem to you as if you are being asked to "give in" to your children in the next few chapters and that they are not being asked to give much back in return, even though they may have hurt you also throughout the years. You will have a chance to talk about these feelings as you explore your relationship more deeply together, but if you do so initially your children are likely to get defensive, and nothing will be accomplished.

The concepts below are important to know about and to use in relationships. Understanding them and applying them to your relationships with your adult children can clear up a lot of misunderstandings and unhappiness. They can help you break down the walls between you.

In this chapter you will learn:

- How to become more understanding and accepting.
- How to distinguish between intensity and intimacy.
- Why it's important to be open.
- The value of humility.
- How to gain increased self-knowledge.

- How to identify genuine giving.
- How to achieve interdependence.

FROM INTOLERANCE TO UNDERSTANDING
AND ACCEPTANCE

The way we treat differences between people strongly influ-
ences the way our relationships develop. We learned from our
parents how to treat people who seemed different, and often
our parents were intolerant of differences in outsiders, in their
children, or in each other. Intolerance may be a family pattern
carried over from previous generations or from our society as a
whole. Usually it is based on fear created by a lack of understanding.

Opposite inherent personality styles can be a source of
continuing struggles or major conflicts if the people involved
are unable to accept and deal with differences in positive ways.
People push each other out to the extreme ends of the con-
tinuum in a given area (polarize each other) because they are
trying so hard to change one another. Each is determined to
prove that her style is the right one.

Four opposing characteristics or preferences that are often
the basis for intolerance and misunderstandings are explained
below. These differences greatly affect the parent-child relationship and they are also a common source of problems in the
marital or primary relationship.

The book *Please Understand Me* by Kiersey and Bates contains comprehensive information about these characteristics as
well as a personality test you can score yourself.*

Extroversion and *introversion* are the first of these pairs of

---

Please Understand Me is based on the Meyers-Briggs Type Indicator originally created in
1943 by Katharine Briggs and Isabel Briggs Myers. This test was based on Carl Jung's
theory of psychological types published in 1923.

potentially conflicting characteristics. Extroverted people are social, outgoing, enjoy a lot of human contact, are fast-moving and comfortable in noisy atmospheres. Introverted people have few contacts, prefer being with people one at a time, are introspective, like to stay home and do projects and are most comfortable in quiet atmospheres. It's easy to see how conflicts can arise in relationships if people are different in this area, especially if they are strong opposites. An extroverted parent who does not understand differences may label an introverted child peculiar and withdrawn and try to force the child to be more sociable. The child may feel pressured and uncomfortable, and a struggle can easily ensue. The introverted child will feel more and more isolated, as if there is something wrong with him, especially since statistically, only one out of four people is introverted. An extroverted child, on the other hand, may feel shut off and unhappy at home with an introverted parent who, preferring quiet, may suppress the child's inquisitiveness and try to hold his energy down.

Sensation and *intuition* are opposing preferences which lead to two entirely different approaches to the world. Sensing people are practical. They like things done in an established way, and they think in terms of past experiences. They are usually stable, like step-by-step approaches to things, and are inclined to be precise and factual. Intuitive people are more innovative. They tend to work in spurts of energy, follow their inspirations, and focus on the future. They often would rather learn a new skill than use it and are frequently impatient with routine details. A sensing parent may get extremely frustrated with the complicated, imaginative, or dreamy style of an intuitive child who, in turn, may have difficulty with a parent who does not value creativity highly. An intuitive parent may have trouble understanding and meeting the needs of a child who prefers things to be concrete and the child may feel frustrated and unloved as a result.

Thinking and *feeling* people also see the world from different perspectives. Thinking people tend to prefer objectivity and analysis over sympathy and awareness. They tend to be impersonal, technical, and logical. Feeling people are usually more empathic and emotional, supportive of others, and inclined to resolve things on an emotional level. Feeling people lead with their hearts; thinking people with their heads. An emotional parent may not understand the needs of an analytical child, and an analytical parent may discount his feeling child's emotions. The feeling child may feel that his thinking parent is removed and distant, and the thinking child might think that his parent is overly emotional.

Perceiving and *judging* are characteristics that emphasize different time frames. Perceiving people are likely to perceive endless options in the world and therefore to prefer leaving things open-ended. They are hard to pin down to commitments, because they prefer spontaneity and want to be able to be open to new possibilities. Judging people are inclined first to make judgments about all of the options, and then make a decision. They want things settled, prefer closure, and like to know what will happen ahead of time. They do not have as hard a time with decisions or follow-through. This difference can be a source of continuing irritation in relationships. A perceiving parent may not give adequate structure to a judging child and a judging parent may get frustrated by the spontaneity of a perceptive child. A perceiving child may feel controlled by a judging parent and a judging child may feel let down by a perceiving parent.

Additionally, four main temperaments and categories of people have been identified through different combinations of these types.

- Those who tend to be the pillars of the community, responsible and traditional, who value being useful (sensing, judging).
- Those who tend to be action- or movement-oriented, and value being in the moment (sensing, perceiving).
- Those who have ideas and visions for the future, and value being unique and significant (intuitive, feeling).

• Those who are technologically oriented and value analysis, competency, and control (intuitive, thinking).

People are not necessarily locked into one type. But, as you can see, people who do fit into these categories have different goals and priorities. If people are only aware of the priorities of their own personality style, and haven't learned to deal with differences effectively, their relationships will probably contain a lot of frustrations and misunderstandings.

With awareness and hard work, people can learn to understand and accept each other's differences instead of tearing each other down. They can also expand their own limited views of the world by moving closer to the other's positions at times. For example, a parent who tends to be serious and responsible can learn about action and freedom in a relationship with an action-type child, and she can teach her action-oriented, more impulsive person about responsibility and structure. However, if they do not respect each other's differences, and instead try to change each other rather than expand themselves, endless power struggles ensue. Ultimately, these conflicts undermine and devastate the relationship.

Do you think you are extroverted or introverted?
Are you more sensing or intuitive?
Do you tend to be more feeling or thinking?
Do you fit the judging or perceiving description above?
Do you prioritize responsibility and tradition?
Do you prefer movement and action?
Do you care a lot about significance and uniqueness?
Is your focus analysis and competency?
Can you tell which categories your parents and children fit into?
What do you think their styles and priorities are?

What are some problems between you and your parents and you and your children that have been caused by your different personality types and your inability to deal with these differences effectively?

_____

_____

What did you learn while growing up about how to handle differences between people?

_____

_____

_____

Having different ways of representing the world often separates people and makes it difficult for them to communicate
with each other. People working in a system called neu-
rolinguistic programming (NLP), originated by Richard Bandler
and John Grinder, among others, have identified differences in
people's preferred representational systems. People tend to
represent the world either visually, kinesthetically (physically),
or auditorily. What this means is that most people tend to favor
one of their senses over the others in representing and understanding the world around them. If people communicate with
those in a different representational system without either of
them switching systems, they can lose touch with each other
rapidly. Both will come away feeling misunderstood and uncared for.

One typical couple who came into therapy represented the
world through different senses. He was highly kinesthetic, and
she was highly visual. He would get extremely annoyed at her
for the physical discomforts she created for him, such as pur-
chasing furniture that was visually pleasing to her, but uncomfortable for him to sit on. It wasn't until we related his physical
discomfort to her visual discomfort, by having her imagine pictures that were crooked on the wall and unharmonious colors
placed next to each other, that she was able to understand the
impact on him (referencing her feelings to understand his) and
became willing to negotiate.

If you pay attention to people's language, you will start to figure out what representational system they use. Visual people use phrases like, "I see what you mean," "It looks fine to me," or "Things are out of focus"; kinesthetic people say things like, "That feels right," "I can't get a handle on this," and "I grasp what you're saying"; auditory people use language like, "That rings a bell," "I hear you," and "That doesn't click." Once you've identified people's preferential mode of representing the world, you can begin to communicate with them in their system if you are having trouble understanding each other.

How do you think you represent the world? Do you think mainly in visual, auditory, or kinesthetic terms? How do you think your children represent the world?

_____

_____

_____

Can you think of problems in communication that have been caused by not understanding or allowing for these differences?

_____

_____

_____

Communication also easily breaks down when people have different symbols for the same concepts. For example, when people want to express their love, they tend to use their own symbols in expressing their love rather than the other person's to demonstrate their caring. If they don't know the other person's symbols of love or caring, they often get a negative response back to their attempts to be giving, and they do not understand why. It is interesting to watch people with different symbols for expressing love, who don't understand this concept, try to be loving and giving to each other. They use their own symbols instead of the other person's and confusion abounds. One woman tried to show her husband how much she loved him by making a big fuss over his birthday, something she would have liked him to do for her, because it was a symbol to her of being loved. She did this year after year, despite his protests that he wanted a quiet birthday. When she finally listened to him long enough to understand that this was not what he wanted, she was able to let go of this tradition. When he finally understood that this was her way of showing her love for him, he was no longer upset with what she had been trying to do for him.

Often parents think they are giving their children what they need and want, while the children have a totally different idea of what their needs and wants are. For example, a father may think that his son should be involved in sports since he loved sports as a child. Meanwhile his child may have a natural inclination or preference for music. The parent may believe he is passing something special on to his son, but in reality he is taking his own past experience and projecting it onto his son without first listening to him and trying to understand him. The concept of being treated as an individual may be completely foreign to this father. In order to shift his relationship with his son he would have to change his perspective entirely. Children are living in a very different world today than their parents lived in. The interests their parents might have had or the songs they sang may not be a part of their children's symbols for happiness or success.

List several special things you have done for your children that you think they really valued and appreciated.

_____

_____

_____

_____

What are some things you did for your children that you felt they took for granted or didn't care about receiving?

_____

_____

_____

What differences between your representations of the world were not recognized or understood?

_____

_____

_____

This section only touches on the many variations that exist between people. In addition to all the subtleties of the above differences, we must deal with differences in appearance, aptitude, intellectual level, physical strength and dexterity, energy, rate of development, gender, race, socioeconomic level, and culture. We must learn to allow for religious preferences, values differences, political ideas, time preferences (day or night people), sensation differences (such as sensitivity to heat and cold), and preferences for neatness or messiness (the world is divided pretty evenly on this one). Whether someone is the oldest, the only, the middle, or the youngest child may affect how he functions in relationships. Personal styles, tastes in music, food, clothing, colors, how and where to spend leisure time, money, choices in friends and entertainment, and sensitivity and awareness differences, are all potential areas of battle if the differences involved are not respected and handled cooperatively.

It is impossible to live with another person and not have areas of conflict. If two people have no conflicting areas, at least one of them is not expressing himself. Allowing for differences is a major factor in creating relationships that work for all the people involved. There are many different ways to live in this world and to forget that leaves us intolerant, righteous, and lonely.

Of course we don't have to form long-term relationships with people we don't get along with. But we don't choose our parents or our children, and for the amount of time we are in each other's presence we can learn honestly to respect and accept the differences between us. Our own view is never the only one. If we focus on being "right" rather than being open to other people's perspectives we will seriously impair our relationships. There is no specific skill that I know of that can teach people to accept and value differences. It seems, though, that the more accepting we are of ourselves, the more open, caring, and respectful our relationships will be. The more we are doing those things we love to do, the less likely we will be to care whether others are different from us or not. If the conflicting style of someone else is in our way, we can learn to negotiate with them in a cooperative way until we find solutions that we both can live with.

FROM INTENSITY TO INTIMACY

In some families, people lead highly intense and chaotic lives. It appears that these family members are very connected and involved with each other but in reality they are quite isolated from each other outside of their roles. In these types of families, people play out repetitive, magnetic, and destructive roles with each other that do not allow for changes to occur in the individuals involved, except from one limited role to another. A pattern that is frequently seen in families that are not functioning in a healthy way is known as the victim, persecutor, rescuer triangle. To understand this clearly, draw or visualize a triangle with the three roles of victim, persecutor, and rescuer at each angle. People who have become entrapped in this system often spend their lives stuck in the angles of this triangle or caught on the perimeter, going across from one role to an adjacent one. People take on one of these roles in the family, for a while, and then they shift the roles around. The people stuck in this system create a lot of high-intensity dramatics, which sometimes has the appearance of intimacy, but it is not true intimacy. There is a lot of blaming and making accusations in these roles. Consequently, the victim acts and feels powerless, the persecutor acts and feels like the bad guy, and the rescuer acts and feels sacrificial and noble. What is missing in this system is real people, with the ability to have a truly intimate relationship, one built on trust, respect, understanding, openness, spontaneity, and growth.

In an alcoholic family, for which this pattern was originally identified by psychiatrist Eric Berne, the alcoholic plays the part of the victim most of the time. The spouse rescues the victim (calling in to work to say the spouse is sick, lying to the children) or persecutes the victim (calling him a drunken slob). The roles sometimes shift when the spouse feels victimized by the alcoholic's actions and the alcoholic becomes the persecutor. The alcoholic may repent and rescue the spouse, and the roles will shift once more. People rarely get off the basic triangle to experience a spontaneous, intimate relationship with each other. The children in these families usually adopt these roles too, and continue to follow these established roles when they leave home, even if there is no alcohol involved. In this way, the pattern goes on to the next generation.

When you approach your children, be careful not to fall into any of those roles. Do not blame your children or try to rescue them or allow yourself to become a victim. There are no winners in this game, and nothing gets resolved. You will be approaching your adult children using the skills you have learned, in a way that makes it most likely that you will be able to create a spontaneous, intimate relationship together.

Have you or your children been involved in the triangle described above? In what role or roles? What have you discovered about the effects of this pattern?

_____

_____

_____

What might you gain by breaking out of this pattern?

_____

_____

_____

FROM SECRECY TO OPENNESS

One of the primary signs of an unhealthy family is that secrets play a large role in family dynamics. Breaking through secrecy can be frightening, but without openness you will not be able to experience anything more than partial relationships.

It's important for you to understand, if your children ask you questions that seem to be prying or painful, that their purpose is not to hurt you, although remembering former times may be difficult for you. Even if your adult children sound angry, their purpose is to learn about their past and to work on your relationship. By this time, if you have been following this book, you have already addressed most of the subjects your adult children are likely to ask questions about, so it will be less painful to deal with them now. Also, you now understand that anger is a cover-up for the pain, fear, and confusion that lie below the surface.

Asking questions may be a crucial part of your adult children's healing process. Sometimes people have been traumatized either because of painful, isolated incidents or because they have lived in a continual state of traumatization and a part of them has become frozen. Frequently that part is attached to memories that are fuzzy or nonexistent and seems to belong to someone else. The end result is that they feel as if they don't have a past. They feel disconnected, as if they don't belong anywhere. It is as if there are holes or missing parts in their minds, feelings, and bodies.

Your adult children are trying to fill in the missing pieces in their minds by asking you to share your memories. It's as if they are trying to complete a jigsaw puzzle whose sections are not understandable without the missing pieces. Left without any solid facts, people create fantasies about their pasts. Often they fill in negative thoughts about their own badness, insignificance, and unworthiness. Not really knowing their past, people feel incapable of living in the present and have no guide for projecting their future. Some become lost souls, feeling rage, pain, and confusion when they allow themselves to feel. Most of the time their lives are based on survival and little more.

The following story shows how important it is to be open. In this family the pattern of secrecy created more harm than the events in themselves.

> Laura, a woman in her forties, was extremely hostile toward her mother, who had been emotionally unavailable and physically abusive to Laura from the time she had returned home from a two-week hospitalization when Laura was four. No one had explained to Laura what had happened to her mother, and from that time on Laura had figured out that she must be a bad girl, because that was the only way she could understand why her mother had become so distant and angry toward her.
>
> When Laura and her mother began to be open about the past, Laura learned that when she was four, her mother, then only twenty-four, found out that she had uterine cancer. She was hospitalized and had a hysterectomy but was not expected to live. She was extremely ill, angry, and depressed for a long time when she returned home. Additionally, at that time, Laura's father began going out with other women.
>
> How different Laura's feeling about herself and her mother would have been if her parents had told her, "Honey, your

mom's real sick and she's scared now. She feels really bad that she can't be a very good mom. Sometimes when Mom feels bad she yells a lot or goes off by herself, but it's because of Mom's feelings. It doesn't have anything to do with you. We're gonna try real hard to get through this the best we can." But no one told Laura anything. They thought she was too young to understand. The result was that she came up with the only explanation she really could: Mom was upset because Laura was bad.

Even though it was forty years later, having her mother explain what had happened during that time and listen to how Laura felt helped a lot. At least the pieces could go together now in a way that made sense. Laura hadn't been a bad kid; and her mother wasn't a bad person either. Her mother had been going through a major battle to survive and the family pattern of secrecy had kept her from talking about her illness and her pain.

You can help your adult children immeasurably simply by filling in, to the best of your ability, the missing pieces of what happened during your own childhood and adult life as well as what happened when they were young that has affected their lives. To do this you have to get beyond denial and beyond the reasons for denial.

What questions might your children ask that you would find difficult to respond to?

_____

_____

_____

How could you deal with your feelings so that you would be able to answer their questions satisfactorily?

_____

_____

_____

What are some things you think it would be important for your adult children to know?

_____

_____

_____

_____

FROM FALSE PRIDE TO HUMILITY

The hardest part of breaking down the wall between people is that it entails a great deal of humility on the part of the person who has made the commitment to change the relationship into a more open and cooperative one. In this case, of course, the person taking this first step will be you, and so again the greater burden initially will be yours.

Unfortunately, humility is often associated with humiliation, although their meanings are very different.

- Humility is the lack of arrogance or false pride; modesty.
- Humiliation is the state of being humiliated, disgraced, or shamed.

Humility is crucial in making peace with others because most people are not likely to be open with you if you are not willing to approach them in a nonthreatening way. This is not limited to your adult children. False pride and arrogance create either more false pride and arrogance or humiliation and shame. Humiliation and shame create more humiliation and shame or false pride and arrogance. Either way, you create a lot of frustration and anger. On the other hand, humility creates humility, which immediately puts you on equal and cooperative terms.

The advantage of approaching someone you care about with humility are considerable. You don't have to carry a defensive posture and you don't have to be perfect. You don't even have to be right. Being right all the time is a formidable, unending burden. You don't have to feel or act righteous and superior, which tends to elicit hostile responses from others. Most importantly, you can be honest with yourself.

Is there any parent who always handles everything perfectly? We have all hurt our children inadvertently or because we were trapped in old patterns, or because we were out of control or we didn't know better, or because we thought it was for their own good, or we were afraid of appearing too weak or too harsh. Why is it so hard for parents to acknowledge their errors, with humility, and say that they are sorry for resorting to hurtful or ineffective behaviors? Why not simply admit that at times they hurt the people they love?

Saying you are sorry you acted in a certain way is not the same as saying that you were bad or to blame. It just means that you regret that whatever was hurtful or ineffective happened. This may sound like an insignificant difference, but in reality it is a major distinction. The first puts you in a subordinate position and the second places you on the same level as the person you are talking to. Don't be defensive but don't act inferior either. Being sorry means that you understand on a profound emotional level that a person you love has been hurt. It must convey that you regret the event happened and you wish you could have prevented it. It means that you care enough to empathize with their pain.

It is important always to keep in mind what your intention is in going through this book and to remember why you are doing all this emotionally difficult work. What is important is that you are trying to make peace with your children, not at the cost of your self-esteem but at the cost of your defenses. Your task is to break down the wall between you and your children—not to add bricks to the existing wall or to do battle.

The way to break down a wall is to simply take down your side of the barrier, with grace and humility. This needs to be done sincerely, not just perfunctorily. This sounds both easy and impossible at the same time, but it is the most straightforward and powerful way to grow personally, repair relationships, and create an atmosphere that will make others want to drop their walls too. We will be going through concrete steps for doing this in the next few chapters.

Most adult children are longing for a relationship with their parents where they can feel valued and respected. If you take down your walls and are willing to work with your adult children on understanding each other, there is a high probability that they will take their walls down too. Eventually you will have a chance to share your hurts and frustrations with them.

What might you lose by taking down your wall?

_____

_____

What can you gain by taking down your wall?

_____

_____

List the resources you have available to help you through any difficult periods that may arise.

_____

_____

_____

FROM DEFENSIVENESS TO CURIOSITY

It will be important for you to be willing to learn how your adult children perceived the past, in order to break down the walls between you. Often what they tell you will not be what you want to hear. They may be harboring feelings from the past that have become very intense because they have not had a chance to be expressed or resolved. They may have a lot of resentment built up because of the hurt they have endured.

It will be difficult to listen to your adult children's perceptions if you get trapped in feeling as if your self-esteem depends on your being right and perfect. It will be a lot easier if you take what your adult children say as information, feedback, and an opportunity for you to learn and to grow.

You will need to:

- Listen to information which may seem intensified or exaggerated to you, so that you will be able to understand the feelings that your children have about your relationship.
- Be open to information about how your adult children perceived you, and to take that as feedback which you can use in the future.

Children often have a much clearer view of family interactions than their parents give them credit for. When we were growing up, our parents rarely wanted to hear our perspective on things. If we tried to express our points of view, we most likely were called impudent or fresh and we ended up going away feeling frustrated and misunderstood. Nonetheless, we were often quite insightful about many things that occurred and we certainly had our own point of view from which to observe things, which was a worthwhile perspective on events.

Interrupting children and shutting them out of discussions has deprived parents of an opportunity to learn and grow that cannot be matched anywhere else. You can learn a great deal from your adult children now if you approach them out of curiosity rather than defensiveness. They have an invaluable perspective on you that no one else shares, since they have seen you behave in ways you probably never showed anyone else. Because of the way we have learned to treat children, they probably saw you at your worst times.

Your adult children may be angry over various things that happened in their childhoods. They may talk to you in ways that you feel are disrespectful. Don't get caught in their manner of talking. Listen to their pain underneath their anger. If you get caught, and cannot listen to them, let them know that you respect their opinions and you want to hear what they are trying to tell you but that you are unable to hear their words. Ask them to try again more gently in a minute or two. If the conversation gets very hostile, continue the discussion in writing or take a break and try again later.

If you can accept your adult children's feedback you will learn more about their feelings and you will learn some important things about yourself as well. You will come away with an increased understanding of how your adult children and perhaps others perceived you in the past.

In our home we generally deal with conflicts with all of us speaking our minds about what we think is going on. A disagreement with my daughter, Kira, brought to my attention that I had asked her to do something but hadn't allowed her to do it without interfering. I learned (again—we learn things over and over) that I have a problem letting people do things in their own way.

This was a lesson from my daughter, not an attack or rudeness on her part. In family therapy sessions I am truly amazed at how clear children can be about what is happening in their families. Even small children know that their dad is unhappy, that their mom is too protective, or that their brother is being treated badly.

Your children know some truths about you no one else does. You know truths about them that no one else can share with them. You have a wonderful opportunity to learn about yourselves and each other, once you break down the barriers between you.

EXERCISES

1. Write down some statements that you wanted to tell your parents that they would have taken as signs of rudeness or attacks on their self-esteem.

   _____

   _____

   _____

2. Write down some comments your children have told you that you felt were signs of rudeness or attacks on your self-esteem.

   _____

   _____

   _____

3. Write down some insights your parents might have gained from you, if they had taken your responses to them as feedback, information, or lessons.

   _____

   _____

   _____

4. Write down some insights you might have gained from your children if you had taken what they said as feedback, information, or lessons.

   _____

   _____

   _____

5. Write down some things your children might have learned from you if they had taken what you said to them as feedback, information, or lessons.

   _____

   _____

   _____

FROM PLEASING TO GIVING

Relationships can get extremely confused if people have not made the distinction between pleasing and giving. People often believe they are being giving to others, when in fact they are trying to please others, which is different. Most people who are trying to please others are doing so because they are trying to satisfy their own needs indirectly. Some people have learned to please others from one of their parents and some people's families required them to fill this role. Usually people try to please others because:

- They crave approval.
- They are afraid of being abandoned if they don't.
- They are afraid of conflict.
- They expect emotional repayment in return.

People who continually try to please others are often "co-dependents" or "rescuers" (who used to be called martyrs). They usually get very little back in return. Sadly, this reinforces their belief that they don't deserve to be loved. They often grow up believing that they are not lovable in themselves: They have to "give" something to get love. They tend to get into roles where they take care of others instead of themselves. They feel guilty if they do take care of themselves because they have grown up feeling unworthy. They often try to make other people dependent on them so that they will not be abandoned, and consequently they do things for others that are not useful for them. For example, it is not useful for an alcoholic to be given more alcohol or to be protected from the consequences of his drinking. Children do not need to be overprotected or over-indulged and tend to resent their parents' overinvolvement in their lives.

People who are giving are satisfying their own and other people's needs openly and naturally. They know that their presence and their energy and the love they have are a gift in themselves and they do not have to add things to themselves to make themselves lovable. They give because of:

- The sheer delight of giving and receiving.
- Their desire to express their love.
- Their desire and need to share and contribute.

When you give you express your love in a way that does not create, assume, or come out of helplessness or dependency. It is heartfelt, genuine, and joyous, and it does not have strings attached to it. People who can genuinely give can also genuinely receive. Relationships work best if genuine giving and receiving come from both parties so that the relationship is not out of balance.

If you are going to give to someone it is important to communicate with each other to find out what each person needs or wants. The classic story is about the realtor who made a fortune in the following way: He takes the woman out into the garage and tells her that her husband would give anything to have a garage like the one on that property. He then takes the man into the kitchen and tells him that his wife would die to have a kitchen like that. The couple is then stuck with a house they both hate because they have not communicated with each other and have been manipulated into trying to give each other what they think the other person wants.

As your understanding and self-esteem increase and you communicate more openly with people you will gradually shift from pleasing to giving.

How have people in your family confused the concepts of pleasing and giving?

_____

_____

_____

_____

What are some ways you tried to please your children? What motivated you to do so?

_____

_____

_____

_____

What are some things you put up with to avoid conflict?

_____

_____

_____

What are some true gifts you gave your children?

_____

_____

_____

_____

When you approach your children, try to separate out what is going on between you in terms of pleasing and giving. This area will be addressed more in later chapters which help you to work on your present relationship.

FROM DEPENDENCE OR ISOLATION TO INTERDEPENDENCE

In families where people have very loose boundaries between them, people's identities become mixed up with each other's and an enmeshed family system is created. In this kind of family, people have difficulty separating their own needs from each other's and their feelings and identities become merged and submerged. Because they are so interconnected, these families are generally very dependent on each other. In Josh's family there is a lot of togetherness, but family members violate each other's boundaries and independence is discouraged. If Josh wants to do something independently, it is considered a betrayal of the family.

When people's boundaries are too rigid, people are distant and removed from each other and a disengaged family system is created. In these families, people are not allowed to enter each other's worlds or feelings. Their needs and identities are kept separate and hidden and the children in these families grow up isolated and aloof. Leaving is treated as a sign of independence but it is actually isolation. In Margaret's family, feelings are not shared and most activities are done separately. When Margaret feels lonely or empty inside she ignores these feelings because in her family weakness and dependence are treated scornfully.

In many families, combinations of enmeshed and disengaged behaviors occur. Perhaps the mother in the family is enmeshed with the children and the father is disengaged from the family; or a parent is enmeshed with one favored child and disengaged from the others; or the parents are enmeshed with each other until there is a conflict and then they disengage from each other and enmesh themselves with the children. This can get very complex and difficult to sort out. What all of these families have in common is that the children do not learn how to create flexible and appropriate boundaries that will allow them to have interdependent relationships.

In a healthy family, people's boundaries are defined but permeable, that is, they shift according to what is appropriate to a given situation. People choose who and what they let into their boundaries based on their feelings, intuition, and reason, and they don't become immersed within other people's boundaries or feel excluded by them. In Brian's family there are appropriate boundaries and also close bonds between the family members. People in this family can come and go without feeling guilty or lost. They check in and communicate with each other because they want to, and they have created a balance of activities participated in jointly and separately. The relationships within the family, such as the relationship between Brian and his brother Arthur, and the relationship between Brian's parents are strong but not confining or exclusive. Roles and needs shift and change without major upset, and people are able to negotiate with each other respectfully when conflicts arise. This family system is interdependent, rather than dependent or isolated.

There are very few families that are as healthy as Brian's. In most families, people unknowingly invade each other's boundaries or cut ties off abruptly, thoughtlessly, and hurtfully.

Did you learn from your family how to set appropriate boundaries growing up? If not, what difficulties did that cause for you?

_____

_____

_____

_____

Did your children learn how to set appropriate boundaries growing up? If not, what difficulties did that cause for them?

_____

_____

_____

_____

If your family was either enmeshed, disengaged, or a combination of both, you will need to create appropriate flexible boundaries with your adult children. In this way you will be able to attain interdependence between you. The first step in this process will be identifying how it was, and then communicating about it. You will then be able to work together with your adult children to form an interdependent relationship in which you are respectful of each other's needs.

There are many concepts in this chapter that are important to know when you approach your adult children. However, they are abstract and difficult to sort out. Do not get overwhelmed by trying to apply them or remember them. Just understanding them will be enough for now. Lasting changes generally come about as a result of internal changes in perceptions and attitudes rather than from trying to behave in the way you think you are supposed to. Be open to new ways of viewing people and relationships, and the power to go forward will come from within.

In the next chapter we will be looking at some ineffective ways other parents have responded to their adult children, so that you can learn from their mistakes and avoid perpetuating them in your family. If they sound like responses you have been using, you will learn why they created problems.

In the following chapters you will be given methods for approaching your adult children that have helped other families reconcile. Using them will increase the probability of your family relationships improving as well.

CHAPTER THIRTEEN

What Not to Do

And in the naked light I saw,
Ten thousand people maybe more.
People talking without speaking,
People hearing without listening,
People writing songs that voices never share,
And no one dare disturb the sound of silence.

"Fools!" said I, "You do not know
Silence like a cancer grows.
Hear my words that I might teach you,
Take my arms that I might reach you."
But my words like silent raindrops fell
And echoed in the wells of silence.

PAUL SIMON, "The Sounds of Silence"*

Parents often get caught in their old patterns of handling confrontations, and cut off their adult children before they have had the chance to fully express themselves. The result is that issues don't get resolved and pent-up feelings do not get discharged. If parents were able to allow their adult children to finish more of what they had to say, the initial feelings could be ventilated, and the deeper emotions and issues could be exposed so that they could be addressed and dealt with openly.

Parents who do not know how to handle grievances from the past usually do not respond to their adult children in a positive and productive way when they are confronted. They defend themselves in the only way they know how. Their primary motivation is to try preserve their self-esteem, but in the end they alienate their children even more. Parents have acquired a negative reputation for being uncaring and unable to change, because of their defensive responses to confrontation.

Claudia Black, in her book *Repeat After Me,* writes, "Unless your parents have experienced a recovery process dealing with their own problems and/or if they feel good about themselves and no longer continue old behaviors, they will not understand what you are saying. They will repeat their own patterns of defense—ignore you, scream, blame, cry, or give you token acknowledgment. Do not expect them to say, 'I'm sorry,' 'I love you,' 'I was wrong.'"

Susan Forward, in *Toxic Parents,* states the same concept in an even more devastating manner: "As I write this I feel a deep sadness at having to warn you that the people who were supposed to nurture, love, and protect you will, in all likelihood, assault you emotionally when you dare to tell the truth."

It is distressing to me how often parents do respond exactly as these authors claim. Equally distressing, however, is the fact that there have been few attempts to understand why parents "assault" their children when faced with confrontation.

The reason parents respond as they do seems very basic and understandable. Parents have no conception of how to respond to what feels like an assault on them: on their lives, their morals, their behaviors, their ability to parent, their marriage, and their beings. People spend a great deal of their lives trying to keep from letting down their guards and being wounded. It is unrealistic to expect them to respond in a positive way without any guidance or understanding of how to do so. Their automatic reaction is to defend their positions.

In one family, three out of the four adult children have been able to get along with their parents. Angie, however, never has. She has been going to therapy, and has discovered some dynamics in the family that have upset her. As a child she had been singled out as the vehicle for her parents' own displaced anger and frustration and she had been subject to severe humiliation whenever she had thoughts that were different from the norm. Not very productively, Angie has harassed and verbally attacked her parents for the past few months in a poor attempt to communicate her pain. Her parents have responded by denying her accusations and calling their other adult children for validation and to complain about how horribly they are being treated by her.

These parents are responding like typical parents who have no idea how to respond to their child's accusations. They defend themselves, attack her therapist's credibility and Angie's sanity, and compare her to her sister and brothers, who they insist have no problems and never had any problems. In this way, they try to prove to everyone who will listen to them that Angie is the problem, not them. The result of this behavior is that no resolution is reached and this battle has only increased the bad feelings between them. (It would have been a lot easier on her parents if Angie had confronted them in a positive way. However, since she did not and your adult children may not, it is important to learn how to handle this kind of confrontation.)

This situation is not anyone's fault. Parents don't know what to do, and adult children don't know how to prepare their parents for the confrontations that are bound to take place. If the adult children are in therapy, they may practice being able to tolerate probable responses from their parents. So they are prepared—sort of. Usually they are not prepared enough. But the parents have no preparation at all and the response they give is rarely what their children need. The exceptions are in those cases when the parents begin to make the same realizations as their children and become open to change. They can then connect to their children's pain in a profound way.

The following are some of the most common responses of parents to confrontations by their adult children. Try to avoid them if at all possible. Read the scenarios so that you can get the impact of receiving these responses and understand not only what not to do but why you should not to do it. I have listed twenty of the most common responses. Although they may seem to be exaggerated, they are authentic.

In the following chapters, some of the adult children will continue their dialogues in letter form, expanding on what they were trying to communicate. This will give you the chance to hear what they wanted to say but couldn't complete because they were interrupted by their parents' defensiveness.

1. The counterattack

ADULT CHILD: I lived in constant fear of your temper.

PARENT: You were always hypersensitive. A little yelling never hurt anyone. Why don't you act like a man?

2. The self-defense

ADULT CHILD: You were always so nervous when we were growing up. I could never say anything to you about my feelings, because I was afraid you'd fall apart.

PARENT: I tried to be a good mom to you. I was just trying to make sure everything was okay. It was so hard to raise you and your brothers.

3. The call to a Higher Authority

ADULT CHILD: In our family there wasn't any life at all. All there were were rules, rules, rules. Your rules, never our rules.

PARENT: It was God's will. If He hadn't wanted things that way, He would have made them different.

4. The implication that the child is crazy

ADULT CHILD: I hated you for being an alcoholic. A bottle was really the only thing you ever loved.

PARENT: What the hell are you talking about? I was never an alcoholic. I like to drink socially . . . everyone does. It must be those crazy shrinks you've been going to. . . .

5. The avoidance of the subject

ADULT CHILD: You pretended that Dad didn't have a drinking problem for as long as I can remember. You just shut your eyes and acted like it wasn't happening.

PARENT: Do you want some lunch? You must be hungry.

6. The cliché-quoting

ADULT CHILD: You and Dad were always punishing me for something. It didn't matter how hard I tried or how much I did. There was always something that didn't meet up to your expectations, and I was spanked or given the belt, or something I cared about was taken away.

PARENT: We weren't trying to hurt you. It hurt us worse than it hurt you. Everything we did to you was for your own good.

7. The philosophical statements

ADULT CHILD: You always thought Janet was so much better than me. She could do no wrong. She was always prettier, smarter, more popular, more lovable. How do you think I felt, always compared to her and always losing? It wasn't fair.

PARENT: Whoever said life was fair?

8. The minimizing of the child's experience

ADULT CHILD: Why did you have to control everything I did? I wasn't ever allowed to have a mind of my own.

PARENT: It wasn't that bad. I just set limits and structure. You're making a big deal out of nothing.

9. The ungrateful child

ADULT CHILD: Why weren't you ever there when I needed you, Dad? How come everything else was more important than being a father?

PARENT: I spent the best years of my life working to support you and your brothers and this is what I get. . . .

10. The denial of the truth

ADULT CHILD: I can't believe I'm confronting you about this, but it's time I did. I've remembered, Dad. I remember you coming into my room at night and touching me in ways you were supposed to protect me from being touched. I was only eight years old.

PARENT: I don't know where you're getting your ideas from but that's ridiculous. I never touched you. What kind of a parent would do something like that?

11. The pain comparison

ADULT CHILD: Dad, I lived in terror of your violence. You would throw things, eyes glassy, face red and hard, mouth clenched. It was terrifying.

PARENT: You want to hear some real troubles, I'll tell you what happened to me when I was a kid.

12. The sarcastic response

ADULT CHILD: I hated it that you always tried to flirt with my girlfriends, putting your arms around them, leering at them. It wasn't right. It was embarrassing to them and to me.

PARENT: Well, what do you want me to do about it now? Get down on my knees and beg for your forgiveness?

13. The shifting of blame

ADULT CHILD: Do you know what it did to me to watch the way you treated Mom? You ignored her, went out on her, treated her like a servant.

PARENT: Your mom was cold as ice. I never would have survived if I'd had to depend on her.

14. Giving unsolicited advice

ADULT CHILD: You and Mom always acted like everything was perfect in our family—everything except me, that is. You never dealt with your problems—all you did was focus on what was wrong with me.

PARENT: What you really ought to do is try exercising and eating properly. Maybe then you wouldn't feel so upset all the time.

15. The defense of someone else

ADULT CHILD: Mom, there are some sexual things that my grandfather did to me when I was small that I need to talk to you about.

PARENT: How dare you say such a thing about your grandfather!

16. The righteous pose

ADULT CHILD: How could you spend so many years going on and on about irrelevant things and ignoring how depressed and defeated we all were?

PARENT: Don't be insolent with me, young lady.

17. Walking away

ADULT CHILD: Do you know what it feels like not to have a mom you can talk to or count on because she's passed out drunk on the couch?

PARENT: I've got to go now.

18. The humiliation or abasement of the self

ADULT CHILD: How come you set it up so that we all had to be parts of people instead of whole? I was more than just a brain, Laurie was more than just a pretty shell, and Tom was more than just a jock.

PARENT: I'm a failure as a mother and a person. I've done everything wrong. You must think I'm contemptible.

19. The "You're saying that to hurt me" style

ADULT CHILD: The hardest thing for me growing up was watching you disintegrate before my eyes.

PARENT: You're trying to hurt me, aren't you. You have to open up old wounds. Why are you doing this to me?

20. The "It was good enough for me" style

ADULT CHILD: I hated you when you threatened to give away my animals if I didn't do what you wanted.

PARENT: Well, my father treated me that way, and I turned out just fine.

All of the above responses are basically defensive maneuvers. It's not surprising that parents are defensive. Most of us have spent our whole lives armoring ourselves against attack. When an appropriate time arrives for us to take our armor off, we don't even know how. When we made mistakes in our childhood we avoided admitting them, for good reason. What were your parents likely to say if they thought they'd caught you doing something bad? "Don't lie about it. Admit it. Admit it." And then if you did admit it, you would get whacked or punished for your crime or at the very least you would get told that you were a disappointment to them. So when our children want us to admit how we hurt them, instead of *aligning with them* against the absurd and hurtful behaviors we have all been subjected to, we dig in our heels, become children ourselves, and guard ourselves with all our might. And of course if the guard goes up, the wall cannot break down.

Mistakes are easily made even in fairly open relationships. My fourteen-year-old daughter, Chanti, was talking the other day about the times that I had failed her in one way or another when I was busy, preoccupied, or moody. I responded, "All you ever remember are the bad things," counterattacking, and thereby discounting her feelings. How much better and more honest it would have been to have acknowledged the truth in what she said, since she was accurate that I had been ignoring her. I could have listened to what she said, reflecting back, "You miss me when I'm not there for you," or I could have self-disclosed, "It's hard to listen to you now. I feel badly that I haven't been there for you in a better way."

Mistakes can be repaired. You can go back and do it right the second time, or the third time, or the fourth. How else can people learn? Dr. Haim Ginnott, author of several books on parenting, writes that kids should be given hundreds of chances. Adults should be given hundreds of chances too. A failure in communicating with your children means that you are learning and that you made a mistake. It doesn't mean anything more. Successful people fail more often, because they continue trying and failing until they eventually succeed. If you don't risk, you don't fail, but you don't learn and grow either.

To sum up what not to do, don't:

1. Counterattack.
2. Defend yourself.
3. Call on a Higher Authority.
4. Act like your child is crazy.
5. Avoid the subject.
6. Use clichés.
7. Use philosophical statements.
8. Minimize your child's experience.
9. Talk about gratitude.
10. Deny the truth.
11. Negatively compare your child's pain to yours.
12. Respond sarcastically.
13. Blame someone else.
14. Give unsolicited advice.
15. Defend another person.
16. Act righteous.
17. Walk away.
18. Humiliate yourself.
19. Say that your child is out to hurt you.
20. Say that you turned out okay with the same treatment.

EXERCISES

1. What were your reactions to the children's statements?

_____

_____

_____

_____

2. What were your reactions to the parents' answers?

_____

_____

_____

_____

3. Would your parents have used any of these responses with you? If so, which ones, and how would you have felt as a result?

_____

_____

_____

_____

4. Can you think of other responses your parents might have made to your confronting them? If so, write them down and consider how you would have felt as a result.

_____

_____

_____

_____

5. Which statements seem closest to ones that your children might say to you?

_____

_____

_____

_____

6. Which responses would be hardest for you to avoid using on your children?

_____

_____

_____

_____

7. Write down any other ways you think you might respond to your children that would not be useful for them or for you.

_____

_____

_____

_____

Now you are ready to go on to the next chapters, to find out what works. The better prepared you are, the more likely you will be to have a successful initial communication, which will set the tone for positive interactions in the future.

CHAPTER FOURTEEN

Letters and Responses

What's past is prologue.

SHAKESPEARE, *The Tempest*

In the complex world of relationships, it is often easier to figure out what not to do than what to do. Sometimes, of course, just not getting in the way of someone's communication is helpful in itself.

In order to find out directly what adult children need from their parents, I have asked numerous adult children to respond to the following questions:

Question 1. What would you say to your parents if you felt you could express your feelings about your childhood to them openly?

Question 2. What would you want your parents to say to you in response?

Some of their answers have been reconstructed and organized into the letters that make up the bulk of this chapter. Their answers to the first question will give you an idea of the kinds of things your own adult children might say to you if they thought you would respond in a positive way. Their answers to the second question will show you how you might respond to your adult children if they did share with you openly.

The responses the adult children wanted from their parents fell naturally into five parts. These were:

1. *To be listened to.*
2. *To have their statements and feelings acknowledged and validated.*
3. *To know how their parents felt.*
4. *To have their parents express regret for their adult children's undeserved pain and struggle.*
5. *To have their parents offer to make restoration, mainly by being willing to work with them on the current relationship.*

The explanations below will help you understand these five components of effective responses. We will be using these five parts in several ways. Keep them in mind when you meet with your adult children to talk in more depth about the issues that concern you both.

1. *Listening to the adult children's feelings.* Recall the parts in prior chapters when you went back to being a child and felt how painful it was to be badly treated. If you skipped over the earlier chapters or exercises, please go back and do them now, so that you can understand this process on a deeper level. Once you have reaccessed these feelings you will be able more easily to say to your adult children, "You must have felt so frightened, angry, humiliated, or confused, when that happened." Often there are several mixed feelings involved and you can let them know that you understand this.

2. *Acknowledgment of the validity of part or all of the adult children's statements.* The importance of acknowledging children's perceptions cannot be overemphasized. Children grow up believing they are crazy when their parents deny what is happening at home. If you or others have been hurtful to your children, it may be hard to admit that you were hurtful or that certain events occurred, but it is important for you to do so. What you will be saying essentially, and it doesn't have to be said in a complicated way, is: "Yes, it was like that. You did not imagine it." Be careful not to minimize their feelings.

The purpose of acknowledging your children's experience is to let them know that you understand what they went through and how they perceive the past. The specific details of what actually occurred do not have to be proven or disproven. Things in the past and even in the present are rarely verifiable, and things are seen from different perspectives. Your purpose is not to discredit your adult children's views; it is to create an open emotional climate for them, so they can trust you and share their thoughts with you.

3. *Self-disclosure about how the adult children's feelings are affecting their parents. Also, self-disclosure about past patterns or events which generated the hurtful behaviors that were involved.* When you respond to your children, you may need to let them know how the interaction with them is affecting you. If you feel yourself getting upset as you listen to your child, it is a good idea to let them know that. You might say, "It is hard for me when I realize how angry you must be. I used to think I was doing a good job as a parent." Or "It hurts me to remember some of the things that have happened. I want to talk with you about these areas, but it is very hard to do." It is also important to self-disclose about those patterns you learned that you repeated when they were small. "I learned growing up that you get hit with a belt if you don't do what you're told, and even though I hated it, I just couldn't help doing the same things to you that my father did to me when I became frustrated," would be one example. Be careful to self-disclose about the past to share information with your children, not to defend your actions.

4. *Regret for the adult children's undeserved pain and struggle.* Regret means that you are sorry for what happened, and wish that it could have been avoided. Regret is not to be confused with guilt and self-castigation. Whatever has been done can't be undone and you did the best you could at the time. If you could have done it differently, you would have. Let your children know that you realize that they did not deserve to be treated badly. You might say, "I wish you had not had to go

through all the pain you experienced," or "I'm so sorry I used to take out my frustration on you by criticizing and controlling you. You did not deserve to be treated like that."

5. *Restoration in ways that are possible.* Express your willingness to do what you can to lessen the hurt your children have experienced. The most useful way is simply to be willing to talk further and to make changes that will help yourself and your relationship now. If you can afford to pay for therapy, and your children cannot, you might offer to help pay for your adult children's counseling, if they want to go.

As you go through the five responses, you will become accustomed to using them. Remember Angie, in the last chapter, whose parents were distraught over her verbal attacks and complained to her brothers, sister, and everyone else how abusive she was? Imagine how much better it would have been for their relationship if her parents had taken this approach.

Instead of defending themselves and pointing to how their other children weren't having problems with them, they could have told Angie gently how hard it was to listen to her when she sounded so angry [self-disclosure]. Then they could have listened to the real pain underneath her anger [listening]. They could have admitted that it had been hard for her growing up [acknowledgment] and said that they felt badly thinking about the times she'd been hurt [regret]. They could have shared some of their struggles and lack of knowledge and understanding of her [self-disclosure], and indicated a willingness to try to do it differently now [restoration].

The arguing would never have escalated as it did. Instead, the barriers would have come down, and the exciting work of communication could have started. That was what Angie wanted. Her intention was not to see them punished or hurt, even though she was angry with them. In reality, of the four children, she was the one who cared the most about a genuine relationship. The others had compromised in order to have a partial relationship, and didn't talk about things that they too were dissatisfied with.

Of course, ideally Angie would have approached her parents in a more diplomatic way. Perhaps your adult children have or will. However, many children do not approach their parents very politely, and it's important not to get side-tracked in demanding that their confrontations be courteous. It will just stop you from getting to the important work that needs to be done to heal your relationship. Be prepared for the possibility that your adult children will express their anger and frustration undiplomatically. That way you will not be caught off guard and you will be able to respond to them effectively.

Here are several letters from adult children and the responses they wish they could receive from their parents.

Note: Letters concerning major abuse are in Chapter Sixteen. Read that chapter even if you think it does not apply to you, since abuse may have happened in your family without your knowledge. Read it thoroughly if you have any suspicion at all that your children have been abused sexually or if there has been severe physical or emotional abuse, extreme neglect, or alcoholism in your family.

LETTERS AND RESPONSES

1. Dear Dad,

Why weren't you ever there when I needed a dad? Why didn't you take being a father seriously—as important as meetings, sports, the newspaper, and the TV? At least once in a while you could have spent time with me—being a father to your son. You never had time to go to any of my games, open-school nights, play ball with me, or help me with my homework. I grew up feeling worse than if you had been gone physically. At least then I wouldn't have had to see you around and feel hurt each time I was unable to reach you. I grew up feeling worse than if you had physically abused me. At least then you would have noticed me. At least then I might not have grown up feeling that you ignored me because there was something wrong with me. I wouldn't have felt that I might as well be invisible. I figured out when I was real small that I wasn't good enough to be your son. It's left me feeling insignificant, no matter what I accomplish, always trying to prove that I'm worth something. That seems absurd now, but it has been a belief I've grown up with that has lasted. I don't understand. Why didn't you want to be with me?

Dear Bill,

You're right. Most of the time I acted as if you didn't exist. I put importance on everything but my children. What you're saying is true, and I realize that I hurt you badly [acknowledgment of child's feelings, without minimizing or defending]. It had to have been hard for you to need a father and not have me there for you, day after day, year after year [listening to feelings].

I feel terrible for what I did, and I don't have any excuses. I didn't even know who you were, I was so self-absorbed. My only sort of justification is the fact that my father abandoned my mother when I was very small and I never learned how to be a dad. I was also always trying to prove myself, to a dad I never had. I felt that I would just be a failure with you, and I never even tried to get to know you. It was easier to watch sports than deal with people [self-disclosure]. I wish that we had gotten help long ago. I needed to understand myself before having kids, but I didn't know how. I feel so badly that I hurt you and that you believed things about yourself that were untrue and that caused you to doubt yourself [regret, not guilt]. I know it's thirty years late, but if we can talk now and I can help in any way I want to try [restoration].

2. Dear Mom,

The hardest part about growing up for me was that you were always so nervous. I never knew why, and I always thought I made you nervous, but I see now that I have left home that you are just as nervous as you ever were. I always felt that I didn't dare talk to you because you would surely fall apart. It's not that you ever said anything . . . it's just that you were like a nervous bird always worried, always trembling. It's not that it was your fault. It's just that I couldn't say what I needed because your needs always came first.

Dear David,

It feels real bad to read your letter, mostly because what you say is true. I have been self-absorbed [acknowledgment]. I want you to know that you're right that it was never your fault that I was so anxious. I would have been that way with any child [self-disclosure]. It must have been hard for you to feel like you always had to keep your feelings suppressed to protect me [listening]. I wish I had gotten help and handled what needed to be handled and gotten on with life. Instead I hurt you sense-lessly, with my constant anxiety and fear [regret]. Let's talk more so you can tell me more about how this affected you and we can try to make things different from now on [restoration].

3. Dear Dad,

The hardest thing for me growing up was watching you disintegrate. You never found a place for yourself, you never laughed or played. You just lived in a despair and depression that will haunt me for my entire life. I had no clue as to how to be a happy person, and for years I was just like you, and I hated myself.

Dear Andrea,

You're right. I've never been able to be happy, and I'm still confused and alone. I've been trapped in unhappiness for years and have been unable to get out [acknowledgment]. I never realized that watching my pain affected you. I wish I hadn't been so self-absorbed and only aware of my own pain [regret]. I don't know if there's anything I can do that can make up for those years but if I can help by listening or talking to you I'll try [restoration]. I'll try to help myself too. I guess you're saying that it would help you to know that I'm doing more with my life than barely surviving [listening]. I want to help myself for me too. There's no use going on like this until I die. I feel as if I am dead already. I have to deal with my problems if I'm ever going to get out of this hole [self-disclosure].

4. Dear Mom,

   I used to be so afraid of your temper, Mom. I never knew when you were going to explode. There never seemed to be any outside reason . . . just the time of the month or the weather. . . . Things seemed to be going along fine, but then your mood would shift and you'd be a different person. You'd flare up at nothing. When I was still pretty young, I stopped trusting you. It was a big problem though because there was no one else I could trust, so I trusted no one.

   Dear Toby,

   My moods have always felt beyond my control, and the outside circumstances didn't matter very much. Little things triggered big ones and I exploded [acknowledgment]. I can see where your trust would be broken which is something that could scar you for life [listening]. I wish I had gotten therapy a long time ago to deal with issues such as my being sexually abused when I was small. Maybe then I wouldn't have brought all of my old problems into my own family [self-disclosure]. I am willing to talk with you more about anything you'd like whenever you want to. I know that I've hurt you and your sister very badly and I am really sorry you were hurt by me [regret]. That doesn't make up for anything in the past, but maybe we can have a relationship now, in the present. Please let me know what I can do to help you to learn to trust me and others so you don't have to continue feeling so alone [restoration].

5. Dear Dad,

   Do you know what it did to me to watch the way you treated Mom? You ignored her, went out with other women, treated her like a servant. You were a lot of fun to be with when we went places together: I was your special daughter, and you loved to show me off. But Dad, you tore mom's soul to pieces. You broke her spirit. And because you broke hers, mine broke as well. My relationships with men have been repeats of your relationship with Mom, because of what I watched as a child. I'm afraid to even get involved in a relationship.

Dear Karen,

It is so hard to listen to what you are saying. I thought we had something special between us, but now you are saying that that doesn't count because of how my relationship with Mom was. It is really hard to hear this, but I guess I had better listen if we are going to clear this up [self-disclosure]. I know that I treated Mom disgracefully. You're right that I went out on her and treated her badly. She did everything around the house and I didn't help her [acknowledgment]. I have to say that I had no idea how much you were hurt by this, or that you felt so resentful of me. I guess you felt connected to your mom a lot more than I knew [listening]. I didn't mean to hurt you, and you may not believe this but I honestly didn't mean to hurt your mother, either [regret]. It didn't work out for us, and I don't mean to justify myself by that, but I basically treated her like my dad treated my mom [self-disclosure]. I know I can never make it up to her. It's too late. She won't even talk to me. But is there something I can do for you, so that the past hurts you less? Can we talk more about this, soon [restoration]?

6. Dear Mom,

You and Dad were always punishing me for something. It didn't matter how hard I tried or how much I did. There was always something about me that didn't meet up to your expectations, and I was spanked or given the belt or something I cared about was taken away. I wasn't such a bad kid. Why did you act like I was? I have so much anger and distrust built up inside because of the way you treated me. This is especially frightening to me, because we are going to have a child in a few months and I don't want to pass all of this on to a new generation. I don't want my child to feel the fear towards me that I felt towards you.

Dear Jerry,

Until recently, I never realized how harsh we were with you. You are right. You weren't a bad kid at all and you did not deserve to be treated the way we treated you [acknowledgment]. It sounds like you have had a hard time in many areas that we really didn't know about, and that this has gotten in your way for much too long [listening]. I feel badly that you have had to carry around so much anger and fear from your childhood but I am so proud that you are working it out now, before your baby is born. I wish I'd had the wisdom and knowledge so necessary to being a parent [regret]. Let us continue to talk with each other and straighten out the past so that it does not continue to harm the future. Let me know what you need from me. I am here for you now, and I hope it is not too late to make things work out for you and your family [restoration].

7. Dear Mom,

You and Dad always acted like everything was perfect in our family, everything, that is, except me. I was the focus of all your attention. You never dealt with your own problems. You both had so many terrible things happen while you were growing up, but all you ever did was obsess about me. You thought that if you did all the right things for me it would make everything inside you all right, but it didn't work. I didn't need you to sign me up for every program in town or to be a part of everything I was part of. I felt engulfed and stifled by your presence and I felt bad and guilty because it looked like you were such "good" parents. In fact, you were overprotective, overpreoccupied, overbearing, and overwhelming. It was too much work for me then and it's too much of a burden now. I can't be enmeshed with you anymore. You have to deal with your own life, and I have to deal with mine.

Dear Tony,

I never would have understood what you are saying if I hadn't read about unresolved problems carrying through to the next generation. It makes so much sense now. Dad and I were so concerned that you looked okay—that is, that we looked okay because of how you were—we focused all our energy on trying to make you into someone perfect [acknowledgment]. We tried to live our lives through you. That way we didn't have time to think about our inability to talk to each other or to have a close relationship. I didn't have to deal with my anger toward my parents for their betrayals and abandonment [self-disclosure]. I can see now how much pressure it put on you and how I prevented you from becoming your own person [listening]. I am sorry that I ended up hurting and burdening the person I most wanted to protect [regret]. Please give me a chance to work with you on this and to straighten out our relationship on your terms [restoration].

Note the commonalities in the parents' responses:

1. The parents validate and *acknowledge* their children's perceptions and feelings.
2. They *listen* to the hurt behind the anger and accusations. They don't get trapped by the accusations into feeling intimidated or humiliated. They don't fall into using the useless attacks listed in Chapter Thirteen.
3. They *self-disclose* about how they feel in the moment and state their intention of continuing to listen anyway. They *self-disclose* about how their own childhood has influenced their actions.
4. They express *regret* for the pain that their children have experienced.
5. They offer to make *restoration* in some way, now that they are aware of the hurt their children have felt.

Next try your hand at responding by yourself to some letters from adult children, using the five steps we have been going over. If you are not sure what to say, look at a completed letter to find appropriate words. There is no one right answer. Your best check of whether the responses are effective is to pretend you are the adult child who has written the letter and see if the response you've written as the parent strikes a positive chord for you as the child.

8. Dear Mom,

There are some things that really hurt me growing up, and if we're going to have an open relationship I want to be able to tell you how I felt back then. When you and Dad divorced my world felt like it was crumbling, and you wouldn't ever talk to me about it. You were so angry at Dad and bitter towards him that it seemed to take over your whole being. Anything I felt didn't seem to matter. I just tried to be good so I wouldn't make any more trouble for you. I know you tried your best and I know it was hard on you to lose Dad after twenty-five years, but the atmosphere in our house during my teenage years was so stiff and tense that I could hardly stand it.

Dear Jackie,

It's true. I_____

_____

_____[acknowledgment].

I feel terrible that I _____

_____

_____[self-disclosure].

You must have felt_____

_____

_____[listening].

I'm so sorry that_____

_____

_____[regret].

If there is some way to_____

_____

_____[restoration].

9. Dear Dad,

 All you ever knew was rules, rules, and more rules. There were rules for sitting, rules for playing, rules for sleeping, rules for living, rules for eating . . . always so many goddamn rules. Your rules were the law. No exceptions. Why no exceptions, Dad? Why were your rules the only ones that counted? How come you were the authority? Because of your obsession with rules, I've spent years of my life trying to fight rules and it's been exhausting. I never should have had to. There should have been warmth and flexibility in our home, not just rigidity and ice.

Dear Pat,

It's true. I_____

_____

_____[acknowledgment].

I feel terrible that I_____

_____

_____[self-disclosure].

You must have felt_____

_____

_____[listening].

I'm so sorry that_____

_____

_____[regret].

If there is some way to_____

_____

_____[restoration].

10. Dear Mom,

You always thought Janet was so much better than me. She could do no wrong. She was always prettier, smarter, more popular, and more lovable. How do you think I felt, always being compared to her and always losing? It wasn't fair. What do you think that did to my self-confidence? How come you never recognized my special qualities and only concentrated on Janet? She was so wonderful that she got all your attention, and I was either invisible or wrong. Do you have any idea how much that has hurt me over the years, in my friendships, in my relationships, in my own self-esteem?

Dear Cindy,

It's true. I_____

_____

_____[acknowledgment].

I feel terrible that I_____

_____

_____[self-disclosure].

You must have felt_____

_____

_____[listening].

I'm so sorry that_____

_____

_____[regret].

If there is some way to_____

_____[restoration].

Now that you have had some experience with other adult children, you will have a chance to try responding to your own children. One way of doing this is offered below. Try writing what you think one of your adult children would write to you if he thought you would listen to him nonjudgmentally. Respond to that letter using the five steps we have been going over. The purpose of these exercises is to identify and clarify some of the things that happened in the past that have had a harmful affect on your adult children and to practice responding to their pain.

In the next chapter there are several methods suggested for approaching your adult children. One of the methods you may decide to use at that time is to bring your writing with you to help you focus on the problems that you want to resolve. The next chapter will help clarify how to do this. What you have written about the past will then be your "prologue" to enhancing your present and future relationship.

In writing these letters, you will probably remember some difficulties your adult children experienced that are from sources outside of your relationship and you will want to acknowledge these areas. However, your main goal is to clear up your own relationship with your children, so your focus will need to be on the barriers between you. Even if your child had a very difficult time with his father, for example, concentrate on the problems between the two of you rather than on their relationship.

You may want to reread Chapters Four and Five to recall the problems your children encountered growing up. Remember: If there was major abuse in your family, your letter will vary in some ways, which are outlined in Chapter Sixteen.

Now, write a letter to yourself from one of your adult children, saying what you think your child would say to you if she felt she could speak freely. If you want to write this letter, but you are having trouble doing it by yourself, ask someone you trust who knows your family to help you. If there is no one available, jot down some notes, or fill in some parts of it.

Dear Mom or Dad,

Part 1: It's hard to tell you this because (I don't want to hurt you, we never talked about these things, I have so much built up anger, I'm afraid of how you'll react)_____

_____

_____

or . . . I've tried to tell you about this before but (you weren't willing to listen, you cut me off, you reacted so angrily, you seemed so crushed)_____

_____

Part 2: Some painful things that happened to me while growing up were:

_____

_____

_____

and/or . . . Some things that you did that hurt me were:_____

_____

_____

_____

Part 3: The ways I felt at those times were: (angry, frustrated, furious, scared, intimidated, lonely, anxious, hopeless, terrified, humiliated)_____

_____

_____

Part 4: The ways these things have affected my life are:_____

_____

_____

_____

_____

    Do not make this letter very long. Now, to the best of your ability, write your caring response to this letter, dividing it into the five steps.

1. Acknowledgment:

_____

_____

_____

2. Listening:

_____

_____

_____

3. Self-disclosure:

_____

_____

_____

4. Regret:

_____

_____

_____

5. Restoration:

_____

_____

_____

Check this response over and see if you have communicated what you want to say, and if you think you would feel good about receiving this response from your parents. Put any finishing touches on the letters that you think will increase their effectiveness if you decide to bring these letters with you when you talk to your adult children about the struggles of the past.

CHAPTER FIFTEEN

Methods for Approaching Your Adult Children

I had no time to hate, because
The grave would hinder me,
And life was not so ample I
Could finish enmity.

Nor had I time to love; but since
Some industry must be,
The little toil of love, I thought,
Was large enough for me.

EMILY DICKINSON

The methods presented here for approaching your adult children have a high probability of breaking down the barriers between you. When you begin talking with your adult children, you will have the chance to apply the difficult personal work you have done. The internal changes you have made and the awareness you have gained will help you in the reconciliation process.

The way you approach your adult child will depend upon the condition of your relationship. If your relationship with your adult child has been fairly positive and open, you may have already shared with her some of the things you have discovered. If so, you are probably listening more deeply to what she is saying and disclosing more of the vulnerable parts of yourself. If you have not yet approached your adult child about these issues and your relationship is generally positive, almost any approach you take is likely to deepen and strengthen your relationship. If you have not spoken with your adult child about the specific things that you feel were problems for her when she was growing up you may want to set up a meeting with her for this specific purpose. This will allow you to break down any barriers from the past that still remain between you. If she seems hesitant to bring up anything negative, it may be because she is afraid that dealing with these areas will hurt you. Bringing up specific problem areas will let her know that you are open to discussing them. You can explain that addressing these issues is important for you, your relationship, and future generations, and worth the initial pain.

If your adult child has given you this book, this meeting will give you a chance to find out more about why she thought you ought to read it. Even if she suggested you read it because of one of your other children, there are probably things that happened in the past that have affected her as well. If your relationship with your adult child has been distant or troubled, and she gave you this book, you will be in a good position to communicate with her, as she has already opened the door for you. It will be important to find out what has hurt her in the past, and the methods below will help you to do so.

If you have bought this book on your own and you are trying to reach an adult child who is distant from you or if your previous encounters have been antagonistic or ineffective, you will need to go slowly. If your adult child has been unwilling to communicate with you, it will be even harder to break through the walls. You may have to try more than one of the options presented here. *If your relationship is in one of these difficult places, read the remainder of this book before you approach your adult children.* That way you will be able to deal with other problematic situations that may arise. Don't be discouraged if your previous efforts have not worked. Certainly you did the best you could at the time. However, you probably did not know that you needed to take the time to explore your memories or feelings or to view your relationship in terms of history and the effects events had on you. You probably weren't prepared to deal with defensiveness or distrust. You most likely were unaware of the types of responses to avoid. And, you most likely didn't have a clear approach to use that would allow you to share your feelings and to listen to your child on a deep level. It may take a while for your adult child to realize how much work you have been doing, so you will need to be patient. But you will be approaching your child differently now, and your chance of breaking through will be greater.

Caution: If your child has been subjected to sexual abuse, serious physical or emotional abuse, extreme neglect, or if you have had little contact with your child over the years, you may need to go even more slowly. Additional guidelines are offered in the next chapter.

It may not be easy to break down the walls between you and your adult children. You will need to be understanding and accepting of differences. You will need to be willing to be intimate. You will need to approach your adult children with humility, but not with arrogance or shame. And you will need to be open to learning about yourself and your relationship. If these concepts seem vague or unfamiliar, go back and reread Chapter Twelve, "Breaking Down the Walls."

This is not the time to bring up grievances that you may have against your adult child. Doing so will be counterproductive to your purpose of giving your child a safe place to share openly about her own experiences and feelings. You will have a chance to let her know the ways she has hurt you, too, but not until later. An exercise for doing this is in Chapter Seventeen.

There will also be a chance to share the positive parts of your relationship. There are several lighter exercises for you to do together later on. For most people, this process will work best if the barriers between them and their adult children are broken down first.

Several methods parents have used to approach their adult children that have been successful are listed below. You can use their approaches as models in order to have a base and structure for your own communication. You may want to practice using these methods in your own mind. This may give you some perspective on how your adult child will react and help you prepare to listen. Your initial contact with your children can be made in person, by phone, or by letter. Talking in person or by phone will give you more immediate results and allow more flexible give-and-take. However, letters are sometimes easier because you can carefully organize your thoughts and because letters give the other person a chance to absorb what you have written before having to respond. Your communication will work fine by phone or letter if distance prevents you from meeting.

No matter which approach you use, communicating about these sensitive areas with your adult child without defending yourself can be extremely difficult. Remind yourself how far you have come in understanding yourself and your history. Acknowledge yourself for having the courage to explore the truth about your past. Think about the chapter on your child within, and hold the child you once were close as you prepare to meet with your adult child. Remember that your adult child will not know how hard you have been working or that your intention really is to make peace with her. If your relationship has been difficult, your child may think you are going to resort to old ways of handling things, and she may not trust you. It is up to you to show her that you have begun to change. You need to let her know that you realize you still have a lot to learn, and that you want to continue your search together with her. Most of all, you need to remember to listen to her. It is up to you to let your love and caring show through.

There are several options below for approaching your adult child. Whatever approach you choose, *make sure you include at least some of the five parts below in all of your communications with your adult child. We've gone over them before, but I strongly suggest you go over them once more.*

1. *Self-disclose.* Self-disclose from your heart your intention to repair the relationship and to deal with the hard issues. Self-disclose why it is important to you. Let your adult child know what your reasons are for going through your own healing process. Ask for your adult child's help in repairing your relationship. If your adult child's responses are very painful to hear, you will probably need to let her know this. Tell her gently that you want to continue but that it is a struggle for you not to defend yourself.

2. *Listen.* Listen carefully. When your adult child begins to share, listen as patiently as you can until she is finished. Keep listening and trying to understand what your adult child's experiences were like. You are trying to learn about her and how she perceives the past. Check with her to see if you do understand. There is no need to feel defensive. You are both struggling together against the enemies of hurtful, repetitive patterns, lack of skills, and misunderstandings.

Remember that listening is something you do with your entire being. Your voice tone when you respond makes a difference. Your adult child will be able to tell if you are truly listening, by your facial expressions, and your posture. *Caution: If you self-disclose to your adult child without listening to her in turn you are actually using her rather than communicating with her. It will not work if you tell her what you learned and how you feel without listening to her.*

3. *Acknowledge your adult child's perceptions and feelings.* When your adult child shares her perceptions with you, find the parts of what she says that you believe and understand, and validate those parts. Don't defend yourself, your history, or anyone else whom she may be angry with or accusing of. Remember that anger is only a surface emotion. Below are hurt, fear, confusion, shame, emptiness, and helplessness.

If what your adult child says seems unbelievable to you,

you will need to take some time to listen more to your child, to look deeply inside and possibly to read more about abuse and your understandable feelings of disbelief. If you need more time to absorb what she is saying, tell her so, and emphasize that you are trying as hard as you can. Even if you feel certain that your adult child is exaggerating or making things up, this in itself speaks to the severity of the problems in your family, which need to be addressed. Especially acknowledge her feelings. Your primary purpose is to understand your adult child's perceptions and pain. You won't lose anything if you acknowledge the parts that you know occurred and recognize that the feelings she had and may still have are real. If you instead try to discredit your adult child's perceptions she will be unwilling to trust you with her thoughts and feelings. If you find yourselves at an impasse on this issue, you will probably need to get outside professional help, separately or together.

4. *Express regret.* Express your regret for the undeserved harm your child has received. Express your regret for the hurt she has experienced. If you wish that you could have protected her from having to go through so much pain and confusion, say so. If you feel that she deserved more love, care, or understanding, tell her that. Tell your adult child you are sorry for things you did to her, as you inadvertently repeated patterns from the past. Tell her you are sorry for times you neglected her as well.

5. *Express your willingness to make restoration.* Express your intention to make whatever restoration is necessary to heal your relationship. This does not mean you are obligated to pay for your mistakes of the past. Penance and penalties will not work anyway. Your restoration needs to be in the form of your determination to repair the relationship between you. You may, however, want to help pay for therapy if there has been a great deal of damage done to your adult child and you have the funds and she does not.

At the end of this chapter, there is space reserved for you to write down your personal plan for communicating with your adult child. It is a good idea to fill it in, as the more prepared you are, the less likely you will be to be caught off guard and act ineffectively.

ALTERNATIVE APPROACHES

Below are several approaches parents have used to reconcile with their adult children. These methods can be adjusted in any way that you think will work best for your family. Most can be done by mail, phone, or in person. They will probably lead to several conversations, in which you will be using the five responses listed above. At the end of each contact, make sure to set up another time in which to communicate.

Note: This book can be used as a bridge to approaching your adult children. The last method in this chapter gives you examples of how to use this book in this way. The parents below did not have this resource.

Basic Initial Contact

Some parents approached their adult children by briefly stating their thoughts and feelings and focusing on beginning the communication process. Their main purpose was to set up an initial meeting to deal with the issues that needed to be handled, not to bring up anything specific at that time.

Stuart called his daughter and said:

Diane, I have recently realized that I've made some serious mistakes as a parent, and that I've hurt you unintentionally. I want to talk with you more about this, and also to listen to your point of view, so our relationship can be more open and stronger. Would you be willing to meet with me for brunch next Sunday to talk about this?

Frank wrote the following to his daughter:

Dear Bonnie,

I'm learning things about my past that are helping me make sense out of our relationship and I'm starting to understand mistakes I've made that I deeply regret. I never realized until recently how harsh I was with you and how much I hurt you. I've always thought everyone else was the problem, but now I realize that most of it was me. It's hard to admit how much of it was me.

I love you and I care about how things have affected you. I never meant to hurt you. You didn't do anything to deserve the kind of treatment you received. I want to make things different and I'm willing to do whatever it takes for that to happen. Please meet with me soon to talk over some of these things. I want to listen to what you have to say. I will call you to set up a time and place to meet in the next two weeks.

Jim wrote:

Dear Chris,

There are a lot of things I have wanted to talk to you about for a long time but I haven't known how to. I want to share some things I've learned about myself that may help us to repair our relationship. I need to do this for myself, so I can grow and understand what went on for all of us. I think it's important for you too, because there is so much confusion and hostility between us.

It is hard for me to approach you, because I'm not really sure how to talk about this. I am afraid you won't understand me or work with me, and I sincerely want to work on our relationship together. Please, Chris, meet with me so I can talk with you about some things I've been discovering about myself, my history, and the way I was as a parent with you. I'm just starting to understand how my past affected you, and ways that I acted that were hurtful to you, even though I had the proverbial best intentions. And I need to hear how you felt and saw all of this. I promise to try to listen to you also—really listen, without being defensive. I really care about our relationship, and that's why I'm contacting you now. I'm willing to meet with you anyplace you'd be most comfortable, for an amount of time that you can handle. I could come to your home, we could meet in a restaurant or you are very welcome over to my house if you prefer. Call me if you get a chance, or I will call you within the next two weeks to talk about meeting.

Sharing an Idea

Some parents began their communication by talking about something they learned that was meaningful to them and tying this concept in with their relationship. For example, Krista began her communication with her adult child by referring to the differences between the partnership model and the authoritarian model.

I realize that growing up we lived in an authoritarian household where whoever was bigger was in control. I am just finding out that there is such a thing as a partnership model, which is based on equality and cooperation. In this system, no one uses or abuses power over anyone else. I want to talk to you about this concept and about how the abuse of power affected our family. I want our relationship now to be one that is equal and caring.

Note: If your being overly intellectual has been a problem in your family, be careful to express yourself on a feeling level.

Caring

A very successful approach parents have taken is to let their children know how much they value them and how proud they are of them. They then address the fact that they realize they have hurt their children and are sorry for the pain they caused.

Nora's dad approached her this way:

Nora, I don't think I've told you this directly before but I want you to know how much I love you and how glad I am that you're my daughter. I am so proud of you and how much you've accomplished. I also want to say that I am so sorry for the ways I've hurt you in the past, not meaning to, but hurting you just the same. My intentions might have been good but you'd never know it from my actions.

Listing Specific Hurtful Experiences

Other parents have opened up their relationships with their adult children by being more specific. They wrote down several things that they believed harmed their children when they were growing up and shared them with their adult children. This approach put the parents directly on the line. However, it allowed them to gain some benefits that more general approaches did not.

- They had a tangible way to convey to their adult children that they cared enough to spend time and effort in trying to understand how they felt as children.
- They directly opened up and confronted areas that their children were afraid to confront or areas their children were unaware of.
- They were able to defuse their children's anger, because they acknowledged up front what had happened and were willing to be vulnerable.

One adult child who had cut off contact with his dad three years previously said: "If my dad had just said that he felt badly about the past and he wanted to talk to me about it, I might've met him and listened, but I would have been on guard. But when he called and told me some of the specific things he'd done that he now realized were abusive and that he was genuinely sorry he had done them—well that took down ninety percent of my defenses. I knew then that he wasn't just talking around things. He was saying what I really wanted to hear. Feeding a very empty spot. I had decided before that I was better off just walking away and cutting my emotional losses rather than feeling bad all the time, but I had still felt terrible. I needed those family bonds intact. It's been really important to me to have our relationship back. A positive relationship is so strengthening for everyone."

Here is one mom's letter to her daughter:

Dear Robin,

I have been working for a long time on handling my confusion about the past and I believe that some things that happened in our family have hurt you badly. I have listed some that I think were harmful to you in a genuine attempt to understand some of the experiences you have had to deal with. I don't know if I am accurate or not. Please let me know where I am accurate, where I am not, and what I have missed. Please simply correct me rather than getting frustrated and angry. This is the best I can do at this time. It may be hard for you to communicate with me like this because you're uncertain as to how I'll react. You may think I cannot handle dealing with these issues or others you have with me, but I can and I want to. These are some of the things that I think hurt you when you lived home:

- My acting as if I were helpless and couldn't make it on my own. Making you feel that you couldn't leave me.
- My going in my room and closing the door for hours when I was upset, and not coming out, even though I knew you were outside crying for me.
- Making you continually take care of your sisters and brothers when you were still a child yourself.
- My treating your sister as if all the family problems were her fault and pushing you to be compliant and good.
- Using you to prove that I was a good mother, even though in my heart I knew it was a lie.
- Having to listen to me talk to you about things that were not appropriate to talk to a child about.
- Being used as my support instead of being supported by me.

I want you to know how truly sorry I am that I handled things so poorly and that you were hurt by my actions. You were treated in ways you did not deserve. Please let me know how we can make our relationship a good one in the present. I want to work with you to heal the pain of the past.

If you decide to write a letter detailing the problems you think your child faced growing up, you may want to reread Chapters Four and Five. The symptoms of trauma and the list of ineffective patterns can help you to remember specific incidents. *Note:* If one of the problems you had in your family is overinvolvement in your child's life, this may not be the best approach to use. Your attempt to understand them may be interpreted as trying to tell them how they feel, and so may evoke negative feelings. In these cases, it is better to choose one of the other more open-ended approaches.

It is not necessary to write a long list of all the grievances you think your adult child has. This letter is simply a way to open up the communication between you. It is a beginning, and your adult child will fill in the missing parts from her perspective.

If you want to approach your children in this way but you cannot write this letter by yourself, try to find someone you trust who knows your family who can help you. Other options are to jot down some notes, or to deal with these issues verbally with your adult child when you meet.

Sharing the Letter You Wrote from Your Adult Child's Perspective, and Your Response to That Letter

Another method which also puts parents on the line but has the benefits listed above is to send letters to their adult children which are similar to those you wrote at the end of the previous chapter. If you decide to approach you adult child in this way, preface your letters with a paragraph that lets them know that this is your best attempt to figure out what their experience was and that you need their feedback in order to know what their childhood actually was like for them.

Stan wrote the following *from the perspective that he thought his daughter had of her childhood:*

Dear Dad,

You attended all the social action events in town and you were everyone's father figure. There wasn't a committee you didn't head. You worried about everyone who was needy: except your own children. I needed you to be there, to listen to me sometimes. I hated hearing about all your political connections, not that I had anything against them, it's just that they got your attention instead of me. I hated hearing people tell me how lucky I was to have you for my father. You didn't have time to tuck me in at night. You never took the time to put your arms around me and just listen if I was upset. Instead you picked up the newspaper or turned on the news. You might have done great things for the rest of the world but you left me feeling unloved and uncared for.

Dear Gail,

It is true that I was involved in everything but my family. I walked out emotionally and acted like if I saved the world my family didn't matter. It was easier to deal with abstract thoughts and to get honors for being an upstanding citizen. I knew I was living a lie every time I looked at you or your sister. I just couldn't face it. And as you know I didn't look very often.

I want to have some time to explain to you how I ended up being as removed as I was. I don't think I was born that way, or that I purposely tried to distance myself from you. I just didn't know how to get close to anyone. I wish there were some way I could start our relationship over knowing what I know now. I never had a daughter and you never had a dad. You deserved to have a father who took you seriously and spent time with you. It must have hurt a lot and been especially hard since people bought my facade. Please get together with me now to try to make our relationship a real one.

Asking Your Adult Child What She Thinks Would Be Best

This approach has worked best in families where the parents have been overly directive and involved in their children's thoughts and feelings. It has not worked as well if it continued the pattern of the adult children doing all of the emotional work.

Lila and her daughter Wendy had the following conversation:

> LILA: I know that you've been distant from me for a long time, and I want to repair our relationship, but I don't know how to go about it. Can you tell me what you need from me, so that I can be here for you in a way that works for you?
>
> WENDY: You mean you're going to ask me what I need instead of telling me?
>
> LILA: I guess that's the first rule, then. You need me to listen to you instead of telling you what I think?
>
> WENDY (*after a pause*): That would be great, Mom. I really would like it if you'd listen to me.

Addressing an Unsuccessful Approach

Some parents who were unsuccessful in prior attempts to communicate with their adult children directly addressed their past approach when they contacted them. They remembered what they had done, why they did it, and thought about why they had been unsuccessful. Some of the most common ways they approached their children in the past were through:

> *Guilt:* You never _____ anymore.
>
> *Blame:* You don't even care about _____.
>
> *Subservience:* Isn't there something else I can do for you?
>
> *Unhappiness:* I'm so miserable.
>
> *Attack:* You've been a problem ever since _____.
>
> *Reproach:* I never thought my own child would _____.
>
> *Righteousness:* You know you should _____.
>
> *Small talk:* So, how's it going? How's the job, kids, _____?

Gloria said to her son:

Aaron, I tried to talk with you before but I realize now that I came across righteous and attacking. I guess that's something I've been good at most of my life. It must have been hard for you to live with a mom who seemed so sure of herself and so critical.

I want you to know that I am not changed yet, but that I am in the process of making some important changes. I realize how difficult I have been, and I can see why you did not want to try to deal with me.

The reason I am approaching you now is to learn more about you and about myself and to straighten out the hurts of the past. I am approaching you now because I want to continue to grow and change and because I want to have a relationship with you that is healthy and strengthening for us both. Please meet with me so we can begin working together.

If you decide to use this method, think about how your adult child felt at the time and why you think your prior approach did not work. Let your adult child know you realize the mistakes you made in your approach. See if this approach was representative of the way you usually acted in your relationship. Tell her you want to know how she sees the problem, and listen to her response. Self-disclose about the importance to you of repairing the relationship.

Addressing an Unsuccessful Approach by Your Adult Child

In some families, the adult children have tried before to communicate with their parents, but their parents responded with one or more of the defensive actions listed in Chapter Thirteen. These parents decided to approach their adult children by referring to these earlier attempts and acknowledging their own defensive reactions. They also said that they now realized that their adult children had been attempting to break through the walls between them.

Paulette told her daughter the following:

> When you approached me a long time ago and told me how much more nurturing you got from your friends than you ever got from me, I felt really defensive and just withdrew. I denied a lot about my own past and about the things that I did that were hurtful to you. I thought you were only saying what you did to hurt me, but now I realize that it was your attempt to communicate with me on a genuine level. Well, I'm not in denial anymore, and I am deeply sorry that I was when you approached me before. I hope it is not too late for us to try again. Please tell me how you felt and I will try my best to listen to you. I may not do a great job at listening but I am willing to try.

Sharing an Article or Book

Some parents approached their adult children by sending them relevant articles or books they'd found or copies of pages from books that they thought were important. They enclosed notes that explained how they thought these items applied to their families. Writing a note explaining your intention is important because your adult child may become defensive if she thinks you are trying to tell her what to do or read. Make sure that what you are sending is not something that is designed to change her.

Daniel sent an article about relationships to his daughter, and prefaced it with the following:

> Dear Lynette,
>
> When I found this, I immediately thought of how similar our family was to the family in this article. It shows how even well-intentioned parents can be harmful to their children. I'd be interested in knowing what your impression of it is, and I'd like to hear more about how you think the ways we treated you might have affected you. I'll call you in a few days, and I hope we can set up a time to get together then.

Current Problem Areas

Sometimes there is a current problem that is blocking the parents' communication with their adult children that needs to be addressed before they can deal with the past. If you suspect this is so in your case, you may want to read Chapter Nineteen, "What's Left" and Chapter Twenty, "Letting Go," before you approach your adult child. Parents who could not figure out what the actual problem was simply asked their adult children to tell them. Those parents who knew what was wrong shifted their perspectives or their actions in order to reconcile and let their adult children know that they had made these changes when they approached them.

James said to his daughter:

> Tina, I really want our relationship to be a good one, but there is something in the way and no matter how hard I try I cannot figure out what it is. I have searched my mind and my heart, and I still draw a blank. I know that there were things in the past that were hurtful to you, and I am more than willing to address those. But there is a distance here which seems to be in the present, and if I am doing something now that is hurting our relationship I want to know what that is so that I can stop doing it. I do not want to hurt you. It's really important to me to repair our relationship.

Emily approached her daughter Heidi in this way:

> Heidi, I really want us to have a better relationship, and I want to deal with the barriers that I have put up between us that have been hurtful to you. I realize now that I have been interfering in your life and that I've been telling you what to do about things that are for you to decide, not me. I have put down your life-style and tried to change you because I thought my way was better. Well, I don't think that now. I just think that we have different needs. Please meet with me so that we can talk more about this, and so that our relationship can work better for us both.

Elaborating on Reasons for Wanting to Reconcile

Another approach has been for parents to let their adult children know why they are determined to reconcile. If you decide to approach one of your adult children in this way, you may be able to find your own reasons from your list at the end of Chapter One, "Why Become Involved."

Matt, who was very ill, approached his son Dave in this way:

Dear Dave,

We've had a distant relationship for a long time now, and it has been painful for me, and I guess it has been for you too. I don't want to leave things like this. It makes me feel unhappy and distressed when I think about the fact that nothing has been resolved between us. It's not good for either of us to continue in this way. As you know, I've been quite ill, and there is a feeling of urgency at this point in my life. I very much want to make peace with you. I am aware that I have hurt you badly, and I want to talk with you and listen to you about those times. I also want us to get to know each other as we are now.

Addressing the Possibility of an Outside Problem

Some parents whose adult children were unreceptive suspected that there was something unrelated to them that was in the way of their reconciliation. If you suspect this is so, you may want to ask your adult child specifically—without being invasive—if there is anything going on that she is struggling with that is keeping a distance between you. Let her know that you are prepared to listen without judging her, overreacting, or giving her unsolicited advice.

Ira said:

I have a sense that you are dealing with something that is pretty difficult for you. I don't mean to pry, but I want to let you know that I am concerned. This has been bothering me for a while now. It may be my imagination—you may just be busy and overwhelmed—or perhaps you are angry at me for something. Won't you please let me know what is going on, so that I can understand what is happening? If it is something to do with me, I want to work it out with you. If it is not, I would like to be there for you, to listen and support you. I promise I won't criticize you or give you advice you don't need or want.

Third-Party Information

In spite of all the work they've done, sometimes parents are still unaware of how they affect their adult children. Some get along perfectly well in other situations, but when it comes to their immediate family or their children they act differently and do not realize it. These are people who are polite outside the home but let their other sides come out with their children. Sometimes only one of their children gets treated badly. Usually the parents are repeating old patterns or are taking out their anger on them. Difficult as it may be, you may want to ask someone who has seen you frequently with your adult child for honest feedback about how you act in that relationship. Someone else in the family may be helpful in this capacity, if you are clear that you want information, not reassurance.

Some people act in a way that creates distance or other problems in any close relationship. Again, ask friends, acquaintances, or anyone you think is aware of your approaches to people, what they think gets in your way in relationships, and listen to their responses.

Doreen could not understand why her daughter, Melissa, had cut off communication with her two years before. She asked her friend Kim for honest feedback and Kim responded by telling Doreen that her rigid and caustic manner were sometimes a problem, even for her. For a while, Kim said, Doreen would be calm and friendly and things were fine, but then she would shift and get rigid, edgy, and sarcastic and be frightening to be around. It didn't matter that much to Kim because they didn't see each other frequently. But Kim told Doreen that she could see how it could be hard to be in a close relationship with her and that her actions could create antagonism and fear.

Doreen wrote her daughter this letter:

Dear Melissa,

I've been approaching you by asking you why you won't communicate with me, and you told me once that you need space from me, but that's all. I haven't understood why, and I guess you've been afraid to tell me. I've been asking people what it is I do that turns them off and the feedback I've gotten has helped me understand at least part of why you don't want to be involved with me. I'm realizing that I can be frightening when I become harsh and rigid. When I'm upset I take it out on whoever's there, with my sarcasm and my temper. I guess with you I've been that way most of the time. I'm trying to grow and change, and to sort out the patterns I've learned. I would really like us to communicate about this, so that we can get beyond this part of our relationship and find the love we have for each other.

Third-Party Intervention

Some parents have asked other people to tell their adult children about the work their parents have been doing. These have been family friends, friends of their adult children, and family members. *Note: Make sure you do not ask a person to help who is likely to use one of the ineffective approaches mentioned in Chapter Thirteen.*

Usually this approach is not necessary unless your adult child refuses to talk with you. It is probably better to approach them directly, if they are willing, so that they will not become upset with you for being circuitous. There is a lot of confusion in relationships when people talk for each other, and it is best to avoid this. Nonetheless, sometimes this approach works.

Peter asked his wife Sandy to approach his son, since his

son was unwilling to talk to him. This fit her role as peacemaker in the family, which was not good for her, but at least in this case she was doing something that could ultimately get her out of the role. In this case she was also willing to take the risk of having her son respond to her angrily.

Sandy said:

> Jimmy, I know you don't believe this, and actually I don't blame you, but your dad really is changing. He's taken a long, hard look at himself and how he's been with us and he doesn't like what he's seen. He wants to stop dealing with people the way he has, and he's willing to put a hundred percent effort into it. He really wants a chance to make peace with you, Jimmy. Please try—for me as well as him and for yourself, because I hate being in the middle like this, and it would be so much easier to get out of the middle if you two had a relationship with each other.

Facilitator

Another way parents have reconciled with their adult children is through asking a family member or friend who was acceptable to all concerned to facilitate their interactions. This approach was useful when the parents knew that there were problems but needed outside clarification of what they were. Sometimes it helped to talk privately with the third person to get clarification before meeting together, so that it wasn't overwhelming to the parent. If you use this approach, be careful not to choose an outside party who will confuse things further. The purposes of the facilitator are: (1) To give information to you neutrally about the barriers you have constructed in your relationship with your adult child; and (2) to have someone help you each understand the other. *Important: Do not ask a third party to be there to gang up on your adult child. Do not ask a third party to help you out and then get defensive toward them. This is an extremely difficult position for them to be in.*

Shelly was able to reconcile with her son through her daughter Valerie's assistance and support. Shelly had a satisfactory relationship with her daughter Valerie, but her son Wayne was hostile toward her and quite distant. First Shelly asked her daughter to tell her what it was about her that had driven her son away. After being reassured that her mother really wanted to know the truth, Valerie told her mom the following:

> Mom, I love you very much and I don't want to hurt you, but if you are sincere about wanting to reconcile with Wayne I am willing to tell you what I think. From what I can tell the reason Wayne is so upset with you mostly comes down to your continually giving him advice he doesn't want. When we were growing up it was so painful for all of us—you were so bright and knowledgeable it was hard to trust our own judgments. Sometimes you wouldn't listen, and would get the problem wrong, and then we felt discounted and misunderstood. And when you were right, we felt like we were idiots when it came to handling the world. I've worked through a lot of this in my own therapy, and it doesn't seem so important to me now. But Wayne—maybe because he is the oldest and had it worse—just feels that he doesn't want to deal with it any longer.

These three people got together several times, with Valerie facilitating. The relationships gradually began to improve for everyone, although everything did not go smoothly. This turned out to be helpful for Valerie too because she was able to be open in her relationship with her mom which she had been afraid to do before.

Therapeutic Intervention

Some people choose to go to a therapist to get through the initial stages of reconciliation. If the adult child goes to a therapist, she usually feels safer meeting her parents with her own therapist, if her therapist deals with intergenerational confrontations. Some therapists may want to set up one or more individual sessions with you first and some may not work this way. *Note: Do not set up an appointment without an agreement from your adult child.* Chapter Eleven offers ways to find a therapist if neither of you have one. A therapist may be able to help you express what you need from each other and help you sort out how you interfere with each other. You can examine family patterns and talk about how they've affected you and your relationship. If your adult child needs to confront you about something from the past, or even the present, but is afraid to, the therapist can function as a support for her, so that she feels safe enough to say what she needs to. Going to a therapist may be your best choice if there has been serious damage in your family, and especially if your family fits the description of major abuse in the next chapter. If you have tried several other approaches and they did not work, therapy may be the last one that will.

Jerome approached his son Jason in this way:

> We've been trying really hard to improve things between us, but we keep getting stuck. I'm feeling pretty frustrated and I guess you are too. I think we'd handle things a lot better with professional help. Do you know of a therapist we could go to together who could help us break down the barriers between us? Or do you want to try to find someone, or should I?

Each therapist has his own style, and each family is unique. You will have a better chance of reconciling if you give the therapist a chance to work in his own way. You may want to try another therapist, if you are doing everything you can and things are not improving after many visits. It's important to realize, though, that often things get worse before they get better.

Use This Book

You will have a resource you can use that the parents mentioned did not have. It may be the easiest, most direct way to approach your adult child. You can use this book as a bridge to communicating and as a lead in to setting up a meeting.

If your adult child has given you this book, or suggested you read it, bring it up in your initial approach. Say something like,

> I've been reading the book you gave me, and I want to get together with you and talk about some of the things that I've been learning.

If you bought this book on your own, you can tell your adult child a little about the book and why you bought it. This is a natural way to begin your communication. You could write:

> I've found a book about improving relationships with your adult children and have learned some things about myself and us that I think will make a difference in our relationship. Can we meet soon to talk about it?

You can also copy and send parts of this book, especially those that you have filled in or that have meaning for you. You will be sharing more of your past when you go on to Chapter Seventeen, "Getting Deeper."

With or without a facilitator, it is usually best to keep serious meetings limited to between one and two hours. If it seems appropriate, do something enjoyable and light together afterward. If the conversation goes on too long and gets very heavy, you may get into a glitch, which is a computer term for getting stuck without a way out. People get into glitches when both people defend themselves without listening to each other. If you do not remember to stop and listen, you may end up in a glitch, and then there will be no real communication or resolution possible at the time. If you realize that you have gotten caught in a glitch, stop the conversation. Explain to your adult child what a glitch is and that it appears as if the two of you have gotten stuck. Often stopping for a while is the best course of action. It gives you both a chance to think about what the other person has been saying and feeling and to resolve to approach the other person more sensitively the next time you meet. Make sure you remember to set up another meeting or plan a time to call to set one up, so you can resume the conversation.

Once again, you do not have to use any of these specific ways in order to make peace with your adult children. Imagining a dialogue with your own parents or your children may spark other ways to go about approaching your adult children. You may want to ask other people how they have reestablished positive relationships, or how they wish their parents would approach them. Use whatever approach you feel most comfortable with, and it is bound to work fine. *Don't let anything prevent you from trying to reconcile with your adult children.*

It is important to realize that reconciliation does not always go easily or quickly. In fact, it often goes frustratingly slowly. Parents often make mistakes and have to try again several times. They are likely to be caught off guard more than once. Reconciliation does not happen at all for some people. In some cases, the children feel that they need to cut off their parents in order to survive. This is especially true if the family system has been extremely abusive or engulfing. Perhaps the adult children cannot forget the pain of the past. Perhaps they have tried to make peace with their parents before and were shut out and they are unprepared to try again. They may be thinking in black-and-white terms, and not realize that they can negotiate a partial relationship. They may not know that their parents are willing to be open and to respect their views and feelings. They may be filled with anger, holding down the pain, fear, and confusion just below the surface. The adult children may have expectations of their parents that their parents are unable to meet. They may not be able to let go of unrealistically high expectations of their parents. They may have problems in their own lives that their parents know nothing about that they feel unable to share. Or they may have placed reconciliation with their parents last or nowhere on their priority lists.

You will be trying, probably more than once, to communicate the things you've learned with your adult child, in a way which does not dictate to her what you think she should do. It will not work to approach her righteously or by trying to induce guilt. Do not use a power trip on her, not only because it is a poor method to use in relationships, but because she has the strongest weapon, if you care more at this time than she does.

If your adult child is unwilling to communicate, how long should you go on trying? As long as you still want to, you continue to have hope and you find new methods that you have not tried before. In Chapter Twenty, "Letting Go," you will read about how one parent goes through her grief at the realization that her daughter is not going to respond to her efforts. As long as you both are alive and able, however, there is some hope left, because people change, and new discoveries are made each day.

In the space on page 239, construct your personal plan for approaching your adult child. Copy this form if you will be approaching more than one child. Answer these questions in your plan:

- Will my contact be by phone or letter?
- What are some options for places to meet with my child?
- What are some good time options?
- Which approach will I try first?
- What will I do if it is not working?
- Who do I want to be there?
- What do I want to self-disclose?
- What harmful experiences has my adult child been through that need acknowledgment?
- Am I prepared to listen to what she has to say?
- Am I willing to express my regret for the undeserved pain she experienced?

- Am I ready to work on the relationship to restore it to a positive place?

MY PLAN FOR APPROACHING MY ADULT CHILD

_____

_____

_____

_____

_____

_____

_____

_____

_____

_____

_____

_____

_____

_____

_____

_____

_____

How are you feeling about the prospect of approaching your adult children?

_____

_____

_____

What additional support can you get if you feel you need it?

_____

_____

_____

What would stop you from following through on this chapter?

_____

_____

_____

What would be the cost to you and your children if you didn't continue?

_____

_____

_____

What is motivating you to go on?

_____

_____

_____

During one of your conversations you will want to ask your adult child if she would be willing to go over some sections that you have completed in this book. When you do and she agrees you will be ready to work together on some of the exercises in Chapter Seventeen, "Getting Deeper."

CHAPTER SIXTEEN

Major Traumas

Man has no choice but to love. For when he does not, he finds his alternatives lie in loneliness, destruction and despair.

LEO BUSCAGLIA

This chapter is specifically written for families in which some form of severe abuse took place. Since you may not know that abuse occurred in your family, please read the entire chapter, even if you think it does not apply to you. People may have been afraid to tell you or anyone that they were abused. They may have blocked out the experience.

Some parents will inevitably find themselves dealing with situations that they never thought could happen in their own families. The most common "unbelievable" actions are those involving sexuality with children. These are the least known and the most difficult to come to terms with for the child, the nonabusing parent, and the abuser. However, the fact is that many children are sexually abused, estimated at one out of three or four girls and one out of seven boys, and someone is abusing them—usually someone known to the victim. It is not just happening to someone else's children in someone else's family. The term *sexual abuse* encompasses all categories of sexual victimization of children. It may begin innocently, as affection, but gradually turn into sexual abuse. It can be violent and involve ritualistic tortures. It can occur without physical contact, as when the adult makes sexually provocative statements, exposes the child to pornography or has the child witness sexual activities. Despite many attempts by family members to discredit children, either because of denial or fear, it has been established that nearly all children who say they have been sexually abused are telling the truth. Most children don't lie about these things because they can't. They know details they would not normally be capable of knowing. (A rare exception to this is in recent cases where the children have been told by one parent to lie about the other parent in custody battles.)

If there has been sexual abuse of children in your family, confronting the abuse is likely to be a traumatic experience in itself. There is no way around that, but it must be done in order to heal your relationship. Read books on this subject. Seek out professional help, groups, and workshops. *The Courage to Heal* by Ellen Bass and Laura Davis is almost mandatory reading. *The Obsidian Mirror* by Louise Wisechild will give you a personal haunting view of the torment created by sexual abuse, as well as illustrating how inappropriately parents can react to confrontation.

Another situation that is frequently denied is alcoholism in the home. People who drink heavily, even have periods of blackouts, deny that they are alcoholic. One woman's mother told her, "I'd rather go out and have a few drinks than spend all that money on therapy." She didn't have the nerve to respond, "Mom, your having 'a few drinks' all the time is a lot of the reason I'm *in* therapy." There are many tests to find out if you fit the description of an alcoholic. Two of the questions usually are, "Is drinking making your home life unhappy?" and "Does your drinking make you careless of your family's welfare?" These are questions you might want to ask the people in your family. If you answer yes to any *one* of twenty items in a basic list, including drinking to feel more powerful, to escape worries, and to satisfy a craving, you may be an alcoholic; if you answer yes to three or more you are definitely an alcoholic. These questionnaires are available through Alcoholics Anonymous if you are not sure you were or are alcoholic.

It's extremely dangerous to remain in denial about alcoholism, or drug addiction (prescription or not). People have killed and maimed countless other people, driving drunk, and have remembered nothing afterward. They have sexually abused their children, or been dragged up the stairs by them, or vomited over them, with no memory of the event.

Below you will find summarized some, but not all, of the specific, severely harmful behaviors likely to leave lasting scars on children. You may have been treated in these ways, acted in these ways, or witnessed these actions. The effects of severe abuse on a child will vary with the kind, amount, and duration of the abuse, the relationship between the abuser and the child, and the age of the child at the time. How the child is treated once the abuse has been recognized will also affect the outcome. In all cases, however, severe abuse of a child is a betrayal of the child's trust and will have profound consequences for the child.

SEVERE PHYSICAL ABUSE

Hitting a child with belts, wooden spoons, or other hurtful objects. Burning a child, or breaking a child's bones. Sitting on, throwing, kicking, or punching a child. Holding a child down for extended periods of time. Forcing a child to ingest food or to have objects such as enemas inserted inside his body.

SEXUAL ABUSE

Attempting to stimulate a child sexually, with or without physical contact. Fondling a child or masturbation by, of, or with a child. Oral sex with a child. Insertion of any items in a child, anal intercourse, or rape of a child. Other bizarre sexual acts with or in front of a child. Allowing other people or animals to perform sexual acts with or in front of a child. Viewing pornography with a child.

ALCOHOLISM OR DRUG ADDICTION

Exposure of a child to an addicted parent who is violent or whose moods are erratic and unpredictable. Exposing a child to an addictive life-style. Putting a child in the position of having to parent the parent, as in picking the parent up at bars or cleaning up after he vomits. Having a child ride in a vehicle with a parent who is drunk or high.

SEVERE EMOTIONAL ABUSE

Frequent name-calling, criticism, or tearing down of a child's efforts. Scapegoating a child or acting as if a child is crazy. Extreme obsessiveness, perfectionism, or fearfulness that cuts off a child's self-expression. Frequent exposure of a child to dangerous, traumatic, erratic, or volatile situations.

SEVERE NEGLECT

Leaving a child alone or forcing a child to stay in isolation for extended periods of time. Abandoning a child. Depriving a child of touch or contact. Not providing sufficient food, clothing, shelter, and other basic physical needs of a child.

This chapter addresses two major populations separately: first, parents who have been abusive; next, nonabusive parents who have been in a family where abuse occurred.

Note: Although the pronoun "he" is used in this chapter, it is important to realize that abusive acts are commited by women as well as men, and that boys and girls are sexually abused by women as well as men.

FOR THE ABUSIVE PARENT

The following letters show what adult children need to say to their offending parents and appropriate responses from the parents. Note that there is a sixth step in the responses: *Taking action*. These four letters are to parents who have harmed their children through alcoholism, violence, neglect, and sexual abuse. Read them as examples of what you may hear.

1. Dear Mom,

Do you know what it felt like to have a mom you couldn't talk to or count on, because she was passed out drunk on the couch? Do you know how it felt to have you humiliate me in front of my friends, staggering around, trying to act like my pal? Everyone was always laughing at you, which meant they were laughing at me. Or they pitied me for having you for my mother . . . which was even worse than being laughed at.

You keep saying you're not an alcoholic, but last time I visited I counted fourteen empty beer cans in your garbage can and I know they weren't left over from before because I took out the garbage the day before. And no one else was there but us. Alcohol is the only thing you really love, Mom, no matter what you say.

Do you know how much I miss having a mom? Do you know how much I need you? And, Mom, I'm starting to follow in your footsteps—not with alcohol but with crack. I'm nineteen years old but I feel totally without hope. I still need you, Mom. I need you to help yourself, so you can help me. I'm really afraid of what is happening to both of us.

Dear April,

You sound so terribly hurt and frightened and lonely, I can hardly believe that I have been ignoring what is so obvious to me now [listening]. Of course you are just repeating what I have been showing you. I am alcoholic and probably have been for the past several years [acknowledgment]. I feel so awful that I have let you down for so long [regret]. I realize that no words of apology will mean much as long as I keep on drinking, and I know that it will not be easy but I am going to stop. I will go to an AA meeting and if you are willing I'd like you to go to an Al-Anon meeting at the same time [action]. Please let me know what I can do to make up for the hurt you have been through and how I can help you keep from being addicted too [restoration].

2. Dear Dad,

I lived in dread of your violence. You would throw things, eyes glassy, face red and hard, mouth clenched, whenever you didn't get your own way. You would beat us with your fists and anything else you could get your hands on when you went into one of your rages. No matter what we did, we couldn't avoid your brutality when you thought someone was thinking something different from what you thought or when someone made a mistake. Who did you think you were, anyway? I needed a father, not a person to be terrified of. We all jumped when you wanted something. We lived in constant fear of your temper.

Dear Pat,

There is no excuse for my violent outbursts. I was cruel and punitive with you far beyond what was appropriate or acceptable. If it happened now, I would fit the category of child abuser, because I beat you with straps and belt buckles that I know left marks [acknowledgment]. I know it must have been terrifying and demeaning for you to live in our household, because of my temper [listening]. I know because my dad treated me exactly the way I treated you. I wish I could say I learned something useful from being beaten, but apparently all I learned was to beat my own children [self-disclosure]. I wish I had realized this sooner and hadn't hurt you as I did [regret]. I know I still have a lot of anger inside and I intend to do something about that. I will go for help, although I am not sure exactly how to go about it [action]. If there is anything I can do to help us have a good relationship, please tell me what that is. I want us to make peace with each other [restoration].

3. Dear Dad,

You abandoned us when I was so small I barely knew what having a father meant. I grew up without a dad at a time when not having a father made you suspect to the other kids, defenseless, and alone. There was no man to look up to, no one to do a man's job, except me, when I was far too little. For as long as I can remember, Mom counted on me to take care of her. I was supposed to help her out and take your place and I didn't know how. I've been furious with Mom for years about her expectations of me. But you are the one that just left your family and took off, thinking only of yourself. Why no child support payments, Dad? Why no letters, Dad? Why no phone calls, Dad? Why no birthday gifts, no visits, no vacation trips? Why nothing at all? And what do you want from me now?

Dear Gary,

You have every right to be furious with me, and to stay furious for as long as you need to. I realize now how much I hurt you by cutting you out of my life so completely [listening]. I never made a real effort to communicate with you, and I had a lot of years to try [acknowledgment]. The result was that you never had a father and I never had a son, and I can't begin to put into words how much I regret that I cheated you and me [regret]. I never did support you then, and at the very least I owe you and your mom child support. I intend to help you out financially because it is a debt I owe that I need to pay off. I can never make up for abandoning you, and I wouldn't even try, but I am here for you now [action]. Please let me into your life so that we can deal with this together and so I can show you that I am sincere in wanting to have a relationship with you now [restoration].

4. Dear Dad,

I can't believe I am writing this, but it's about time I did. You probably think I don't remember what happened to me and you would have been right until two years ago. I didn't remember. But I do remember now. I remember things I can barely stand to remember. I remember you coming into my bed at night and touching me the way fathers are supposed to protect their daughters from being touched. You touched me inside my pajamas, inside my body where you weren't supposed to ever touch me. And you made me touch you, telling me how good it made you feel. I feel sick even writing this letter. You took away my childhood with your body and your smells. It's taken two years of therapy to even be able to write this letter and I'm scared to death you will deny it and make me feel like I'm crazy. But I'm not crazy and I'm not making this up. I have had to pay for your abuse with my childhood.

Dear Jen,

There are two ways to answer a letter like yours: I could lie and say you are crazy or lying; or I could admit that what you are saying is the truth [acknowledgment]. It is frightening to say that, but I guess it's not any more frightening than being a child and being sexually abused by your father. It must have taken a huge amount of courage for you to have confronted me about this now [listening]. Thinking about what happened so many years ago makes it seem unreal and I wish I could make it all disappear, for me but especially for you [regret]. Since I can't, I'd better deal with this now. I will go with you to your therapist if you want me to, or to a group, or for family counseling. I want to reimburse you for the therapy you have had and any costs in the future [action]. This was not your fault, it had nothing to do with you. Sometime I'll tell you more about me [self-disclosure], but for now I just want to do whatever I can to take this burden off you [restoration].

If you wish to, write a letter to your adult child that is

similar to those described in Chapter Fourteen. You can use the format for writing this letter as well as the outline provided.

In your response letter you will need to let your adult child know that you resolve to take action to stop any abusive behavior that is still occurring, if you have not already done so. In the case of child sexual abuse, part of the necessary action may involve filing a police report, if it has not already been filed. Taking action is difficult, but it is the only way to clear things up with your adult children, or yourself. It is never too late to stop destructive or self-destructive behaviors. Many resources are available today that did not exist before. Now is the time to utilize them.

APPROACHING YOUR ADULT CHILD

You will want your children to feel comfortable and safe with you when you make contact with them, and this may be difficult if they have not been safe in the past. They will need to believe that you are sincere and that they can trust you not to hurt them. This may take a lot of time, and you will want to let them know that they can take as much time as they need. For this reason, in most cases, your best initial approach is through letters. The distance will give your children a chance to integrate your intention to make peace with them and your willingness to take action to clear things up, without your having to confront each other directly.

The purpose of your first letter will be simply to begin communicating. This letter needs to be brief, and your approach can be similar to some of the approaches outlined in Chapter Fifteen. It can refer to the abuse, but initially it is best not to elaborate on the hurtful experiences your adult children have undergone. It is best to deal with the abusiveness of the past slowly. You may choose to approach your adult child by letting her know that you are prepared to take action or that you are already taking action. For example, you might say, "I have been going to Alcoholics Anonymous," "I am learning ways to deal with my violence," or "I am not drinking anymore."

It will be especially important to let your adult child know that you realize that you have been abusive, that you do not intend to minimize the harm you have done to them, and that you realize that they are not to blame for the abuse.

Here is Mark's letter to his daughter, Jen.

Dear Jen,

I have realized that the things that happened in our family can no longer be denied and kept hidden. I have been sexually abusive and I do not want to pretend any longer that I was not. I do not want to act like it was not a big deal, because I know now it was. I especially want you to know that there was nothing that you did that deserved abuse.

You probably do not trust me at this point and that is understandable. If you need to tell me how furious and how hurt you are I will do my best to listen to you. I will also take whatever actions are necessary, personally and legally, to help us both.

I would like to meet with you to talk about this, wherever you feel safest, with a therapist or any other person you choose. If you feel safer or more comfortable just writing for now, I will communicate with you in that way.

Please respond to this letter so that we can begin this process together. I'll write again or call if I haven't heard from you in the next three or four weeks. It is really important to me to repair our relationship.

Acknowledging the abusive acts will be an extremely important part of your reconciliation. Let your child know clearly that he is not responsible for any of the abuse that he was subjected to. Children are never the responsible party, no matter how difficult they are or how they behave or how mature they seem. Children are not responsible for the actions of adults. You did not deserve abuse as a child, and neither did they. Do not minimize what you did to your child. It is hard to face the emotional scarring and devastation that abuse leaves on children, but it will help in the healing process if you can both talk honestly about its impact.

The following letter was sent by a man to his seventeen-year-old daughter. Her mother never gave the letter to her, and the daughter did not find it until after her father's death. The daughter had not known how to reach her father all these years, as he thought she had.

Dear_____,

You were still a baby when I left and I have not been in contact since that time. I would have liked to have known you better but circumstances and life did not make it possible. I want to know you now, all about you—to see you, to hear you—I want to know that you are alive and well.

I do not know what or how you feel about me but I assume that if you wanted to communicate with me you could have done so. I have been living here since you left and your mother has always known how to find me. Your mother kept your addresses concealed and I accidentally found out where you lived only recently.

I guess that at best you have mixed feelings for me, or perhaps strong antagonistic feelings towards me. Even so, I feel that we should see one another, to speak to each other, in order to better decide on what to do about our future relationship. I do not want to ignore or postpone meeting for the rest of our lives. We should not be afraid or hate so much that we cannot face one another.

If you do, however, decide that you want me to stay out of your life completely, I'll do so, much as it will hurt. There must be a mutual desire to have a good, healthy relationship—that is what I want.

Life is short and often by the time we realize we need to do something, it is already too late. That is why I am doing what I am. The doors to my heart and home are open to you. I believe our lives can be enriched in knowing one another and any misunderstandings can be cleared up. It is worth the attempt.

If you decide you do not want to meet, please answer this letter anyway. I wish you happiness and fulfillment, in a life enriched with the best that the world can offer.

QUESTIONS ASKED BY PARENTS WHO HAVE BEEN ABUSIVE

1. What will happen in therapy?

If you go to your adult child's therapist, you may initially be subjected to a lot of anger and bitterness, because your adult child is the client and the therapist's main concern is your child's welfare. This will be difficult to take, but eventually you will be able to share more of your perspective and feelings and repair your relationship. If you go to a therapist who is new for both of you, it may be somewhat easier for you at first, because there will be more neutrality. However, it may be more difficult for your child. It is wise to let your adult child make this decision.

2. What will happen to me if I have sexually abused my child and I report myself or am reported by someone else?

This will vary depending on the state you live in, the extent and duration of the abuse, prior criminal records, how long ago it happened, how many children have been affected, your remorse, your willingness to follow through on treatment, as well as variables such as your presentation of yourself and the particular people you deal with in the justice system. The laws change continually, so what is true now may not be true next week. If the abuse happened a long time ago, chances are that you will be covered by the statute of limitations in your state, and you will not be prosecuted. If you have recently been involved sexually with a minor or are currently involved it will be more difficult. Whatever your personal situation, it is important to get legal advice and, if necessary, legal representation before you do anything, so that you can go through this process in a way that is least detrimental to you and your family.

3. Can I reconcile with my adult child without reporting the abuse if I have not been abusive to anyone else and this happened a long time ago?

Possibly, but this may not be feasible from a practical standpoint. If you get counseling the therapist may be mandated by law to report the abuse if it happened recently. Since it will be difficult to reconcile without going to therapy, either individually or together, not reporting the abuse may not be an option. If this happened a long time ago, it is unlikely that anyone will press charges if they have not already done so.

4. What if I am being sexually abusive with minors but not with my own adult children any longer?

Please get treatment *immediately.* The effects of sexual abuse are devastating to the victim. If you are still an offender, you need to stop this cycle before it goes any further. See Chapter Eleven, "When It's Too Hard To Do It Alone."

5. Can I repair my relationship with my adult child even if I do not stop my abusive or addictive behaviors, for example, violence or alcoholism?

If you do not stop the abusive behavior, you are asking people to accept you in a way that is not good for you or for them. They will then be allowing or in a sense enabling you to act in a way that is harmful to yourself and others. This is not the kind of relationship that is beneficial to anyone. You need to stop being abusive to yourself or others now, whatever it takes, and move on with your life.

6. What if I can't change?

Family therapist Virginia Satir wrote that the main thing she learned from her mother was that if something broke or a mistake was made you were better off approaching it from the perspective of how to fix it than of whether or not it could be fixed. You can always grow and make changes and "fix" yourself. Believing you can and being committed to change is half the battle. It takes time and support but it happens all the time.

7. What if I don't want to change?

It's not unusual for people not to want to make changes if

their behavior is self-gratifying and gives them immediate satisfaction. Many people with highly addictive behaviors won't change until they experience a loss that hurts them more than their abusive behavior satisfies them. Others will change if they find a substitute behavior that is sufficiently satisfying or if they find something more valuable to them than their addictive behaviors. Some people change when they find the roots of the addictive behavior and are able to cut them off at the source. If you are not willing to change your behaviors, you may have a marginally reconciliatory relationship with your adult child, but you will not be able to create a real relationship.

8. What if my adult child accuses me of something major that I have no memory of?

You may have blocked it out through denial or you may have been drinking and blacked out. This is not uncommon, and it is a serious and dangerous problem for you and your family. You may have a part of your personality that is separate from the rest of you that you are unaware of. It is important to consult a therapist who is experienced in this field. Sometimes it is helpful to find a therapist who is trained in hypnotherapy. Retrieving painful memories will be traumatic, but you can integrate these memories into your life. There is a chance your child is lying or mistaken, but this is extremely unlikely. If you have been severely abusive and may be abusive now or in the future but you do not realize this, believe your adult child, or take action, your relationship will be impossible to fully repair.

FOR THE NONABUSIVE PARENT

The following letters are written by adult children to their nonabusive parent in families where abuse took place. The parents' responses contain the five parts described in Chapter Fourteen and also the sixth part: *Taking action.* The first letter is written to a mother who protected her alcoholic husband. The second is written to a father who did not stop his wife's physical abuse of the children. The third is addressed to a mother who does not yet know that her own father had sexually abused her daughter.

1. Dear Mom,

You pretended that Dad didn't have a drinking problem for as long as I can remember. You just shut your eyes and acted like it wasn't happening. Have you heard the word co-dependent? Well, if you haven't, let me give you a quick lesson. A co-dependent is someone who allows or encourages someone else's addiction. Does that ring a bell? If it doesn't, it should. But then maybe you're so deep in denial you don't even know it's about you. You probably don't even understand why I'm writing this letter. Well, here's why. No matter how much Dad drank you just shut your eyes and acted like it wasn't happening. He did the most frightening things: Once he broke a door down, once he took a knife out on you—do you think because I was a child I don't remember or have feelings? God, Mom, how could you just pretend nothing was happening and that it would go away without you having to do anything? You just cleaned up his messes and he never had to do a thing about it.

Dear Sherry,

Pretending nothing is happening is what I do best [acknowledgment]. My dad drank and ran around on my mom and she went about her business as if nothing out of the ordinary was going on and I learned to do the same. When I was fifteen my grandma came to live with us, dying of cancer, and I was the one who was supposed to take care of her and watch her die. Any ideas I had of being my own person died in the two years I took care of her. So I married your dad, and I shut my eyes and I did what I thought was my job. Yes, daughter, I have recently heard the word co-dependent, and yes, I know that the pattern fits me well. I want to change this, but I don't know if I can. I want to change it for you almost more than myself because I feel sort of hopeless about myself [self-disclosure].

I know how hard it was for you to live with Dad. I can say

that honestly, because I lived with a father like your father, and then with your dad for thirty years [listening]. I feel really sorry that I put you through that. I know I am responsible for not taking any actions to stop him from abusing alcohol [regret]. I don't know what to do now, but I am willing to go with you to Al-Anon meetings, if you would like to, or work on these issues with you [restoration]. It will be difficult but I will confront Dad about what he put us through [action]. I love you, even though I haven't shown you that in the ways you needed. I want us to work this out.

2. Dear Dad,

Mom used to torture us when she got into her horrible moods, and you didn't even try to stop her. Once she almost drowned my sister in the bathtub, holding her under the water until she could barely breathe, because she wouldn't do what she was told. I witnessed that scene and so many other nightmares when I was too little to talk. And you were there, you were a grownup, and you never stopped her. She would turn into someone we barely recognized, and force us to do what she wanted. Food would be her weapon as she made us eat everything that she had set out, whether we wanted it or not. I remember vomiting, and her making me eat a full plate of food that she put out, saying I was rotten to the core and that I was going to kill her with my stubbornness. You were there at the table, Dad, watching. Why didn't you say anything? Why didn't you stop her?

Dear Dawn,

I was afraid of your mother, and I know that sounds ridiculous but it's true [self-disclosure]. You and your sister went through hell and back, and I just sat there as if I was oblivious to it all [acknowledgment]. I remember the times in the kitchen and I remember thinking how awful it was for her to scream and scream and to force you kids to eat regardless of what you wanted and you looked so terrified that I knew it was about killing you [listening]. I wish I had done something to protect you and your sisters when you needed me to [regret]. Tell me what I can do or give you now that I couldn't then [restoration]. I am willing to talk with your mother about this now [action].

3. Dear Mom,

There are some sexual things that my grandfather did to me when I was small that I need to talk to you about. I know this is a huge shock to you, because he is your father, but I have to tell you now because I have been keeping this secret for so long and it has been tearing me up inside. Maybe if I tell you the truth some of the feelings I have of being dirty and bad will go away. Maybe some of the guilt and shame that I still have, even though I know in my head it wasn't my fault, will go away. Maybe the five-year-old that I was will be able to live in the light again if you will listen to me and believe me and try to understand how much this has battered me and destroyed big pieces of my life.

Dear Alison,

I don't know what I can possibly say to you that can even begin to express how shocked and horrible I feel. I am bewildered, because you are talking about my father and even though I wasn't close to him I never thought he would be capable of what you are describing. Not with his own grandchild [self-disclosure]. I see that what's much more important, though, is how you must feel, how you must have felt going through this and not having anyone stop him [listening]. I don't want to believe you but I do believe you. I know you would never make up anything like this [acknowledgment]. I wish that I had been aware of what was happening to you and that I could have stopped it right away [regret].

If you want to prosecute him, I will stand behind you. If you have not reported him I will help you or do it for you [action]. God, how could I not have realized this was happening? I have so many questions to ask you, but I guess the best thing I can do now is just be here for you and let you tell me what you want to at your own pace [restoration].

Write a letter from your child's perspective about what you know or suspect he experienced. Follow the format in Chapter Fourteen. Then write your letter of response, including a statement of your willingness to take action if you have not yet done so.

When you approach your adult children, you can use one of the methods listed in Chapter Fifteen. You might want to let your adult child know immediately that you are not going to protect the abusive person anymore.

Here is how Gary approached his daughter, Dawn:

GARY: Dawn, I've realized that a lot of things I've done have been very damaging to you. Especially not protecting you from your mom's abusiveness.

DAWN (after a pause): Are you saying that you're willing to talk about how Mom really was?

GARY: Yes, I am.

DAWN: I'm completely stunned.

GARY: I guess you're shocked that I'm willing to finally stop protecting your mother and myself. I want to get together with you soon to talk more about this. I am determined to break the abusive cycle we've set up in our family. I'd like to meet with you at whatever place you want to, in the next couple of weeks. Can we schedule a time and figure out a place now?

If you find out in your initial contact or your first meeting with your adult child that there was sexual or other major abuse that you did not know about, you will probably need time and help to adjust to the truth. This will be especially difficult if the abuser is someone close to you, such as the child's other parent, stepparent, or grandparent. A trusted friend or other adult relative may have sexually abused your child. Sexual abuse by older or more powerful siblings is not uncommon. Many young children have been sexually abused by adolescent sisters and brothers. It may take time for you to absorb all this, and you need to let your child know that you need time to get beyond the confusion you will likely feel.

It will be crucial for you to believe your adult child if you want to reconcile. You will also need to spend a lot of time listening, and to be willing to deal with the abuser, especially if the abusive behavior is still going on. The issue of sexual abuse will probably not be quite as difficult to handle if the abuser is someone you do not know well.

If you were a nonabusive parent in a family where abuse occurred; if you were told by your child that an abusive act occurred and you did not believe your child; or if you did not know that an abusive act occurred, and you find out when you meet and begin to share openly, remember to do the following:

Listen to your child's anger and pain. This will not be easy, but your child needs you to care about how dreadfully he has been hurt, and to understand the struggle he has been going through just to survive.

Apologize to your child if you did not recognize the abuse, if you did not believe him, or if you did not stop the abuse. Do not try to excuse or justify yourself. Just tell him that you are sorry that the abuse happened and that you did not stop it. Do not suggest or imply that your child was responsible for the abuse. Adults have no right to abuse children, no matter how difficult the child is, and it is crucial for your child and for your relationship that you let your child know that you realize this. Do not minimize what happened to your child. Abuse is not to be taken lightly. It is extremely painful and deeply scarring.

Take whatever action is necessary to stop the abusive situation if it is still going on. You have the rest of your life ahead of you. Don't think that you cannot change or that it isn't worth it. It is. If you are still with the abusive person, and the person has not changed and may be dangerous to others, get professional help immediately. Al-Anon is an essential support if your spouse is alcoholic. Other resources are listed in Chapter Ten, "When It's Too Hard to Do It Alone."

COMMON QUESTIONS ASKED BY NONABUSIVE PARENTS WHOSE CHILDREN WERE ABUSED

1. Why didn't my child tell me he was being abused?
Some of the major reasons children don't tell are:

- They are afraid to tell, because they have been threatened directly or covertly. Children have been told that if they tell they will be killed, maimed, or given away. They may have been told the abuser will abuse a younger child if they tell, or will kill their other parent, or any number of frightening things.
- They are told that no one will believe them, and that everyone will think they are liars and despicable.
- They feel as if it is their fault that they are being abused and that they must have done something bad to make the abuse happen.
- They are too small or innocent to know the events are wrong, at first. Sometimes they are bribed, or are getting attention they can find nowhere else. Then they become too deeply involved to say anything.
- They do not remember. Some children dissociate so effectively they can have sex with Daddy at night and not remember it in the morning. Parts of them split off, sometimes creating dissociated states or multiple personalities.
- They tried to tell, but either because of the way they spoke or the people they spoke to, the message never got across.

2. If the person accused by my child of sexual abuse says it never happened, is it possible that my child is lying or mistaken?
There are cases of people who have been falsely accused, but this is extremely rare. Children usually don't lie about abuse. In fact, even people whose abuse has been documented often doubt themselves because they so much want to believe that the abuse never happened. Again, it is much more likely that the abusive person is lying. He would have many good

reasons to lie, especially if the behaviors are still occurring. He may not be telling the truth because:

- He may not remember. If he was drinking he may have blacked out and have no memory of the abuse.
- He may have a dissociated part that is not in his consciousness.
- He may not be able to admit his actions to himself.
- He may not be able to admit his actions to anyone else.

3. What will it do to my relationship with my adult children if the abusive person is unwilling to change and I can't leave him?

At best, your relationship with your adult child will be limited. As long as you stay with an abusive person without requiring him to change, you are enabling that person to remain as he is. You are continuing to provide your adult children with a negative role model, both of abuse and of allowing people to continue to be abusive. Therapy can be very helpful in strengthening your independence so that you can draw limits on what you will accept in your relationships—that is, that you can clearly say and mean that there are some things you do not deserve to live with.

4. Do I have to leave the person who has been abusive in order to reconcile with my adult children?

Not necessarily, and especially not if the person is no longer abusive, wants to deal with the reasons for his abusiveness, and is willing to make amends. There are many groups that will help you both along the road to recovery.

RECOMMENDED READING

Outgrowing the Pain, Eliana Gil
The Courage to Heal, Ellen Bass and Laura Davis
The Obsidian Mirror, Louise Wisechild
Contrary to Love: Helping the Sexual Addict, Patrick Carnes
Adult Children of Alcoholics Syndrome, Wayne Kritsberg
Codependent No More, Melody Beattie

CHAPTER SEVENTEEN

Getting Deeper

Love . . . the wrenching emotion that floods over you when you finally become willing to accept the whole person, the dark sides, the light sides.

TONY HAYDEN, *Murphy's Boy*

After the initial confrontations, you and your adult children will be sharing a lot of intimate information with each other. This chapter gives you a suggested format for doing this. Choose the exercises or parts of the exercises you want to do together and work on them during several meetings. Going through the exercises in this chapter will accomplish several things:

- It will give you a structure for learning about each other on a deep level in a way that you may not have had a chance to do before.
- It will give you a chance to create a more meaningful and caring relationship together.
- It will help you to deepen your understanding of each other as people who are connected through history but are also separate individuals with different thoughts, perspectives, and feelings.
- It will give you a chance to share with your adult children some of the relationship concepts you have learned, and to learn things from them.
- It will enable you to recognize, interrupt, and alter negative patterns that were passed down intergenerationally.

If your adult children have given you this book or suggested you read it, or if your relationship with your adult children is basically positive, they will probably be open to going through these exercises with you. If your adult children have not given you this book or suggested you read it, or if the rift between you is still large, they may not be anxious to work with you. In this case, it may be best to go through parts of Chapter Nineteen, "What's Left," with your adult children first to find out if there are any current problems that need to be cleared up before your children are willing to explore the past any further with you.

Your children may already be involved in the recovery or personal growth movement. Ask them if they would be willing to share some of the things they've learned or would recommend some books for you to read. Remember that you can still learn a lot from your children and showing interest in their personal work can give you a chance to share their world with them in a way you couldn't before. They will probably also be curious about the work you have done on your own and eager for details about their past history.

If your adult children are unresponsive to your efforts, no matter how many times or ways you've appealed to them, answer the first questionnaire below and send them a copy of it along with some other parts of the book that you feel are relevant. If you receive a positive response, listen carefully, and then ask them again to work with you on your relationship. If you do not get a response, go on to Chapter Twenty, "Letting Go."

If your adult child is addicted to alcohol or other drugs, abusive, criminally involved, or severely impaired mentally, you may not be able to deal with him at all, and certainly not by yourself. If he is willing to get help or is in the process of getting help, do what you can to support him. If not, you will have to get outside support for yourself, by going to a group such as Al-Anon or a co-dependency group. These groups will help you clarify the boundaries that you must set up between you. It can be worthwhile to try a process called an "intervention" which sometimes helps an addicted person realize that he has a chemical problem. In an intervention, family members and other important people in the addicted person's life unite and confront him. The book *Dare to Confront!* by Bob and Deborah Wright, will show you how to go about setting this up. If nothing works, you will need to let go of your unrealistic expectations, grieve for the adult child you have lost, and create a life for yourself separate from him. We all have to let go and move on as our children grow older, but it is very difficult to do so if you have to remain helpless and watch a child continue in self-destructive patterns. The guidance and support of a professional is often necessary at this time.

Some of the exercises which follow are straightforward, some are complex, some are serious, and some are in the form of games. Which ones you decide to do and how you handle them depends on the state of your relationship, how your initial meetings went, what results were accomplished, and your individual styles.

Your adult children may want to read this chapter to get a sense of what you are trying to do, and you can then work on this entire process together. A suggested sequence for working together is as follows.

EXERCISE 1

Answer the questionnaire below about *yourself*, before you meet with your adult child. This is different from the exercise in Chapter Eight, "Unfinished Business," in which you answered these questions about *your parents*. Again, these are ideas for you to take off from. Do as many as you want to or write your own questions and answers, which may be more relevant to your family.

Bring this questionnaire with you to your next meeting

with your adult children and go over it together. It is important to share openly what life was like for you, because your adult children probably do not know a lot about your experiences.

1. What kind of home did you grow up in?

_____

_____

_____

2. What did you think of yourself while you were growing up?

_____

_____

_____

3. What traumas did you undergo during your childhood?

_____

_____

_____

4. What kind of social, political, and economic environment did you live in?

_____

_____

_____

5. What attitudes were you exposed to, in important areas such as the work ethic, money, sexuality, roles, parenting, the reasons for living, beliefs about dying?

_____

_____

_____

6. What were your relationships with your brothers/sisters like?

_____

_____

_____

7. Were you or others in your immediate family put into certain roles such as "the responsible one," "the black sheep," or "the person who tries to make everyone get along"?

_____

_____

_____

8. Were there harmful behavior patterns in the home such as sexual abuse, alcoholism, severe physical or emotional punishment or neglect?

_____

_____

_____

9. How were differences between people treated in your home?

_____

_____

_____

10. If you were to say that you knew your parents loved you but you can't say how, just how did you know? Did you know, or are you in denial?

_____

_____

_____

11. Why did you marry, if you did? Convenience, money, security, attraction, love (not the same as attraction), planned marriage, pregnancy, to escape your home, familiarity (repeat of the circumstances of your childhood: for example, coming from an alcoholic home and marrying an alcoholic), timing?

_____

_____

_____

12. How prepared were you to marry and raise a family? Had you resolved your childhood issues? Did you have any skills? Did

you know how to resolve conflicts or understand and value differences? Had you grown up yourself?

_____

_____

13. What about your sense of personal achievement? Did you focus mainly on survival or did you find out what you wanted to do with your life and follow through on it?

_____

_____

_____

14. What traumas did you undergo as an adult? What deprivations or losses did you endure?

_____

_____

_____

15. What dreams did you have that you've given up?

_____

_____

_____

16. What issues overwhelmed you when you were in your twenties and thirties, trying to raise your children?

_____

_____

_____

17. What historical events that took place while you were a parent of young children and teenagers affected you and influenced your attitudes?

_____

_____

_____

18. What patterns did you repeat from your childhood in trying to parent your children?

_____

_____

_____

19. If your parents were hurtful to you, what did you learn about hurting? What events created your ability to hurt others?

_____

_____

_____

20. Imagine you are able to start over. What do you think your life would have been like if you had the resources that are available now?

_____

_____

_____

Show your adult child this questionnaire after you have filled it out. Talk to each other about how it feels to share these details. Listen to your adult child if he also wants to share his past at this time. If you are somewhat uncomfortable with each other, be assured that this is a normal and expected response. Talking about why you are uncomfortable should help diminish the discomfort. Then continue with the exercise.

Ask your adult child the questions below. He may want to write down his responses rather than respond verbally.

How do you think my past has affected you?

_____

_____

_____

_____

How do you think my past has affected your interactions in your family or in your other relationships?

_____

_____

_____

_____

What did you think and feel toward me before I shared the parts of my past with you that I haven't shared before?

_____

_____

_____

_____

What are your feelings after reading my responses to the questions we just went through?

_____

_____

_____

_____

If you resent me for not breaking away or not changing sooner, can you conceive of a time in the future when your feelings will change?

_____

_____

_____

_____

EXERCISE 2

Show your adult child the personal history questionnaire about *your parents* that you completed in Chapter Eight. Go over it together. Talk about similarities, differences, and how you've all been affected.

EXERCISE 3

Imagine you and your adult child are the same ages. It's unusual to think of each other in this way, but it narrows the generation gap between you. Don't take this as a way to judge where either of you was or is in your life. The purpose is to detach yourselves from being parent and child and to get a real sense of each other just as people.

Debbie tried this exercise with her daughter, Sharon, for the ages they actually were at the time, although you can pick any age. Through sharing, Sharon realized that when her mother was Sharon's age, forty-one, she was in an unhappy, unstable relationship with Sharon's father, was having problems with her children that she had no idea how to fix, and was stuck in a job she didn't like. This reminded Sharon of how much unhappiness her mother had experienced and she empathized with her more. Imagining herself her mother's age, sixty-seven, made her realize how insensitive she was to people in her mother's age bracket who were dealing with issues that she did not have to face yet. Debbie and Sharon imagined how it would have been if they had met and become friends with each other, when they fantasized they were the same age.

To do the game below, pick an A and a B.

Person A: What were you doing when you were age____?

Person B: When I was age____I was _____

_____

_____

How about you?

Person A: When I was age____I was_____

_____

_____

Person B: When I think about you as the same age as me, I feel

_____

_____

Person A: When I think about you as the same age as me, I feel

_____

_____

Person B: If we had both been at the same place at the same age, I

imagine_____

_____

Person A: If we had both been at the same place at the same age, I

imagine_____

_____

EXERCISE 4

Describe for your adult child what you were like when you were small. Try to convey the unique qualities of the child you once were. Choose several things from the activities listed in Chapter Nine (pp. 104–105) that you both love to do, and for a few moments pretend you are children doing them together. There is no need for you to be parent and child or different ages during this time. Choose at least one of these, and set up a time to do it in reality. For example, Jill wanted to try makeup on her mom. Her mom was more than happy to be made up and they had a delightful time trying on colors and styles. Bob and his dad went sailing together, as Bob had a boat and his dad hadn't gone sailing in years. They spent an afternoon relaxing on the water. Gene and his mom took a picnic lunch to the river and they skipped rocks in the water, and Andrea and her dad played some old card games that they hadn't played since Andrea was small.

EXERCISE 5

Read the chapter on "Nurturing and Effective Parenting" together. Go through the scenes, so that your adult child can

understand how conflicts can be handled gently and effectively. Go through some scenarios from your children's past and
together put them in the framework of the parent listening,
self-disclosing or resolving conflicts, or even just understanding and letting things go. Share how it would have been different if you had been able to use these skills during your early
parenting years.

Have your adult child choose an incident to talk about that
she felt was not handled well. Using the format below, have
your child describe the event and how it affected her. Anne
filled in the blanks with her dad in this way:

> Do you remember when: <u>You forbade me to go out at
> night?</u>
> What I did was: <u>I used to sneak out of the house.</u>
> I felt: <u>guilty but determined to do what I'd planned.</u>
> What I learned that hurt me was: <u>to lie to you and to keep
> my distance.</u>
> If instead you had: <u>respected my judgment and just told
> me you were worried instead of yelling at me.</u>
> Maybe then we could have: <u>negotiated a compromise that
> would have worked for both of us.</u>
> Then I would have felt: <u>relieved and good about myself.</u>
> What I would have learned that would have been helpful
> was: <u>that things can be negotiated and that you were
> on my side.</u>

Now try having your adult child fill in the blanks:

Do you remember when:_____

_____

What I did was:_____

_____

I felt:_____

_____

What I learned that hurt me was:_____

_____

If instead you had:_____

_____

Maybe then we could have:_____

_____

Then I would have felt:_____

_____

What I would have learned that would have been helpful was:___

_____

EXERCISE 6

Discuss some of the patterns that have been repeated in your family. This will help you gain increased empathy for each other, to understand the powerful role of modeling on a personal level together, and to identify patterns you do not want to have repeated in the next generation. For example: Jane married at 23 and had two children and so did her daughter, Judith. Harry was very passive and married a dominating woman and so did his son Jason. The relationships looked different at times, but the underlying structure was the same.

Try the following format several times.

It's strange to realize that you: <u>were a social worker</u> and that I also: <u>became a therapist.</u>
It's strange to realize that you: <u>married someone who abandoned you</u>
and that I also: <u>ended up marrying someone who left me too.</u>

It's strange to realize that you:_____

and that I also:_____

It's strange to realize that you:_____

and that I also:_____

It's strange to realize that you:_____

and that I also:_____

EXERCISE 7

Game: What kind of person is "X"?
The purposes of this game are:

- To find out how differences in personality styles have added to your confusion about each other as well as other people in your family.
- To grasp again the fact that there are definite differences in how people perceive the world and process information.
- To realize that no one way is the only way.
- To understand that how we deal with differences plays a large part in whether we create harmony and closeness or battlefronts and isolation.

Using the following codes, fill in the chart below for yourselves and for any members of your family that you wish to. Go back to Chapter Twelve, "Breaking Down the Walls," to find more detailed explanations of the terms. For a more in-depth look at personalities, and a self-scoring questionnaire, read the book *Please Understand Me*, by Kiersey and Bates, together.

Some people will be easy to place and others will be more difficult. Of course, most people do not fit exactly into any of the categories. If you wish to, ask other family members to try out their perceptiveness in figuring out which categories people best fit into. This is a good way to introduce other family members to the work you have been doing.

Codes

I = introvert (introspective) or E = extrovert (gregarious)
N = intuitive (imaginative) or S = sensing (concrete)
T = thinking (rational) or F = feeling (emotional)

J = judging (structured) or P = perceptive (spontaneous)
Style = one of the following four combinations of the categories below:
    SP = action-oriented
    NF = visionary
    NT = ingenuity
    SJ = responsibility
K = kinesthetic
V = visual
A = auditory
Nt = neat
M = messy

Jim and his daughter Suzanne used this chart to figure out some differences between them that had added to their problems. Jim and Suzanne identified their styles by placing their preferences on the chart below. The main differences were Jim's structured, traditional, thinking style and Suzanne's intuitive, future-oriented, feeling style. Realizing that these were simply differences between people, not positive or negative characteristics, helped them understand, value, and learn from each other.

Fill in the following chart for your family as Jim and Suzanne did below. Then discuss the results together to better understand each other.

Person X	E or I	N or S	T or F	J or P	Style	K or V or A	Nt or M
Jim	E	S	T	J	SJ	V	N
Suzanne	I	N	F	J	NF	V	N
_____	___	___	___	___	___	_____	___
_____	___	___	___	___	___	_____	___
_____	___	___	___	___	___	_____	___
_____	___	___	___	___	___	_____	___
_____	___	___	___	___	___	_____	___
_____	___	___	___	___	___	_____	___
_____	___	___	___	___	___	_____	___

EXERCISE 8

Take a comprehensive look together at the hurt that has occurred and the patterns that have been handed down. This is probably a good time to share some of the work you have done in the earlier chapters of this book. Let your adult child know that you are willing to answer any questions he may have about his history, even if it is difficult. His willingness to ask you questions will show that he is beginning to trust you enough to ask. If you can confront the past as an investigative team working together to identify and stop the hurtful patterns of the past, this work will be less ominous. You may have access to information and people that your adult child does not have. Be willing to do research for him if he thinks it would be helpful.

You may both have to deal with a lot of anger and pain during this process. It is a good idea to negotiate a way to handle things beforehand if they get overwhelming for either one of you. A stop sign or signal, a five-minute break, or writing down what you want to say so the other person has time to incorporate it are some ways of protecting you both. It is crucial to take turns in talking and listening, for each of you to make a resolution to listen as much as possible, and to set limits by self-disclosing when what the other person says hurts too much. If you get stuck, here or anywhere else, find a neutral third party to help facilitate.

EXERCISE 9

Share with your adult child any of the drawings of your childhood that you have done. If you haven't done any yet, try doing them now. Remember that the purpose of these exercises is to express your feelings, not to test or prove your artistic ability.

- Ask your adult child to draw his childhood years from his perspective, and draw these years from your perspective.

- Draw individual pictures of how you each perceived your relationship during his childhood.
- Next draw pictures of how you each view your relationship right now.
- Last, draw pictures of how you each want your relationship to be eventually.

Discuss what the pictures represent about the past, your relationship, and what you each want in the future. Observe and discuss any differences you find in your perceptions. Remember your purpose in these exercises is to understand each other better, not to change each other.

EXERCISE 10

Write separate lists of the positive things you've done for each other. Divide these lists into two parts: those things you felt recognized and appreciated for and those things you felt went unappreciated.

Discuss these lists and clarify with each other how you felt at those times. Share what you would have liked to receive from the other that you did not get.

You can use the format below for this exercise:

For the parent:

What are some things I did for my family that I thought were positive that I felt appreciated for?

_____

_____

_____

_____

_____

_____

What are some things I did for my family that I felt were misunderstood?

_____

_____

_____

_____

_____

_____

Ask your adult child:

- What did you think I intended by what I did?
- What are some better ways I could have shown you I cared?

If you wish, tell your adult child: "I am truly sorry for the times I wasn't able to be there for you in the way you needed me."

For the adult child:

What are some things I did for my family when I was growing up that I felt were positive and that I felt appreciated for?

_____

_____

_____

_____

_____

_____

What are some things I did for my family that I felt were misunderstood?

_____

_____

_____

_____

_____

_____

Ask your parent:

• What did you think I intended by what I did?
• What are some better ways I could have shown you I cared?

If you wish to, tell your parent: "I am truly sorry for the times that I didn't understand how hard you were struggling and inadvertently made your turmoil greater."

Talk about those things that you were not appreciated for in a new light: as attempts to show your love, even though they were not effective at the time.

EXERCISE 11

If your relationship has stabilized and you are still unresolved about some things your adult child did that hurt you in the past, you may need to tell him about the pain he caused you so he can understand how you felt at the time. Be ready to let him know how you need him to respond to you—which will probably be the same way he wanted you to respond to him. You might want to say that you need to get something off your chest and that you want him to acknowledge that the event happened and that you were hurt by him.

Harold was still carrying resentment toward his son Tommy, because when Tommy was addicted to street drugs he stole a great deal from his father. Harold felt that he needed to share his feelings with his son so that this would not remain a barrier between them. This worked fairly well because Harold did not place more value on material goods than he did on his relationship with his son.

This is how Harold's conversation with Tommy went:

DAD: Tommy, I want everything to be okay between us, but I still feel hurt because of some things you did when you were on drugs. You stole some important things of mine and I need to talk to you about it so it's not in the way of our relationship.

TOMMY: I wish you didn't have to bring it up. I feel so horrible when I think about how I was and how I acted. I guess you have a right to, though. I actually don't even know for sure what I did, or what I took.

DAD: Well, you took some jewelry that my parents left me, and a lot of money. And you stole my credit cards and got several thousand dollars that you never repaid.

TOMMY: I don't know what to say. I'm sorry. I feel terrible that I did it. I don't know if I can make up for it. I don't have the money to pay you back.

DAD: I don't want to be paid back, Tommy. I just needed to say how I felt, to clear the air for myself. I love you, and I'm grateful that you're not doing drugs anymore and that we can talk like this. I can't make up for the ways I've hurt you either—so let's not even try.

If you wish, use this format:

Parent:

The way you hurt me was:_____.

The way I felt was:_____.

The way I need you to respond to me is:_____.

Child:

When I _____it hurt you a lot.

At that time you must have felt_____.

I'm sorry that I caused you to feel_____.

If you are following this book sequentially, and your adult children have been receptive to your efforts, by the time you share this chapter with your adult children you will have a clear picture of how they felt growing up, because you were able to:

- Listen to your adult children's experiences of their childhoods.
- Acknowledge the validity of their perceptions, without minimizing their feelings.
- Share your own experiences, memories, and feelings.
- Express your regret for the hurt your adult children have experienced.
- Find out if there is anything you can do now to repair your relationship with your adult children.

If you listen to your adult children share about their present in the same way you let them explore their childhoods, you will continue to discover a wealth of information about the children that you have brought into the world. Listening and caring will be a great support to your children, even at this late date. As you share your own current experiences with them in turn, understanding and compassion can continue to develop between you.

To find out about your adult children's lives now, approach them with curiosity and respect, without preconceived ideas. You may find that most things are going fine for your adult children or you may find that although their lives look good on the outside, they feel lonely and desperate on the inside. You may find out that there is abuse being repeated in their families, either by them, their spouse, or between their children. You may find out that your adult children have been in therapy for a long time, perhaps with many therapists. Be ready to listen and accept what you hear. Whether your children's problems are major or everyday, you will find out, if you listen carefully, that your children still have a deep need inside to be loved, accepted, and valued by you.

It is easiest to share if you have clear and specific questions to answer. The following list of questions will help you and your adult children find out more about each other in the present. Use those you think are appropriate for your family or make up your own. If these questions are asked in a loving and accepting way, and you listen nonjudgmentally, without blocking their communication, your adult children will want to share their answers with you. Go through the questions together, first for your adult children and then for yourself.

- What is your life really like now?
- What is most important to you?
- What do you want to have happen to you in the next year? The next five years?
- What dreams of yours have you attained?
- What dreams have you left behind?
- How do you feel about these losses?
- Do you still want to try to realize these dreams?
- What do you need to have happen in order to attain them?
- What struggles are you still having?
- What burdens are you still carrying from your past that hold you back?
- How do you see yourself in relationship to others your age?
- What do you think you could have done with your life if you'd had a family that was more supportive?
- What are some of the things you love?
- What are some things that upset you?
- What is your perspective on life and relationships?
- What are your spiritual beliefs?
- What are the things you're afraid of?
- What do you pretend is true that you know isn't?
- What are some issues you want to resolve?
- What makes you happy?
- What gives your life meaning?

In the last few chapters you have explored various ways to break down the walls between you and your adult children. You have learned several methods for understanding and approaching them. You have considered how your adult children felt in the past and what issues need to be spoken about and resolved in order to improve your relationship. You have focused on ways to deepen your relationship and to interact with each other.

The last section of this book deals with letting go of the past and moving into the present and then the future. You will be exploring the concept of forgiveness; learning ways to resolve issues in your current relationship; and dealing with loss. Finally, you will be exploring and discovering ways to grow individually.

PART FOUR

The Way It Can Be

CHAPTER EIGHTEEN

The Limitations of Forgiveness

Great Spirit, grant that I may not criticize my neighbor until I have walked a mile in his moccasins.

St. Francis Indian Mission, North Dakota

Don't judge any man until you have walked two moons in his moccasins.

The Indian Committee of the National Council of Churches

Whether your adult children have been hurt mildly or severely, there isn't any way you can take back what happened in the past. Conversely, if you have been hurt by your adult children there isn't any way your hurt can be erased. If one or both of you believes that either of you should feel ashamed of what you did and that you are in need of forgiveness, it will weaken your relationship. You do not need your children's forgiveness and they do not need yours. Forgiving implies blame and guilt which are irrelevant after the fact. It's important to understand each other's experience, not to judge each other. Instead of dealing with forgiveness, you can work together to create a safe atmosphere where the past can be dealt with, understood, and made up for symbolically. (The way forgiveness is dealt with here does not include forgiveness in a religious sense, only in a human one.)

The dictionary provides three definitions of forgiveness. Let's look at the three definitions closely and consider them from the perspective of reconciliation with your adult children.

FORGIVENESS

Definition 1. To Excuse for a Fault or Offense; to Pardon

In order to pardon someone, the person doing the pardoning has to be in a position of superiority. For example, in order to pardon you, your adult children would have to consider you beneath them. This would enable them to become your judges, with the right to condemn or excuse you. But they haven't "walked a mile in (your) moccasins" or experienced your history and how it affected you. How can they claim superiority when they might have acted similarly or worse in your position? You could not have behaved any differently than you did, given who you were and the context of your life (see Chapter Six: "Imperfect People in an Imperfect World"). You will certainly be sorry that harmful events took place, and you will feel genuine regret about actions you've taken that have been harmful, but you do not need to be judged or forgiven. What is the point of forgiving? Forgiveness labels the person being forgiven as wrong and shameful. Shame diminishes one's sense of worth, and low self-worth increases the chances of repeating abusive cycles.

For example, Heather was extremely bitter toward her father for his abuse of her throughout her childhood, and she was sure that she could never forgive him for what he had done to her. This is a common response to hurt, but in reality, it didn't matter to her father whether she forgave him or not. He didn't need her forgiveness. He needed her understanding, so they could move on. Even if Heather had decided to forgive her father, it would not have meant anything to their relationship. The actual effect on Heather of being unforgiving was that she remained distant and self-righteous, hurting herself more than anyone else. As Heather and her father began to communicate openly with each other, she began to reach an understanding of her father as he shared the history of his own abuse, his awareness of his ignorance and his sense of failure. Slowly she became convinced that he was truly sorry that she had been hurt so badly because of the patterns that he had repeated and she felt connected to him in a new way. She was finally able to see him as a separate and equal person who was struggling, rather than as someone unworthy and criminal who was out to hurt her. Once Heather realized all of these things, forgiveness became irrelevant.

Self-forgiveness has the same limitations as forgiveness of others. What happens in self-forgiveness is that a part of your personality separates from the rest and plays out the drama of absolving another part of guilt. In a sense, one part of you acts as the judge, while another part of you takes the role of the part that feels repentant. This tends to be a long-term process and seems like a real waste of time. Instead, you could have sorted out what you did, why you did it, and taken steps not to do it again. All the energy that went into the sin and pardon drama could have been put into learning how to take more effective actions in the future. As a friend of mine once said to me a long time ago, "Don't ask for forgiveness: just don't do it again." You will be better off gaining awareness, understanding, and respect for yourself instead of your forgiveness.

Definition 2. To Absolve from Payment

To forgive another we are technically supposed to absolve the person who was hurtful from penalties. However, reconciliation may work better if some restoration is made or some action is taken. Willingness to work on the relationship, to make changes, and to help with payments for therapy if necessary, are all ways that you can help restore your relationship with your adult children. This is contrary to the part of the definition of forgiveness which refutes the value of payment. But it can be an important and necessary step toward completing and healing your relationships.

Jerry and his son Richard have done a lot of work together dealing with the past. Jerry's father had been a heavy drinker, just barely surviving until he was killed in a farming accident when Jerry was eleven. The designated man of the family, at an age when he was just beginning to develop into an adolescent, Jerry's attempt to create an identity of his own was abruptly halted. He worked through his teenage years to support his family, then married and worked to support his new family of five children. Jerry was a perfect example of someone who missed out on realizing and expressing his own needs and desires and becoming his own person.

As Jerry's children developed into individuals themselves, Jerry had no idea how to relate to them. Closed off from his feelings for as long as he could remember, he remained physically and emotionally distant from everyone.

Jerry's son Richard, not surprisingly, grew up feeling alienated from Jerry and negative about himself, believing as children do that if they were only smart enough, strong enough, good enough, or worthy enough, their parents would love them. As Richard learned more about his past and his father's, he realized that his father's isolation was not a reflection on him.

As the walls continued to break down between Jerry and Richard and as they got to know each other more deeply, the subject of forgiveness came up. This is a section of their dialogue:

JERRY: I feel terrible about what I did to you all those years. I must have been blind not to see that you needed me. Is there anything I can do to make you forgive me?

RICHARD: There's nothing to forgive, Dad. I know now that you did the best you could. But what you are doing now is what I have needed from you all my life. You are willing to deal straight with things that are hard to face, to make our relationship work. You're willing to change. I really can't express how important that is to me.

Definition 3. To Renounce Anger or Resentment

If you understand what conditions contributed to a person's acting in a hurtful way, you will not need to condemn or pardon them. Nonetheless, you may still feel anger and pain, even though you understand the circumstances that led to the hurtful behavior. We all have to do our own grieving for the traumas and losses we have sustained. This entails going through stages of anger, fear, and pain before we can integrate the events and feelings into the rest of our lives. A major problem for victims of child abuse has been people telling them to forgive the person who abused or molested them. They were unable to do so and felt as if they were bad for not forgiving. This concept also got in the way of their connecting with and integrating their emotions.

Many of us will utilize our anger and pain as part of our work to create a better, more civilized world. Anger can be converted into powerful energy that can help us do our part in creating or supporting legislation, grass-roots movements, or groups designed to create change in areas that are unjust and harmful. Anger can be used in our lives as a signal that we are in a situation in which we need to protect ourselves or others who are being abused. The energy we gain from the emotion of anger can be used to leave situations that are harmful to us.

For example, Darlene, who was beaten severely by her father and her first husband, kept just enough anger at them to invoke that anger when she became involved with people who were potential abusers. If she had lost that energy completely, she might also have lost the signal that reminded her that she deserved to be treated respectfully and gently, and that numbing out her feelings was not going to keep her safe. It helped her to stand up for herself, rather than be a perpetual victim.

To harbor anger beyond the point where it is part of a healing process simply embitters us, which is not useful to us or to anyone else. We need to deal with the anger by letting out enough so that it is not mistakenly displaced onto others or left festering inside us. We also need to remind ourselves continually that we have all been hurtful and realize that we are all human and we all make mistakes. We need to do what we can to minimize our own destructiveness as well as the destructiveness around us, and move on.

It is important to realize that though traumas may have happened to us, and we may have contributed to the traumas experienced by others, the trauma is not who we are. If we conceptualize a small circle inside a much larger circle, and label the small circle "ourselves" and the large circle around it "the traumas in our experience" we become overwhelmed and lost. If we conceptualize the small circle as "the traumas in our experience" and the large circle as "ourselves" we can handle what has happened to us.

EXERCISE

Write about a situation in which you were hurtful to one of your adult children.

_____

_____

_____

What types of feelings provoked you into being hurtful (fear, anxiety, humiliation, loss, confusion, helplessness?)

_____

_____

_____

What patterns from your past history did you repeat?

_____

_____

_____

If you had known then what you know now, what might you have done that would have been helpful rather than hurtful?

_____

_____

_____

Can you understand how you were trapped at the time and could not have done things any differently than you did?

_____

_____

What would you say to your adult child now about that situation, if you could?

_____

_____

_____

If you and your adult child both understood why you acted as you did, would you still need forgiveness from your adult child?

_____

_____

You may have negative feelings toward your adult children, and these feelings need to be dealt with too. You will need to understand your adult children's experiences and how circumstances affected their way of viewing and acting in the world.

Maude had very negative feelings toward her daughter Carrie for the way she had acted when Maude had major surgery at thirty-six. Carrie was thirteen when Maude came home from the hospital, weak and in need of a lot of support and assistance. Carrie seemed totally oblivious to her mother's needs, and went off on her own without helping with laundries, dinners, or anything else. Maude had to handle things that were extremely difficult for her, and consequently her healing was slow and painful. Maude felt that she could never forgive Carrie for the way she had acted during that time.

Looking closer at this family, we find that Carrie was in as much emotional pain as Maude was in physical pain. Maude and Carrie had never had a very positive relationship. Maude had transferred a lot of the rage she had felt growing up toward her sister, who had been abusive to her, onto Carrie, who reminded her of her sister. Carrie, like Maude's sister, was more active and less verbal and intellectual than Maude. At thirteen, Carrie had very little self-esteem, was having difficulty understanding her school work, had become sexually active and was living in terror of becoming pregnant. She was also experimenting with alcohol and marijuana. It wasn't that she was being cruel to her mother; she simply didn't notice her mother's needs. She was just as unaware of her mother's needs as her mother was of hers. Who needs to be forgiven in this family? Everyone needs to be understood.

List some times and ways you feel your adult children have been hurtful to you.

_____

_____

_____

_____

What types of feelings provoked them into being hurtful (fear, anxiety, humiliation, loss, confusion, helplessness?)

_____

_____

_____

_____

What patterns did they repeat?

_____

_____

_____

_____

Can you understand how they were trapped at the time and that their behaviors mirrored their circumstances?

_____

_____

What would you want them to say to you, now, if they could, that would help to repair the hurt feelings of the past?

_____

_____

_____

_____

Do you still feel the need to forgive them?

_____

_____

If you still feel that forgiveness has a place in your life, deal with it in a way that works well for you and your family. If you do decide to forgive people or ask to be forgiven, either personally or with another, be sure to deal first with your anger, fears, confusion, humiliation, or pain. Also, be sure to have a deep understanding of the circumstances that surrounded the hurtful behavior, and to reach a state of compassion before you address forgiveness. If not you will just be covering over feelings that need to be dealt with, and you will be using the concept of forgiveness to remain in denial.

CHAPTER NINETEEN

What's Left

> Nothing endures but change.
> HERACLITUS

We go through many changes over the years. The young adults we were when we raised our children and the people we have become are probably very different. For most of us, the years when our children were growing up were chaotic and overwhelming, as we struggled to grow and survive. Anne Morrow Lindbergh in *Gift from the Sea* uses the image of an oyster, "with small shells clinging to its humped back" to represent those years: "Sprawling and uneven, it has the irregularity of something growing. . . . It is untidy, spread out in all directions, heavily encrusted with accumulations . . . It suggests the struggle of life itself." Even if we weren't working outside the home, we were overwhelmed with the duties of caretaking: taking care of houses, cars, bills, and other impersonal matters. A lot of energy was also spent trying to deal with or hide from our own unresolved problems from childhood. There was rarely time for caregiving, that is, spending quality individual time with the people in our family. There were very few times when feelings could be shared and relationships explored.

Our children are also clearly very different now than they were while they were growing up, although many of their dysfunctional patterns, like ours, may be familiar and seemingly intractable. Some adult children tend to regress to their childhood roles when they are with their parents. Take a moment and think of how you feel or felt being with your own parents. You will probably reactivate the same feelings you had when you were their small child. You might fall into the role your family created for you: perhaps the super-responsible child, the compliant child, the problem child, or the peacemaker.

The core of the person as well as some survival patterns remain, but a quick look at a photo album or two and a long look in the mirror will show you that the years have taken their toll, and that you and your children are no longer the way you remember yourselves or each other. Seeing yourselves clearly in the present will give you a chance to understand that you are both independent people struggling to do your best in a difficult world. When you can see yourselves and each other clearly, you will be able to explore whether or not you want to have a close relationship with each other.

The ultimate form of the relationship between parents and adult children will be different for each family and no one form is better than another. Some parents and children will eventually drift apart and find their needs met elsewhere; others will have a more intimate relationship. The form may be flexible and shift from year to year. The form depends on the needs, desires, and abilities of the people involved, not on an abstract model of how a family ought to be. The important thing is for the past to be cleared up so that it will no longer haunt either of you or repeat itself interminably through the generations.

It's possible that in terms of personalities, you and your adult child are very compatible and would have picked each other as friends even if you had not been related. It is just as possible that your personalities do not fit together very well, and that your main bond is the history that you have shared and continue to share. If your relationship was not very positive in the past it may be unrealistic to expect it to flourish now. Your expectations or your children's may be impossible to fulfill for each other, even if your relationship is a positive one.

Deciding *together* how close you would like to be and how

involved you want to be in each other's lives is an important key in creating a relationship where you can each evolve and grow. If you don't work out the parameters of your relationship together there is a high probability that inaccurate assumptions will be made. Frequently, one person makes decisions based on what he thinks the other person wants or expects, and he has figured the other person out incorrectly. Part of the reason most relationships originally got into trouble was because people didn't communicate clearly with each other. There is no point in bringing your relationship this far and then perpetuating the same cycles you have been working so hard to break. Sometimes working with a therapist briefly can be fairly simple and helpful: This part is about listening, self-disclosing, and negotiating. Feelings may get hurt temporarily as you work things out, but the time you ultimately spend together will be of a far greater quality. Just working out these parts of your relationship together effectively will draw you closer.

Boundary setting can be especially problematic in relationships between parents and their adult children. People who have been raised in families with enmeshed or disengaged boundaries often have difficulty creating healthy boundaries in their adult relationships. Negotiating your relationship with your adult children can also be difficult because of the tendency to confuse pleasing and giving. Remember, pleasing is done to meet your own needs indirectly; giving comes from your heart, does not have strings attached, and is appropriate to the needs of the other person. Healthy relationships have appropriate, permeable boundaries and a fairly balanced amount of giving and receiving between the people involved.

In the example below, a family pattern of enmeshment and pleasing keeps people in a bind and stops them from having a positive relationship.

Though Matt is thirty-four years old, his mother, Rebecca, is preoccupied with what he does and where he goes. She has not created a life for herself, and denies her own needs by focusing on what she thinks Matt needs and should have. She calls him up daily, quizzes him on everything he does and says, and insists that he come over with his wife, Beth, every Friday night for dinner. The conversation at the dinner table is contrived and lifeless as Matt and his wife Beth try to act polite and grateful.

This family system is quite enmeshed, and each person is trying to please someone else, instead of communicating clearly about his own needs. Rebecca has felt since childhood that she has to try to meet people's needs in order to be included. She is trying to get Matt and Beth to fill in the missing parts in her life while pretending to herself that she is giving Matt and Rebecca one night a week off from cooking because she is concerned about their welfare. Matt and Beth go along with Rebecca's program because they want to avoid the conflict that will arise if they say they prefer to be elsewhere and because they would feel guilty if they said anything negative to Rebecca who is trying so hard. Rebecca really cannot give very much to Matt and Beth in her current situation. She first has to fill up the emptiness inside herself. Only after she has grown personally will she have the capacity truly to be unselfish and aware of other needs besides her own. Everyone in this family is perpetuating a useless and exhausting pattern because they do not believe that they can state their real needs and find a way to have them met in a positive way.

In the following example, a pattern of disengaging has kept this family from having a positive relationship:

> June has built very thick walls around her as a result of her extremely abusive childhood and countless abandonments. She has considered anyone who tried to enter her world a potential violator of her boundaries, and almost anyone was, as her boundaries were so extensive. She did not allow her children close to her, and they grew up feeling empty and unloved. June rarely had any interactions with her adult children, or anyone else, for that matter, except on a very removed superficial level.
>
> One of June's adult children made a dent, however, by convincing June to go to his therapist with him, at least once. June returned alone to the therapist for several visits and she

was able to recall and talk about some of the terrors of her own past. Her walls began to soften as the pain was released.

When she and her son worked on their current relationship together, enmeshment was not an issue. June needed to learn to trust closeness and she and her son had to search for some common interests so that they could begin establishing a relationship. Pleasing was a problem that needed to be worked out in this case, as both June and her son had grown up believing that pleasing people meant leaving them alone. In that way they could remain protected and avoid conflicts as well. June didn't believe she had anything to give any more than Rebecca did. She too needed to expand her interactions and belief about herself so that she would be able to give and receive on a genuine level.

As parents and their adult children try to sort out their present relationship, they will need to figure out whether these patterns apply to them and their families, communicate about them, see if the patterns they've learned are working for them now, and then negotiate necessary changes gradually.

EXERCISE

In what ways might the model for relationships you learned affect your relationship with your adult children now?

_____

_____

_____

_____

What are some things you have done to try to "please" your adult children?

_____

_____

_____

_____

Which needs of your own were you trying to meet indirectly?

_____

_____

_____

What are some things you have freely given to your adult children?

_____

_____

_____

_____

What would you like to give to them now?

_____

_____

_____

_____

As you work through your present relationship, the events, feelings, and attitudes that belong in the past may become confused with those in the present. That is normal, but you will be able to deal with the present better if you stop the conversation when this occurs and separate the two. It is fine to continue talking about both, but it gets difficult to understand what is going on if they get too entangled. For example, Lenora and her daughter Eleanor, who was sexually abused by her father, were dealing with what they needed from each other in the present. *In the present* Lenora talked incessantly, and Eleanor felt overwhelmed by the constant noise. Eleanor needed her mother to allow them to be silent together some of the time. Lenora needed to realize that this was not related to her daughter's being overly sensitive because of *her past* history of sexual abuse. It was something that she was doing, now, that was irritating her daughter. They could then deal with the fact that Lenora would get anxious when there was silence, and would talk to fill up the void. Also, Lenora needed Eleanor to separate her helplessness as a seven-year-old and her neediness then from their relationship in the present, which gradually needed to evolve into one of equality.

In assessing your relationship with your adult children, one of the things to remember is that although a bond will always exist between you, you are not obligated to them for life. By the same token, they are not obligated to you either. If your children need a parent now, perhaps you're not the one that can best fill this need. You may not want to. Perhaps they can find other people to meet some of their parenting needs. If you need a close relationship, maybe it's not your adult children who can supply it at this juncture in time. They may not want to. If you decide to meet some of each other's needs it is important to do so out of choice, not obligation. Obligation tends to lead to resentment and then guilt about being resentful. There also tends to be dissatisfaction on the part of the receiver because he can sense the resentment. The issue of obligation is not so easily resolved in cases of extreme illness. If the person is disabled and incapable of negotiation, you will have to weigh your needs against the other person's without his input. Remember to reach out for resources designed to offer support and alternatives for dealing with these difficult areas.

Answer the following questions together to help you communicate openly about what you each can or want to do for the other. Discuss and define each one fully and carefully. Many of the needs listed below can be met in other ways than through each other. If you decide that you want to meet some of each other's needs, it is a good idea to go through the basic conflict-resolution format used below. If you identify needs that you do not wish to meet for each other but you cannot find any other ways to get them met, trade-offs can be agreed upon in a cooperative and balanced way.

In this way you will be shifting from a parent-and-child relationship to an adult relationship, if you have not yet done so. This shift and this process will take time, and small steps are important. Talk about the changes that take place, and reach agreements as you go along.

If your role and your adult child's were reversed when your child was growing up because of your needs, it is important to find out if this pattern is continuing and to stop it if it is. You may want to try to make up for this reversal by meeting some of your adult child's needs for parenting now. That is fine if you can, if your adult child wants you to, and if you can negotiate together how that will happen. It is not necessary to do so in order to have a healthy relationship in the present. However, it is necessary to discontinue the emotional role reversal, even if you must negotiate some caretaking from your adult child. Discuss this entire issue openly together.

For the parent: What needs of your own do you wish your adult children would help you meet?

_____a feeling of closeness
_____a sense of belonging
_____companionship
_____a sense of history
_____contact with grandchildren
_____someone to help you with rides, food, or caretaking
_____feeling needed or significant
_____a chance to parent in a positive way
_____other_____

For the adult children: Which of the following needs do you want your parents to help you meet?

_____a feeling of closeness
_____a sense of belonging
_____companionship
_____care of grandchildren
_____help with food, caretaking, driving, etc.
_____a chance to be parented differently
_____other _____

Discuss your ability and desire to meet each other's needs. Before you try to negotiate them, read the following examples of how some families have worked out these issues.

The following examples illustrate how several issues can be handled using the basic conflict-resolution format, *Common Ground*, described in Chapter Ten. The form is on page 140. The issues are: helping out with childcare, spending time together, and family functions. You may think that the solutions in these scenes are found too easily, and that the families are functioning too perfectly. You will be right. The examples given are models of how these skills can be used most effectively in families who have been working together to resolve things for quite a while. Your negotiations, especially when you are just starting out, may not turn out as well, and they don't need to. In order to make this process work, you need the determination to persist no matter how many complications get in the way. Keep on self-disclosing, listening, and going back to try again. Don't hesitate to get outside help if needed.

PROBLEM ONE: HELPING OUT WITH CHILDCARE

Sarah, twenty-six, has two children, Amy, four, and Joey, two. She works part-time and her mother, Lois, who is fifty-one, has been baby-sitting for her for the past several months. Lois and Sarah have been working on their relationship and they have been talking fairly openly. Lois does not want to offend her daughter, but she feels trapped in the house with Amy and Joey three days a week, and gets tired and cranky. She also feels that she is not doing a great service to the children by watching them out of obligation which makes her feeling resentful and guilty. The children, who have picked up her resentment, have become more demanding. Thus a negative cycle has begun. Sarah does not have a problem at this time. The childcare arrangement is working just fine for her. However, as Lois feels unhappy with the current state of affairs, she is about to give Sarah a problem. If one person in a relationship has a problem that involves another person, the problem really belongs to both of them. If they work as a team to solve their now joint problem, many solutions, acceptable to both, will emerge.

Putting this through the process we have been using for conflict resolution, "Common Ground: A Friendship Model for Resolving Conflicts," Lois and Sarah worked this problem out through the following steps.

Step 1: They set a positive tone by agreeing to make sure that they both ended the process feeling good about themselves and each other, their relationship, any solutions they decided upon, and their ability to resolve conflicts together.

Step 2: They identified what was important to each of them.

Important to Sarah

To keep her job.
To know that the children were receiving good care.

Important to Lois

To have less time with the children when she gets overtired.
To know the children were receiving good care.
To be with the children some of the time.

Step 3. Lois and Sarah agreed to create from ten to fifty possible solutions to this problem, in a lighthearted and friendly way. They were determined to have this process strengthen their relationship and to find a solution that both could live with. During this process, evaluations were kept to a minimum since evaluations stop the creative process. Right at the beginning, they put in the solution, "Leave things as they are," so that they could remember, when they were crossing things out, that it was unacceptable to go back to the way it was.

Some creative solutions Lois and Sarah arrived at were:

- Leave things as they are.
- Either Lois or Sarah join a baby-sitting cooperative.

- Lois watch the children from eight to two instead of eight to five.
- Lois take a parenting class to deal with children more effectively and not get so stressed out.
- Better organization of Lois's house so there are more things set up in advance.
- Lois stay at Sarah's house in the afternoons so children have their own toys and environment.
- Children be kept up later at night so they can take a nap in the afternoon.
- Preschool three mornings or afternoons a week.
- Lois attend a preschool that has parent participation.
- Add more playthings to the backyard, such as sandbox, swings, so kids can care for themselves.
- Get a neighborhood teenager to help out after school from three to five.
- Sarah trade some other chores with Lois so that Lois has more leisure time on the other days.
- Lock children in a room for two hours.
- Get a VCR and rent quiet tapes for one and a half hours in the late afternoon.

Step 4. They crossed out any unacceptable or unworkable solutions to be sure that no one would agree to anything they couldn't live with.

Step 5. They then found a combination of solutions to try from those that were left, and a backup solution as well.

Step 6. They imagined how it might work, and dealt with potential problems. They finally arrived at a workable solution.

This problem was resolved by Sarah's finding a parent-participation preschool that both of her children could attend three afternoons a week. The parent (grandparent in this case) needed to participate one day every other week and the other days were free. Since there were two children, Lois participated one day each week. This still left her two afternoons a week free. It wasn't necessary to use the backup solution, which was to find a neighborhood teenager, but it was a relief to know it was a possibility in the event this solution didn't work.

This solution worked well and in fact had extra benefits. Lois became involved in an environment which was much different than the one she had been exposed to when her own children were small. She met people who expanded her interests and increased her self-esteem. The new exposure increased her energy level and her involvement. This turned out to be a very positive solution for the children also.

PROBLEM TWO: DECIDING ON TIME
SPENT TOGETHER

Frank lives alone a few blocks away from his son David and David's family. Frank's current problem is that he feels that when he goes over to David's house he is ignored most of the time, and that he is treated as if he were a burden. Frank was tired of the uncomfortable feelings, and decided to begin working on this issue. He asked David, "How come you act like I'm in the way all the time when I come over? I feel as if I'm unwanted and just a burden to you."

If David hadn't wanted to straighten out his relationship with his dad, he would have avoided conflict by giving Frank his usual placating lines: "No, Dad, things are just fine. We love you. We'll try to make you feel more welcome." This would have been dishonest, made Frank feel crazy, and kept them from resolving things. Instead David took a deep breath and said, "You're right, Dad, it is awkward a lot of times when you come over. I really like seeing you, especially since we've been talking about these things, but it's a problem for me when you drop in without any notice and expect me to stop what I'm doing and entertain you. I can't always do that and I really don't want to. It's a problem for me, too, because if I drop everything I resent you and if I ignore you I feel guilty and bad about myself."

Frank felt hurt and defensive, and his first instinct was to say what he would have said just a short while before: "I'm not blind, you know. I can tell you don't want me over. What can I expect anyway, nobody wants to see me. Well, forget it then. I just won't come over anymore unless you think I'm worth inviting over once in awhile." Instead he continued self-disclosing. "Well, I just want some company, some human voices, ya know. Living alone isn't exactly what it's cracked up to be. I guess it's too much to expect you to make that up for me. But I'm not sure what else to do when I get so lonely."

Frank and David then decided to work on this problem together. They set a positive tone by agreeing on the importance of each person's feelings, their relationship, being able to resolve conflicts, and finding a solution that worked well for everyone. They then figured out what was important to each of them.

The conversation highlighted Frank's loneliness, which had been an undercurrent but had not been dealt with. David and Jeanette, parents of three children, ages five, nine, and fourteen, were overburdened and there were some real ways that they needed help. Frank could contribute to the family rather than just hanging around, unintentionally acting needy and demanding. David and Jeanette felt that more privacy was important to them and that being notified or asked before Frank came over was not an unreasonable request. However, Frank did not want to have to call each time he came over, so they had to come up with a solution which did not require Frank to phone all the time.

It was important to Frank to feel involved, useful, and wanted.

It was important to David and Jeanette to have some privacy and control over their environment and not to feel enmeshed with or burdened by Frank.

They created the following solutions:

- Leave things the way they are.
- Have certain times reserved for privacy for David and Jeanette.
- Have times Frank is included in family activities.
- Frank never come over.
- Frank move in.
- Have a meeting with everyone, including the kids, to see how Frank could help them out on things, since he wanted to be involved.
- Frank take a class in history, an interest that he had never pursued.
- Frank get involved in a political organization.
- Frank get involved with their fourteen-year-old in environmental issues.
- Frank join Senior Gleaners, a group that collects overstocked food from supermarkets and gives it to the needy.
- Frank help out with the kids, for example, driving them to soccer.
- Frank join a group of seniors who travel to various places at reduced fares.
- When Frank comes over without notice he participates or does his own thing without expecting anyone to entertain him, realizing that does not mean he is not welcome.

After crossing out unacceptable solutions, this family came up with a combination of solutions that worked fairly well, and a back-up plan. They imagined how it would work and took out a few snags. Frank found ways to reach out into the community. David and Jeanette reserved times they could count on to be with their immediate family without interruption. In this situation it was critical to find out what was really important to each person. Frank's loneliness, unaddressed, would have made any solutions useless which did not take into account his need to participate.

PROBLEM THREE: FAMILY FUNCTIONS

Dealing with the holidays can be a source of constant irritation, with people going through all kinds of contortions to maintain a tradition and illusion of togetherness that does not fit with their present feelings or life-style.

Marian, in her sixties, has been making Christmas dinner for her four children and their families for more years than she cares to count. She likes to know that she will see her children during the holiday season, but she also feels burned out after all the preparation. Her children have offered in the past to bring parts of the dinner but she has been trapped by her belief system into feeling that she has to do it all by herself. Additionally, gift buying has created more pain than pleasure, and most people were not even happy with the gifts they received. Marian has been watching a lot of talk shows lately, and doing a lot of reading, and has become aware that all her life she has been trying to gain approval and love through taking care of people. She is also realizing that this doesn't work very well, so she has decided she will do things differently this year. She probably could have simply asked each person to bring a part of the dinner, and not to bring gifts, but she decided to do something else. Here is how she approached this dilemma:

Marian wrote the following letter and sent a copy to each of her children:

Dear_____,

I know I have been the one to keep tradition alive in the family for many years by having a big Christmas dinner at my house, but I have gotten tired of it over the years and until now I haven't been able to admit it. Well, I'm admitting it. It just isn't any fun for me anymore, and I suspect it isn't that terrific for you either. Some of you have conflicts with other family members that you have to hide and feel uncomfortable with and others have other places you also feel obligated to go. I'm sending this note out to all of you kids to find out what you would really like to do this Christmas. Think about what's important to you and how you really would like to spend the holidays. Also, think about any ways we can handle gifts to make it less expensive, wasteful, and burdensome. It's important to me to feel relaxed and unstressed, and I want to enjoy the holiday. That's about it. What's important to you? Here are some ways I've thought of that might work. Please check all those that would be acceptable to you and add any others you can think of. Then we'll find some ways that will work for all of us.

_____Leave things the way they are.
_____Have a potluck dinner at my house.
_____Have a potluck at your house.
_____Celebrate Christmas on another day.
_____Each of us have our own dinners.
_____Go on a trip somewhere for Christmas.
_____Have a prepared dinner made by the supermarket or caterer.
_____Order pizza.
_____Go out to a restaurant.
_____Work at a soup kitchen.
_____Skip Christmas dinner and donate the money to feed the hungry.
_____Skip gifts, and donate the money instead.
_____Have a fund for gifts to be divided and each family receive one gift.
_____Pick names out of a hat and then buy for the person whose name you pick.
_____Write letters to each other instead of giving gifts.
_____Gifts only for the children.
_____Make gifts for everyone.
_____Make gifts for children.
_____Do gift-exchange within each family only.
_____Everyone buy themselves a gift.
_____Buy yourself a gift ahead of time and wrap it up.
_____Trade off cooking Christmas dinners at each family each year.

_____Spend more time on the religious aspects of Christmas and less on the commercial.

_____Other_____

After several letters and phone calls, the agreed-upon solutions were:

- For this year, each family be responsible for bringing a part of the dinner.
- Buy gifts for the children only.
- Talk on Christmas day about each other's values and have their communication be the gift they give each other.
- Make it a new tradition to decide about future Christmases on the prior Christmas.
- If a family did not want to come on a future Christmas they could participate in the decision-making from a distance or they could all meet for that purpose at a different time.

Four things all three of these families needed in order to succeed in negotiations were:

- To have resolved a large percentage of past issues.
- To be willing to be honest with each other about what they felt was really important.
- To be determined to solve their problem rather than keep it around.
- To work together as a team, making sure to remember that their intention was for everyone to feel good at the end and for their relationships to continue in a positive way.

DELICATE AND AWKWARD AREAS

There are other areas that will be more difficult to negotiate. Some are not really negotiable, such as choices of life-styles, politics, and religion. These areas are addressed in the next two chapters. Some partially negotiable areas are addressed here. These include visitation with grandchildren, dealing with spouses, ex-spouses and remarriages, and differing parenting styles.

Visitation with Grandchildren

Grandparents often fill a special and important role in their grandchildren's lives, sometimes even if they weren't able to parent their own children very well. This may be because: (1) As grandparents, their self-worth is not as wrapped up in how the children turn out as it was when they were parents; (2) they do not have the pressures of being primary caretakers; and (3) they are at a different stage in their lives than they were.

Many conflicts take place between parents and grandparents over who makes the final decisions about the children. Loyalty issues and power struggles often take place between the adults, and sometimes visitation issues arise because of this.

It will work best if grandparents negotiate openly as much as possible with the children's parents to assure that they have continued access to their grandchildren, if they want a relationship with them. In today's society, because of the many short-term and serial relationships couples involve themselves in, there are many ways you can end up being a grandparent. The possibility of losing contact with your grandchildren increases with each relationship change. Because of the increasing numbers of separations, divorces, and remarriages, you could have a grandchild for many years who is not biologically related to you with whom you establish a close bond. If your daughter is not the biological parent and subsequently divorces the child's natural father, you may be left without visitation rights. Rivalry sometimes occurs between the biological grand-parents and the nonbiological grandparents.

This can become extremely entangled and destructive to everyone. It's important to make sure that all of your rela-tionships are working well. You are less likely to be cut off if your relationships with others have been well maintained.

In confusing situations such as these, self-disclosing di-rectly to the other adults involved, listening to their feelings, and trying to come to workable agreements will increase the probability that visitation schedules will be worked out fairly. In some states there are grandparent groups and legal rights organizations for grandparents. You may find that you need to consult an attorney to determine your rights. Be sure that you have the children's best interest at heart as you go about this process. If you must lose contact, you will need to deal with your grief, even though this may be very difficult to do. The next chapter will help you deal with your feelings and offers a list of available resources to help you further.

Sometimes adult children will not let their children visit with one of their grandparents, if the grandparent has a history of being abusive. This is especially true if the offender has lost memory or is denying that he did anything abusive. This is a difficult situation, but, unfortunately, many abusers, especially sexual abusers, are repeat offenders. If the adult children's par-ents have sexually abused them, they may never let their chil-dren be with their grandparents, even under supervision. It seems too risky to them. The same problem arises if the grand-parent has been abusive in other ways and the parents are not sure that the grandparent will not physically or emotionally abuse their child. After all, it is the parents' job to protect their children. Alcoholism is another major problem. Most parents do not want their children left with a grandparent who may have a blackout or decide to take them in a car when they are drunk. Unfortunately, if you are still abusive, you may lose your privileges with your grandchildren. If you have read this far, you are probably making positive changes, and perhaps your adult children will gradually trust you. If they do not, you will have to deal with your grief. Ways to do so are given in the next chapter, "Letting Go."

In some cases the grandparents are awarded custody of their grandchildren and the adult children receive visitation rights through the courts or they have to negotiate them. In these cases, the grandparents function as their grandchildren's parents. Negotiation can be difficult and often professional intervention is necessary.

Spouses, Ex-spouses, and Remarriages

This is another complicated and sensitive area which holds infinite potential for confusion and hostilities. It can become a source of great conflict if, for example, you do not get along well with your daughter-in-law but you get along fine with your son's ex-wife. You may not get along with one or both of your daughter-in-law's parents. You may not get along with your son-in-law's children from a former marriage.

Your personal relationship is between you and the person you are relating to, and really isn't anyone else's concern. You have a right to see anyone you want to and they have a right to see you. For example, if you have a relationship with your son's ex-wife, you do not have to end that relationship because his new wife is jealous. However, be careful that you are not being used by your son's ex-wife, or using her to hurt his new wife. In one family the grandparents were very close to their son's ex-wife and their grandchild from their son's first marriage. The current wife was jealous, and she needed to resolve jealousy issues from childhood in order to accept that relationship.

However, the grandparents also needed to stop comparing her unfavorably to his ex-wife, which they were doing partially because they were being manipulated by their son's ex-wife whom they had allowed to become very dependent on them. Openness and communication in this complicated area are essential.

You may sometimes want to see your adult child without his wife—or his wife without him. Again, each relationship is unique and does not concern anyone else, as long as it is not used to undermine anyone else. You don't need to have a great relationship with everyone, but you will want to be open to making it as good as it can be. It is also important to realize that your immediate family is not your only resource. There are many other people with whom you can have intimate and lasting relationships if you will reach out to find them.

Parenting Styles

Differences in methods of parenting the grandchildren create problems in many parent/adult child relationships. It is important to deal with different ideas together, probably many times throughout the years as relationships change and the grandchildren get older. Most likely everyone who relates to the children will have different ways of dealing with them. There are many ways to parent, and people are often very defensive about the way they've chosen to do it. I think that the best way to raise kids is using the principles outlined in this book. But those principles include allowing people to choose their own style of parenting.

There are no simple answers for how to deal with this issue. A general rule, to minimize dissension, is: unless you are asked for advice, think hard and seriously before you criticize someone else's parenting style, as long as the way they are handling the children does not directly affect you or qualify as child abuse. If what they are doing directly affects you, you will need to initiate the basic conflict-resolution process we have been using. If you suspect child abuse or neglect, you must discuss this openly so that the children will be protected and the family will receive the assistance it needs. Reporting the problem to Child Protective Services may be necessary.

If your problem with your adult children's parenting does not affect you and is not abusive, but you feel that your ideas are important, think of a gentle way to share them. Perhaps you could demonstrate another way of parenting that will show them how to get better results. You may want to self-disclose about how you are feeling and offer to give them advice and see if they are interested. Your adult children may be receptive and you will be able to show them methods that they may not know. Remember, though, that one of the best ways to teach your adult child anything about parenting is by example. Be the kind of parent to them that you think they should be to their children. If you are getting a hostile response from them, you may not be acting as effectively as a parent as you think, and any advice you offer will be undermined by your own actions.

If your children ask you to do something differently in your parenting of the grandchildren, listen to their reasons, and if it isn't a significant issue, go along with it as a way of demonstrating your respect for their way of parenting. Perhaps it is important to them that their child have a story at night, or go to bed at a certain time, or not have excess sweets. It is helpful to be open to alternative methods of parenting, and your adult children are the primary caregivers of your grand-children, and so expect to have the last word. One possible way through this difficult area is to agree to share the same books as your adult children or to sign up for the same parent-ing classes together. If your adult children's methods seem de-structive or impossible for you to do, and they are unwilling to learn from you, you will have little recourse but to listen politely, negotiate when possible, and make your own decisions on how to grandparent.

FOR THE BRAVE: ASKING FOR FEEDBACK

This chapter is mainly about changing, and you cannot change if you have no choice. If you are still controlled by old patterns or fear, your choices are very limited. By now perhaps you have worked through your old patterns enough to realize that many of them are no longer useful or in your best interests. In that case, you are probably eager to try new methods for dealing with your relationships. As you change in ways you need to, you will start to experience more intimate and rewarding relationships.

Keeping a relationship based on old pathology is detrimental to you and to your adult children. There are many different ways to do things if you are willing to risk trying them out. This is the only way you can learn, grow, and become truly connected to others.

Habitual negative patterns can be broken once they have been identified and once you have made a commitment to break them. If you are willing to risk asking your adult children to help you identify those habits that get in the way of your relationship, they can give you invaluable feedback about how you are affecting those around you. If something correctible is getting in the way of your relationships, you may as well find out what it is. Then you can decide whether you want to change your behavior or not. If you decide to ask your adult children for feedback, you will need to make it clear that you need them to talk to you respectfully. If you find that you are being spoken to offensively, say something like, "It hurts when you talk to me in that way. I want to hear what you have to say, but I can't listen if I feel attacked. Can you try again, more gently?"

Here is how one person successfully and bravely asked her children for honest feedback and made positive changes within her family as a result.

Joanne made phone calls to each of her three adult children and asked them to give her an unusual gift for her birthday. Instead of the cards, gifts, phone calls, or restaurant dinners they usually gave, she asked them to come over to her home on the Saturday afternoon closest to her birthday, with the grandchildren who were twelve and over, and have an open talk about their relationship.

At this meeting, Joanne said openly, "Other people's kids spend time with them, and I don't understand why you don't want to spend time with me. I know it's not my imagination, so please don't tell me that it is. I want to have a better relationship with you and I need to know what the problems are so I can try to correct them."

This meeting was painful in parts for Joanne, but also very constructive. When everything was brought out into the open, there were actually only three things that bothered Joanne's children and grandchildren. The first was her giving them advice when they were not interested in receiving advice. The second was taking the conversation away from the person speaking. One son showed her how both of these affected him: "When I told you our refrigerator broke down you interrupted me in the middle of my sentence and told me about how great your refrigerator was and how we should have bought a different brand. I just needed you to listen to me, not tell me about your refrigerator or give me advice." Another example of how she turned conversations back to herself was given by one of the teenagers, who said, "Well, when I try to talk, you don't listen very well and you tell me the same things that I've heard over and over. I want to listen to you, but it's hard to have a conversation. I don't mean to be rude." The third problem that family members had was that Joanne didn't understand that when they were busy it was best to leave them alone. For example, her daughter said that when Joanne called and she said they were on the way out Joanne would ask innumerable questions like,

"Where are you going?" "What are you going to do?" and "How come you're going there?' instead of just saying, "Bye, talk to you later."

It didn't feel great to Joanne to hear these things, but it felt like a relief to know that there were specific behaviors of hers that were bothering her family and that it wasn't that they didn't like her as a person. For the first time, she had the option of changing some of these behaviors if she wanted to.

Another thing that became clear during this meeting was that this family was extremely busy and that this was a societal and generational time problem that didn't have anything to do with Joanne personally. Because of their fast-paced and overextended life-styles they rarely even had time for their own small family units, and didn't even include each other in their activities as often as they wanted to. Additionally, the adolescents in the family were off in their own worlds a lot of the time, forming their individual identities. The fact that Joanne's friends seemed to have children who spent more time with them was interesting, but didn't necessarily mean that their relationship was better. They might be getting together often because they were all trying to avoid conflict. Or that type of relationship might suit their life-style better. It didn't really matter, because what was important was what worked for Joanne's family, not anyone else's.

Everything in this family wasn't resolved as a result of this meeting, or even after subsequent meetings. What did happen was that the underlying negative currents were brought out into the open so that they did not fester and make people feel more distant from each other. Some things were resolved by Joanne agreeing to be reminded when she fell into old patterns. When she forgot, it didn't annoy people as it once had, and it could now be talked and joked about openly. Specific times when Joanne would be included in family events were organized. She was everyone's link to the past and played an important part in her family's lives once she was willing to listen, share, and be open.

You may feel that you don't want to be around your adult children because of some of their behaviors. If they are open to feedback, you can serve an important role in their lives by identifying those problems you've noticed.

Steven found himself avoiding his daughter, Theresa, and wanted to straighten out the relationship rather than withdraw. He told her he wanted to talk about a problem between them and she agreed. He then told her that he had been avoiding her because she usually borrowed money from him when they saw each other, and he felt that this was the real reason she wanted to see him. Theresa told her dad that she had noticed that he had not seemed pleased to see her recently. As a result of their conversation, Theresa admitted to her dad that she was having financial problems since she had returned to school and asked him directly if he would be willing to lend her some money, which she would pay back with interest. Her dad agreed to do this, since he could afford to and he trusted her to use the money wisely and to return it when she could. They were both able to enjoy their relationship again once the ambiguity and manipulation were cleared up.

Many of these issues can be dealt with if the problems are brought out into the open. However, if your adult children will not talk with you about issues which are in the way of your relationship, you may have to say "The Serenity Prayer" by Reinhold Niebuhr, and work toward letting go:

God, give us grace to accept with serenity the things that cannot be changed, courage to change the things which should be changed, and the wisdom to distinguish the one from the other.

CHAPTER TWENTY

Letting Go

Your children are not your children.
They are the sons and daughters of Life's longing for itself.
They come through you but not from you,
And though they are with you yet they belong not to you.
You may give them your love but not your thoughts,
For they have their own thoughts.
You may house their bodies but not their souls,
For their souls dwell in the house of tomorrow,
Which you cannot visit, not even in your dreams.
You may strive to be like them, but seek not to make them like
you.
For life goes not backward nor tarries with yesterday.

KAHLIL GIBRAN, *The Prophet*

After you have worked on the past and done the best you could to create a better relationship with your adult children, you may need to let go of some expectations that are unlikely to materialize. Letting go can be extremely difficult and painful, because it forces you to go through a process of breaking through denial and giving up false hope. Here you will find some ways to go through the necessary stages of grief if you have experienced either a partial loss or the actual loss of your relationship.

There are two different kinds of losses you may have to deal with. The first kind of loss does not include the loss of the relationship with your adult child, and is therefore a partial loss. It involves grieving over the fact that your preconceived ideas of how things were going to be are unlikely to happen.

This kind of loss can be minimized if you are willing to grieve over the way you hoped it would be and become more accepting of how things are. If you had fantasies that did not materialize of how your children were going to turn out or how your relationship with your adult children was going to be; or if you find that you are unable to get your needs met by your adult children, you will experience this kind of loss. If you have not let go of unrealistic views of how you hoped things would be, it may not be easy even to consider the necessity of letting go of them now. It may seem senseless or unfair to have to give up your dreams of how things were supposed to be. However, your relationship with your adult children is likely to improve if you can abandon these hopes and appreciate what you have instead of focusing on what you do not have.

The second kind of loss you may experience involves the ending of your relationship. This kind of loss may be unalterable and irrevocable. In these situations, changing your patterns or your perspective will not improve your relationships. There are some losses we experience that cannot be retrieved. Some mistakes are not correctible. Some failures are not stepping-stones on the way to successes. A loss of this kind may occur if one or more of your children or grandchildren is inaccessible because of chemical dependency, serious criminal activity, active psychosis or other impairment, disappearance, or death. It also may be an irrevocable loss if you are ready to work things out with your adult children, try to tell them of your willingness, and they refuse to work on your relationship or to communicate with you. Several ways to grieve and integrate your losses are offered here. If these exercises are not enough to complete the process of grief, be sure to seek further help.

PARTIAL LOSSES INVOLVING
UNFULFILLED EXPECTATIONS

One of the hardest things for many parents to realize is that their children are individuals with their own ideas, attitudes, rights, and values. You have had an affect on them mainly as a role model and by your treatment of them while they were growing up. Once they are grown, however, your influence is severely limited. Children need roots, but they also must have wings if they are to survive on their own. If you do not let go of your adult children, and let them create their own lives, you have not completed the second half of your job as a parent.

We all have fantasies of how we want our children to turn out. We see them as a reflection of ourselves, our values, our self-worth, and our ability as parents. Because of this, we often believe that we should be involved in their decisions of how they run their lives. Many parents therefore try to control their adult children's choices of: life-style, career, marital status, friendships, political and religious beliefs, morals, and sometimes even the clothes they wear and the food they eat.

Letting go of your expectations of how your children were supposed to turn out means that you may have to accept the fact that you will never have the children you wish you'd had. You may be faced with adult children who have chosen a different religion than the one they were raised in, or no religion at all. Your adult children may be involved in a radical political organization or may be extremely conservative, while your loyalties are to the opposing political camp. They may go on to be perennial students or they may drop out of school early and never return. They may choose a job you don't approve of or choose to live in another country. They may decide to remain single, to marry, to divorce, or to live with someone. They may marry someone of a different race or religion or someone you do not like or approve of. They may have a sexual preference that is different from the norm: about ten percent of the population does, and many people who are gay or lesbian are unwilling to keep their relationships a secret. Your adult children may decide to have only one child or six children. They may not have any children, adopt, or take in foster children. They may decide to have children without getting married, in this society of seemingly limitless options. Your adult children may decide to educate their children at home or in a public school even though you are convinced that they would do better in private school. Regardless of what you think, they may parent their children in a way that you think is harmful or ineffective. They may not take care of themselves well. They may smoke, drink, or eat excessively. As difficult as these situations may be for you to accept, they are decisions that your adult children have a right to make on their own. Even if you think they do not have this right, opposing their decisions will only alienate them and further impair your relationship. Your input may be valued, but only if it has been asked for, and only as advice which they can consider but are not obligated to take.

One of the most difficult things for children to do is to separate from their families. Yet this is the task we must all accomplish as we go through our life stages and move on to create our own families. Individuation, that is, becoming an individual with our own ideas, beliefs, and attitudes, is a task that we do all our lives, but perhaps most intensively in our adolescent years. It takes enormous emotional energy as adolescents to become separate people with our own identities. During a relatively brief period of time, our bodies undergo major changes and we experience the loss of our childhood selves. Adolescents experiment in various ways and try on different styles to see if they fit. This is the time to begin getting used to the idea of leaving our families and beginning a life of our own, where responsibilities and unknowns abound. This is the time to make mistakes and still know we have a place to go back to where we are understood and loved.

Ideally, parents will help their children through this stage, resolving some things together and allowing increasing independence, so that the relationship can evolve into a more equal one. However, parents often have several conflicting emotions of their own which keep them from being helpful at this time. First, they are going through their own life stage, which also involves losing the family they have been accustomed to for so many years. This may bring up all kinds of feelings, from the loss of a beloved child to a guilty relief that the children are gone, to the realization that they have no idea what they are going to do with their lives or their spouses once the children leave. If parents are single, they may or may not look forward to being alone. Additionally, unresolved conflicts and fears rooted in their own pasts may reemerge while the parents try to deal with their adolescents. All of these issues are not directly related to their children, and get in the way of their being able to assist their children to become independent. These are all outside of the genuine and realistic concern that parents have about their children going out into a world that can be difficult and dangerous.

Mainly beginning in the adolescent years and moving into adulthood, adult children will make many decisions without their parents. Parents are bound to disagree with and disapprove of some of these decisions. However, it is not up to the parents to decide how their adult children should handle their lives. Parents who are enmeshed with their adult children sometimes have difficulty with this concept, but it is very important to remember.

You will need to accept your adult children and their choices if you are to have a positive relationship with them, even though it will be difficult if they have made decisions you disagree with or disapprove of. Let us take the example of a parent who disapproves of the fact that her adult child has married someone of another race. If the parent considers her problem with this marriage less important than the relationship she has with her adult child, their relationship can continue to grow. However, if she considers her problem with the marriage more important, the relationship between her and her adult child will become damaged. How you choose to view the problem you are dealing with is up to you. Your life and relationships simply work better if you view them from an angle that keeps things in a functional perspective. If you can let go of a judgmental stance and consider your children teachers who can teach you about "the house of tomorrow that you may not enter" you will learn much about a world that will likely be going on without you. We cannot force everyone to be like us, nor would we like it if we could. Once we realize that our children are autonomous people rather than extensions of ourselves, we can let go of our need to control them. We may become more separate from our adult children as each of us moves on, but that does not mean that the love and care we hold for each other is any less.

In what ways have your children failed to live up to your expectations?

_____

_____

_____

How would you have liked them to have been?

_____

_____

_____

What prevents you from accepting them as the individuals they are?

_____

_____

_____

What is the cost to you of having your expectations be more important than your relationship?

_____

_____

_____

Like our unrealistic fantasies of romantic love, many of us have unrealistic fantasies of how our relationships with our children should be, based on scenes from television, movies, or storybooks. We may have had a special relationship with one of our parents, or another elderly person, that we want to recreate. We may have seen other parents with their adult children who seem to have the perfect relationship. We may have had a person who functioned as a mentor for us and envision ourselves assuming that role for our adult children as we teach them our craft or skill or share our business or profession with them. We may have memories of reading stories of days gone by where generations of families all lived together in the same home as a great extended family.

The actual relationship you have with your adult children may not be what you envisioned, but it can improve if you let go of your fantasy and accept the relationship you have. It is possible that your adult children will do well in the restaurant business you have established, and want them to work in, but it is more likely that your children will have other interests that they would prefer to pursue instead. Your loss in this case will need to be experienced and integrated, as you learn to establish relationships that fit the needs of the people involved.

If you feel disappointed in your adult child or with your relationship and want to change your perspective and feelings, but you are having a hard time doing it, try the following exercises:

1. Imagine that your adult child is doing whatever it is you want him to be doing. For example, if you wanted your son to be a doctor, imagine him as a physician. If you wanted your daughter to go to your church, imagine her attending with you. If you wanted to have a wonderful close relationship with your adult child where your needs for a family were met, imagine that.

Now imagine the wished-for circumstance, but with perfectly conceivable flaws. Your son is a doctor, but he is so busy he neglects his family or becomes addicted to prescription medicine. Your daughter goes to your church but embarrasses you by coming in drunk. Your relationship with your adult child is close, but she does not grow up and establish her own family. How does it feel now? In Mark Twain's book,

The Mysterious Stranger, the main character complains because of his fate until he is treated to a spectacle of several
fates that he narrowly missed, which were much worse.
Sometimes reality is not as bad as it seems, except compared
to unrealistic fantasies.

2. Imagine your adult child being the perfect child you've
always wanted. Get this image clear and bright, and place it
to your left. Now get a picture of your adult child exactly as
she is. Place this picture on the right. Now make your choice.
You can have your picture which is only a fantasy or you can
have your adult child as she is in reality.

Imagine your adult child meeting all your needs and
place the picture to your left. Now imagine your adult child
meeting those needs she is able to meet now and place the
picture on the right. Again, make your choice. You can have
your fantasy of how the relationship could be or you can have
the relationship as it is in reality.

It is important to realize that your needs may not be able to
be satisfied through your adult children. If you need closeness,
a feeling of belonging, to be useful, to have help in managing
day-to-day chores, or any of the other needs outlined in the last
chapter, and your children cannot or will not help you, you will
have to do some grieving and then you will need to move on.
You may believe that your children owe it to you to interact
with you in certain ways, but although you may be able to
control their actions to some degree, through guilt, threats, or
fear, you will lose the opportunity of having a healthy relationship if you do so.

It can be a great loss to parents when their children leave if
they have invested a lot of themselves in the role of protecting
and nurturing their children. Parents sometimes continue to
hold on to this familiar role with their adult children because
they don't want to experience their loss and are unsure of how
to fill the emptiness that will remain. I asked one person to
describe his mother and he answered casually, not com-

prehending the poignancy of his statement, "My mom? I guess the way to sum up my mom is that our lives are her life." In the film *New York Stories*, Woody Allen caricatures the overpreoccupied and overprotective mother who monitors every move her son makes. There are many parents who preoccupy themselves with their adult children's lives and feelings and are unaware of and unconcerned about their own. If you are trapped in this role, it is necessary for your well-being and for the well-being of your adult children to say good-bye to the children you no longer have and to create a more equal and independent relationship with them. Then take the time to notice yourself and your own needs, and begin developing your own abilities and life. The next chapter offers several ways to do so.

How is your relationship with your adult children different than you hoped it would be?

_____

_____

_____

What are the advantages of the relationship as it is?

_____

_____

_____

What changes do you need to make to improve your relationship?

_____

_____

_____

How did you imagine your relationship would be with your children once they grew up?

_____

_____

_____

Is that fantasy realistic? Is it in the best interests of both you and your children?

_____

_____

_____

If you realize that you have been preventing your adult children and yourself from growing individually by being overinvolved in their lives, what would it take for you to begin distancing yourself from that role?

_____

_____

_____

IRREVOCABLE LOSS

If your adult child is totally inaccessible, your anguish will be more profound and more difficult. Recovering from the death of a child usually takes longer than any other loss, including the death of a spouse or a parent. Your child may be lost to you, even if she is still alive, if she is inaccessible, and your grief will be similar to that over a death. Even if you have already completed the mourning process, you may find yourself going through renewed grieving as a result of having gone through the exercises in this book. In addition to letting go of expectations and fantasies, you will have to let go of the relationship and the person. Ultimately, there is only so much you can do as a parent and as a human being, and you will have to hold on to your best memories of what you had and let go of the rest. You will need to go through several grief processes in order to integrate your loss and move forward. *Caution: All of the following processes may bring up extremely intense emotions. Be sure to reach out for support. While you do need to go through grief to get beyond it, deep grieving should not be done alone.*

Workshop leader and author Sidney Simon designed a

three-part completion exercise* which can be very helpful if you are unable to continue in your relationship with your adult child because of the severity of her problems. Read what you have written to someone you trust. The following example shows how this exercise works:

Gordon, whose son was addicted to narcotics and was unwilling to go for treatment, joined a support group for himself and eventually broke off relations with his son. He went through the exercise in this way. He wrote down:

What I will miss about you is:

Your gentle ways
Your voice
Talking to me about your hopes and dreams
Going to games together
Going fishing
Having a son I was proud of
Watching you grow
Your curiosity
Working on cars together

What I won't miss about you is:

Having you con me out of money
Having you steal my things
Having you disrupt my life
Watching you destroy yourself
Listening to your lies
Feeling helpless
Feeling guilty around you
Being angry and unable to talk about my anger

What I have learned from our relationship is:

That I should have worked out my problems before I had children
That I have hurt you and that there is no way now to make up for that hurt

*Reprinted by permission of Dr. Simon, whose most recent book is *Forgiveness: How to Make Peace with Your Past and Get on with Your Life* (New York: Warner Books, 1990).

That I have to set boundaries to protect myself
That I am only human
That loving and enabling are quite different
That I need to grow and change for myself
To let go

Afterward, he read the list to his support group. This allowed him to express his feelings and begin to integrate them.

Use the space below, if you wish, to work through this part of your relationship with your adult child:

What I will miss about you is:

_____   _____

_____   _____

_____   _____

_____   _____

_____   _____

What I won't miss about you is:

_____   _____

_____   _____

_____   _____

_____   _____

_____   _____

_____   _____

What I have learned from our relationship is:

_____

_____

_____

_____

_____

_____

_____

_____

Find someone you trust or a group you can go to where you can read this list and express your feelings openly. Your purpose in grieving is not to forget the person. It is to integrate the positive things you had together and the lessons you have learned into your current life.

The following stages show a breakdown of the grief process. People do not necessarily go through each stage, nor do they go through them in a neat, organized way. However, most of them do need to be experienced in order to move on with our lives.

In the beginning stages of grief most people go into shock, a brief initial protective mechanism to keep them from feeling pain. Disbelief then sets in, as they find it too difficult to incorporate the painful information. Denial keeps things in place, as they unconsciously hold onto the belief that if they don't recognize reality it doesn't exist. As the reality of the situation sets in, disorganization follows, and they find themselves in a state of confusion and disorientation. Then anger comes to the forefront—anger at the people involved, at one's self, at the circumstances, and at the universe. Guilt is often the next painful stage in which they berate themselves for their perceived failures. The hardest part is feeling and expressing the deep pain that accompanies serious losses.

In the later stages they will go through a process of restabilizing, where they will come to an acceptance of the way things are, integrate the loss, readapt and restabilize. These are all normal stages which people need to go through in order to heal and move on with the rest of their lives.

The grief process often takes at least two years. Holidays

and specific associations often bring back our losses for many more years. If you have not gone through this grief process you may be holding back a lot of pain and be numbing your feelings. It would probably be good to deal with it now, possibly with professional help. If you are feeling extremely intense grief, clinging without relief to sorrow, anger, guilt, or depression, over a long period of time, you may be stuck in the middle of the process of grieving. If you find yourself going over and over your memories, to a point where your entire life has lost its meaning, you may be trying to keep the inaccessible person present by holding on to your anger, guilt, and pain. Consult a professional or join a support group if this is so. There are healthier ways to keep part of the person close to you.

If you have experienced a major loss of this kind, read through the parts of grief which have been described, which are listed below, and see if you have expressed them.

Beginning stages (destabilizing)
   shock
   disbelief
   denial
   disorganization
   anger
   guilt
   pain

Later stages (restabilizing)
   acceptance
   integration
   readaptation
   restabilization

Letting go does not mean forgetting the person you have loved. Whether the person has died or has distanced himself or you have had to end the relationship, you will want to keep the memories of the person that are significant to you.

There are several concrete things you can do to keep parts of a loved one present for you. You might make a photo collage of the person you lost, or write a poem for him, or create a box full of memorabilia. Planting a section in a garden can be a way of keeping him there for you, or you can make something to represent him that he would have loved. Some people find they have already incorporated part of the lost person into their own personality, such as a style of clothing, a preference for a certain kind of entertainment, a skill, or a way of viewing the world. Realizing that this valued part has become part of you is a positive way of holding onto the person you've lost.

One exercise for grieving which can be very powerful is to write a letter to the person you have lost, expressing your love and your wishes that things could have been different. If you can find a supportive person to read this letter to out loud, it can help you through the grieving process.

A way to make meaning out of your loss is to use what you have learned in your relationship to help others. Many people who were addicts or lost their children to drugs are now helping others who are trying to break their addictions. Candy Lightner began MADD, Mothers Against Drunk Drivers, after her daughter was killed by a drunk driver. The energy you would have liked to have given your child can be utilized to work on the specific tragedy you have been a part of. Some concrete ways to do this will be addressed in the next chapter.

This is how Anna went through the process of grieving, from the realization that her daughter was not going to reconcile with her, to creating some meaning out of her family's tragedy:

Anna's daughter, Maria, now twenty-six, was first abused sexually by her father when she was thirteen. Anna, blind to her daughter's pain and deeply in denial at the time, did not believe or protect her daughter when Maria tried to tell her about it. Maria did not have the strength to try again or to tell anyone else. As a result, she was subjected to sexual abuse by her father until she finally left to live with her aunt and uncle when she was sixteen. As soon as she could, Maria cut off all contact with both her parents.

Many years later, Anna absorbed what happened to Maria, when her then ex-husband was accused of child sexual abuse in another state. Anna tried to contact Maria, but did not receive any response. She went through a deep self-evaluation and examination of her feelings and her life in therapy. Anna determinedly tried again to contact her daughter. She sent letters, made phone calls, and asked other people to speak with Maria. Despite all her efforts, Anna's letters were returned unopened. Maria refused to speak with Anna, and no one was able to convince Maria to reconcile with her mother.

Anna's feelings were very volatile throughout this time. Her grieving process was like this: First, Anna went through a brief state of shock when there was no response from Maria, no matter how hard she tried. She remained in a state of disbelief, and proceeded to deny the truth about what was happening, long after it was apparent that Maria was not going to respond. When the realization eventually hit her that she would not be able to reach her daughter, no matter what she did, she felt agitated and disoriented, not knowing what steps to take next. Then anger set in, anger at Maria for not being willing to try to reconcile or at least to hear her out. She also felt tremendous rage at her now ex-husband, who had initially created the estrangement by his sexual abuse of Maria. Most of her anger was directed at herself. She felt furious at herself and extremely guilty for having failed her daughter when she had needed her. Finally she completed this first stage of grief by getting underneath her anger to the deep anguish and emptiness inside for the daughter she had lost.

Slowly, Anna moved through her feelings and began to accept that she only did what she was able to at the time. She started to accept the fact that she was not likely ever to have a relationship with Maria. She then moved into the process of integrating what had happened and making it a part of who she now was. She wrote the following letter to her daughter, as part of her attempt to restabilize, telling Maria of her grief. She did not intend to or need to mail it.

Dear Maria,

It's so hard to accept the fact that you really won't communicate with me. And yet it makes more sense that you won't than that you would. Coming to terms with my loss of you is the hardest thing I have had to do. I keep going over and over the past. I don't see how I could have been so ignorant and blind that I believed that you were making it up when you told me your father was being sexual with you. Why didn't I check it out? Why didn't I ever ask you about it again? How could I allow it to go on? How could I stay with him and pretend it was you that was the problem? Why didn't I help you, my own daughter, when you needed me? God, how much worse it must have been for you.

Going through this work of trying to reconcile has ignited my hopes but then let me down inconsolably, because it is too late to reach you. I see so clearly how I hurt you, and yet there is no way to apologize to you or to make it up to you. The steps for reconciliation are useless for us. I cannot make things different.

I know that I have to let go of my sorrow, and I am doing better than before. I will never let go of my love for you. It's time for me to say good-bye to you, and put my pain to rest, but I don't want to. I don't want to accept that I will never have you in my life again. You were so special to me, and it doesn't matter anymore.

I need to say good-bye. I need to move on for my own survival. I miss you, Maria, and I will always carry you close to my heart.

Anna made a photo collage of Maria and hung it in a place where she could see it so she could have a small part of her daughter near her on a daily basis. Anna then decided that she would use the lessons she had learned to do some work for children who had been molested. In these ways, the past became integrated for Anna, and the best of her relationship with

Maria stayed with her as she moved on to make some meaning out of the tragedy of her past. Anna still has a small bit of hope that she and her daughter will someday reconcile, but she realizes that she cannot control whether or not this ever comes about.

It's important to recognize when a life stage or a relationship is over, and to let go. We need to leave the past behind, without denying its meaning to us. We do not lose these experiences; they have become a part of us. Life is inevitably about process and change. It works best if we learn to move on into the future gracefully.

Community Resources

> Mental health services
> Bereavement groups
> Places of worship
> Al-Anon, ACA and co-dependency groups

RECOMMENDED READING

Necessary Losses, Judith Viorst
A Conscious Person's Guide to Relationships, Ken Keyes, Jr.
Life After Loss, Bob Deits
The Courage to Grieve: Creative Living, Recovery and Growth Through Grief,
    J. Tetelbaum

CHAPTER TWENTY-ONE

Moving On

There is a vitality, a life force, an energy, a quickening that is translated through you into action, and because there is only one of you in all time this expression is unique. If you block it, it will never exist through another medium. . . . The world will not have it. It is not your business to determine how good it is nor how valuable it is nor how it compares with other expressions. It is your business to keep it yours, clearly and directly, to keep the channel open.

MARTHA GRAHAM, as remembered by AGNES DE MILLE
in *Dance of the Piper*

As you have worked through the processes in this book you have examined your life and the family and society that helped shape you. You have faced painful experiences and ineffective patterns. You have increased your understanding and acceptance of the child you were and the person you have become. You have learned many new concepts and skills and have attempted to make things right with your adult children. You have been grieving for and letting go of those things you cannot hold onto.

Even if you have gone through only parts of this book, you have learned, grown, and changed. You have reached a deeper understanding of yourself and others, and have gained a rare sensitivity to the human condition. In these ways you have increased your self-expression and your contribution to your family, to society, and to future generations.

This final chapter deals with exploring the amount of satisfaction, happiness, and meaning you have in your life outside of your adult children. It can be difficult for people who have focused on their families for a long time to consider the fact that we are all part of one family and one world. There are many people besides our own children who need understanding and nurturing. Sometimes the realization that we are not connected to our biological family alone helps us to get past the grief and losses we have had, and to expand ourselves in ways we have been unable to before.

Methods are offered here for expanding your personal self-expression in a way that contributes to the world at large. Whether we are in our thirties or in our eighties, contributing to something beyond ourselves allows us to feel useful and significant. It gives us a sense of belonging and connectedness and increases our sense of meaning and our enthusiasm for life. Some of us will contribute through furthering our own dreams or simply by appreciating life in the moment, thereby contributing by adding to the peace, tranquillity, and happiness in the world. Some of us will contribute by becoming involved in a community effort, committed to making changes in a specialized area. Some of us will contribute by being willing to receive graciously from others: Receiving is another form of giving. Here you will explore ways to contribute that are appropriate for you and that are the natural expression of yourself at this time.

The purpose of this exploration is not to put expectations or demands on you. It is to encourage you to express the unique person that you are, and to share your special talents and abilities with others. This is an important part of the process you are going through, because if your life as a whole isn't satisfying, it will be harder to sustain the gains you have made so far. If you have no substitute that feels as good or better than a familiar entrenched pattern, you will find it hard to stay on a new path.

The middle and later stages of our lives can be productive and exhilarating, or unproductive and impoverished. The path we take in our earlier years affects the later ones. If we have not achieved what we hoped to, we often feel a sense of stagnation and bitterness, which turns into despair as we grow older. If we have been fulfilling our dreams and reaching our potential we have a better outlook on ourselves and our place in the world.

As we age, we experience many losses besides the loss of our adult children. We lose our youth and people we love; our physical abilities deteriorate and our health often suffers; our jobs, income, and living situations may be lost or changed. We need outside connections, dreams, and interests in order to tolerate these losses.

No matter what life stage you are in, with awareness, commitment, and a vision of where you want to go, you can take steps now that will enhance your present and your future.

You may feel that you are doing all that you need and want to do in life and are content with that. If so, read this chapter as validation of the hard work and effort you have made and how much it has paid off. Reading the rest of this chapter may bring to mind friends or relatives who would find value in doing some of the exercises which follow.

It is important to validate ourselves for what we have already achieved; positive feedback is essential for growth. Many of us are extremely self-critical rather than self-affirming. We tear ourselves down for our mistakes or imperfections and casually dismiss our successes. It is exceedingly difficult to grow under these conditions. Change comes faster and easier if we accept ourselves as we are, with all of our strengths and weaknesses, as people who are doing the best we can. For many of us, just surviving has been an incredible triumph. Getting up day after day when we barely could, working when we didn't want to, getting through the myriad disappointments and losses life handed us, has been nothing short of heroic.

If you are still experiencing major problems that prevent you from moving forward, such as alcohol or drug addiction, depression, anxiety, panic attacks, eating disorders, or other untreated physical or emotional problems, please get help now.

You will be taking a large step forward simply by taking care of yourself. Asking for help is not a luxury; it is a necessity if you are living a life which is painful or unfulfilling.

Many of us had few opportunities to identify our own needs and desires or to figure out where we could best contribute our energies and talents. We were prevented from growing personally because of obstacles such as feelings of inadequacy, lack of energy, lost opportunities, and insufficient guidance or support. It was hard to move forward without positive role models. An inordinate amount of energy was expended in being trapped in unsatisfying and repetitive patterns. It is not easy to go beyond an impasse, but it is possible.

Many of us have been prevented from growing because of negative beliefs we've had about ourselves and our lives. The exercise below will help you identify those beliefs that kept you from attaining what you wanted. Check those beliefs that apply to you. Put an asterisk by those that you believe apply in the present.

Negative self-evaluations

____I'm not smart enough.   ____I'm not attractive enough.
____I'm not creative enough.   ____I'm not interesting enough.
____I'm not disciplined enough.   ____I'm not good enough.

Feelings of scarcity

____I don't have enough   ____I don't have the time.
    money.   ____I have no support.
____I don't have enough
    energy.

Outside obstacles

____I can't because of the kids.   ____I can't because of my
____I can't because of my   partner.
    parents.   ____I can't because of my job.
____There's too much
    housework.

Old tapes

___It's too much work.   ___It's too much trouble.
___I'm too busy.   ___I'll just be used.

Age-related obstacles

___I'm too old.   ___I've put in my share.
___I'm too tired.   ___I can't see or hear well.
___My mind isn't like it was.   ___Nobody would want my
___I don't have any strength.   help.
___I can barely get around.   ___I'm just putting in time
___My arthritis.   until retirement.

_____   _____

_____   _____

Now see if the items that you checked are statements about reality or distorted negative tapes that are replaying in your mind. You will probably find that many of them are exaggerations or distortions of reality. Just realizing that they are not about reality can help to minimize their power. You can also use the method for changing unreality statements to reality statements that was described in Chapter Nine, "Accepting the Child Within You" (pp. 106–110), to help you move on.

Even if some of the items you checked are based on reality and are real handicaps, they need not be limiting. Most handicaps can be overcome and sometimes even used to contribute in an individual way. A severely handicapped individual said that for most people there are a hundred thousand things you can do. When you are handicapped there are ten thousand things you can't do, but that still leaves ninety thousand things that you can.

It is only emotional disability that keeps us from attaining what we want. If you feel emotionally disabled, reach out for help. Take one small step and tell someone that you want to do something different but you don't know how to begin. Talk to your adult children, talk to a therapist, join a group, or go to an event. You are bounded only by your belief in yourself.

Well, you may say, it's not that easy. You're absolutely right. It's not. On the other hand, it won't get easier as you grow older, so why not begin now? A man who wanted to be a lawyer thought it was too late for him, since he was already forty years old. "It'll take me six more years of school," he said, discouraged. "I'll be forty-six by the time I get there." The question that turned his perspective around was: "So how old will you be in six years if you don't go to law school?" It isn't easy to follow your dreams, but the process can be exhilarating as well as difficult.

Contributing and belonging are vital to an individual's well-being. Milton Erickson, the psychiatrist and hypnotherapist, was once seeing a patient who was diagnosed as a paranoid schizophrenic and believed that he was Jesus Christ. Erickson gathered information about the man and found out that he had been a cabinet maker. Since Jesus was a carpenter, Erickson utilized this information in the following conversation. "I heard you used to be a carpenter," he said. "Yes," replied the man, speaking as if he were Jesus. "Good," said Erickson, "We have construction on the charity wing over there in the hospital and we need your help." The man became part of a carpentry team that didn't care if he thought he was Jesus or not as long as he could do the work. The man was able to leave stagnation (repetitious behavior that goes nowhere) through using his abilities and contributing.

The following exercises involve identifying the dreams you've had, assessing your skills, and finding places in the community you want to become involved with. You will be working on realizing your dreams in a form that may be different from the form you originally imagined but still contains the parts that are essential to you.

It is important to create a vision that draws us forward, energizes, and inspires us. Without a vision we tend to wander aimlessly or to feel as if we have to force ourselves forward.

With a vision we feel as if we are being drawn magnetically toward our goal. You will need to find a vision that you feel capable of reaching and that has personal significance for you. If your vision doesn't include both of these, your energy will be tied up in the struggle, because part of you will interfere with your completing your vision. For example, one woman created a vision of helping children who had been through traumas that were similar to those she had experienced. She decided that taking in a foster child would be one way she could achieve this vision. However, though she believed that raising a foster child was a significant job that she wanted to do, part of her felt incapable of handling a child on her own and she was unable to follow through on her goal. She needed to find a less consuming way of creating her vision. You will need to make sure that you create a vision that you can follow through on.

The exercises below will help you clarify your values and interests as well as the skills and talents you have developed. Do these exercises leisurely, in a quiet and relaxed atmosphere. Go to your favorite spot and take several half-hour blocks of time to complete them.

1. Write down some of the things you loved to do using the natural abilities you had when you were growing up. (Some examples would be: running freely, spending time with friends, daydreaming, going to the beach, drawing pictures, collecting things, building things, playing house, watching people, participating in sports, being with animals, helping people, playing with trucks, experimenting, watching TV, reading books, writing stories, being in charge, organizing people or things, wondering, learning, listening to music, singing songs, playing an instrument, or dancing.)

---

2. Recall one or more of the dreams you've had of what you wanted to be and do, and write them down in detail. If you cannot think of any, create some for yourself now. (Perhaps to be an artist, a veterinarian, a police officer, a musician, a teacher, a movie star, a political figure.)

_____

_____

_____

3. Write down those things you have now that you love and the parts of your dreams that you have attained. (Perhaps you loved animals and have cared for several, or you wrote poems, even if you never shared them. Perhaps you enjoyed organizing things, and created an organized home or you dreamed of being a mom and had children.)

_____

_____

_____

4. What needs do you believe would have been fulfilled if your past dreams had been met? (For example, being a police officer might have met your needs for power, belonging, structure; being an astronaut might have met your needs for recognition, excitement, and uniqueness; being a political figure might have met your needs for involvement, helping others, and meaning.)

_____

_____

_____

5. Some of your old dreams are unlikely to materialize at this time. Partially let go of unrealistic expectations by writing about your loss below. (You may never be: a professional

ballet dancer, a baseball all-star, an astronaut, a concert pianist.)

_____

_____

_____

6. List some areas of competency that you have achieved in your life that are not related to your dreams. (These can be as diverse as being competent at changing diapers to driving to another city. Typing may not be something you dreamed of, but you may be a fair typist. Don't forget things like fixing appliances, working on the car, writing letters, and taking care of finances.)

_____

_____

_____

7. What are some things that have become important to you since you have grown up? What have you learned from your individual experiences that you have found to be valuable that you want to expand upon now? (Perhaps you have been through a personal crisis and want to share what you have learned with others; perhaps personal connections have become most important; perhaps you serendipitously found a career that you love.)

_____

_____

_____

8. Write down the names of five people you have admired, respected, and wanted to emulate. Then list several admirable characteristics they represent that you either have or wish you had. You can use heroes or characters from books as well as

people you knew personally (for example, a teacher who was intelligent, caring, responsive, and appreciative of others; a neighbor who was open, sensitive, helpful, and interested; an artist who was innovative, committed, self-expressive; a political figure who was powerful, involved, and socially conscious.)

_____

_____

_____

_____

Your goal now will be to match your interests, dreams, and abilities with the needs of the outside world to create a concrete and specific vision for yourself. Whether your personal loves and interests involve politics, law, ecology, children, art, writing, building, languages, sewing, or sports, you can find ways to use your skills in those areas. Your enthusiasm in itself will help others by adding to the positive forces in the world. If you have been through a personal crisis you may decide to share your own experience with others who are going through a similar crisis. You may want to contribute by using your interests to help a specific disadvantaged population. We can't help with everything, but it is important not to ignore the rest of the world and remain uninvolved. Sometimes it seems that one person cannot do very much, but that is not true. Each individual contribution adds to the whole and takes us one step closer to improving the conditions on earth and leaving the world a better place for future generations.

You may want or need to be paid for your endeavors. You can get adequate pay in a field in which you can contribute and which you feel passionate about if you are committed, willing to learn, and responsible. You may have worked in paid positions all your life and want to take the time to do artistic or other expressive work that may not give you income. You may want to volunteer your time helping others. There is an enormous need for even part-time commitments which will benefit others.

WHERE TO START

You have already started this process by doing the exercises to help you explore what you love to do. Books like *What Color Is Your Parachute*, by Richard Bolles, and *Wishcraft*, by Barbara Sher, will also help you clarify your goals. A good place to get individual assistance is at the counseling department in a community college in your area. Most community colleges have reentry programs specifically designed to meet the needs of adults who want to return to the labor market. You are not required to go to college or get a job in order to use their resources, and this is an excellent way to take a personal inventory. The career counselor will give you a battery of simple tests to help you determine your skills and career interests and computerized lists of vocations and avocations that are available that you would do well in and enjoy.

WAYS TO CONTRIBUTE

There are many ways to contribute and the ideas presented here only include a few. Your contribution can mean simply being a whole person who contributes by being a role model to others for finding peace and happiness. If you have an illness or handicap you can help yourself as you help others through participating in a support group of people dealing with similar issues. Another important way to contribute is by working on your primary relationships and friendships and adding your love and warmth to the lives of those you touch.

You can contribute by working in an area that you love and by sharing your enthusiasm. You may be able to find your area of interest by glancing through your local newspaper. This morning's newspaper yielded jobs in: accounting, administration, art, auditing, bookkeeping, childcare, clerical work, computer work, construction, cosmetology, counseling, decorating, dental work, electronics, finances, hairstyling, handymen, healthcare, installation, insurance, legal help, marketing, mechanical work, nannies, nursing, paramedics, photography, real estate, teaching, technical support, sales, secretarial, social work, and writing, to name a few. *The National Business Employment Weekly,* published by *The Wall Street Journal,* lists job opportunities and workshops for career planning.

You may be concerned about returning to the job market when you are past your youth. However, many employers today are looking for more mature people who will be dependable and will not be interrupted the way younger people may be because of their other commitments. They are also realizing that the skills people have attained outside the job market are valuable. Banks, hotels, and travel agencies are just some places that are giving preference to more mature people when hiring. If you are over fifty-five, there are several organizations that can help you, including The National Council on Aging and the American Association of Retired Persons (AARP) with headquarters in Washington, D.C. *The Job Search Manual for Mature Workers* lists career opportunities.

You can return to school to follow your dreams part-time or full-time at any age. People in their seventies and eighties are learning for the sake of learning, or getting degrees, or acquiring the skills for vocations. Many of these people are an inspiration to those around them. A few of the areas listed in a community college catalogue are: aeronautics, anthropology, art, astronomy, biology, business, chemistry, communications, computer information science, cosmetology, dental hygiene, drafting, early childhood education, Chinese, economics, electronics, engineering, English (literature and writing), ethnic studies, family and consumer science, French, geology, geography, gerontology, health education, history, human services, humanities, Japanese, journalism, library technology, management, marketing, mathematics, mechanical-electrical technology, music, philosophy, photography, physics, psychology, real estate, sociology, Spanish, speech, theater arts, and women's studies.

You can also contribute by concentrating more attention on an interest you have always wanted to pursue. Classes and workshops are often held on how to start a business or how to earn income from your endeavor or just earn enough to support its cost. Talk to people who are doing what you want to do to find out how they got started. Some hobbies or dreams people have expanded upon are: pursuing a collection, such as dolls, baseball cards, stamps, or coins; opening boutiques, bagel shops, ethnic restaurants, bookstores, or pet shops. They have done needlework or woodcarvings, they have made stained-glass windows, designed or built homes, renovated houses, restored antique cars, set up landscaping or interior design businesses. They have joined baseball teams or softball leagues, written cookbooks or romance novels, moved to the country and raised animals, vegetables, or bees, and opened up day-care centers or bed-and-breakfast inns. Again, these can be done for your own satisfaction, and you will be contributing by helping others through the service you provide and by adding your own enthusiasm in a positive way.

There are some groups that especially need help. Those who can fit their interests in specifically with the needs of these groups find that there is a lot they can do and that they receive a great deal in return. Here is a brief compendium of groups that are grateful for support, and always have room for help, generally on a volunteer basis, but sometimes for pay. Even a few hours a month is appreciated. There is help needed on every level, from disarmament to day care.

Political: Political help is needed in many areas and you can help the political party, candidates, or programs of your choice. You can travel to other countries, befriend people in other cultures, write letters for amnesty, and help initiate or pass legislation in your area of concern. You can focus on women's rights or a particular ethnic group. Contributing in these ways allows you to meet a wide variety of people of all ages. You can join the Peace Corps, which expects to double its number of volunteers in the nineties and to offer work in the United States as well as overseas. (The average age of a Peace Corps volunteer is thirty-one, 12 percent of volunteers are over fifty, and there is no upper age limit.)

Children: Help can be given to children through foster care, Big Brother and Big Sister programs, child abuse programs, children's homes and children's hospitals. Programs that give children increased self-esteem and skills in communication need to be designed and taught in the schools. Our nation's youth need direction from adults in order to participate in peace and environmental work. Peer counseling is effective for teenagers, and adults are needed to coordinate programs. Teenage alcohol and drug programs are usually in need of volunteers and paid personnel.

Places of worship: You can get connected with many causes through your religious affiliation. In this way you can become part of a group that shares your interests. Religious organizations also need support, and have fund-raising events which are enjoyable to set up and to attend.

Seniors: Many senior groups are active and exciting to participate in. The Gray Panthers and Grandmothers for Peace work politically. The Senior Gleaners bring food they get free from supermarkets to needy people. Many communities have networking for retired people who want to share their abilities at a reduced fee with those who need services.

Environmental: Fears for the environment and the planet have created many groups with a strong energy that need people in all areas of endeavor. Friends of the Earth, Greenpeace, and the Sierra Club are a few. Books abound with titles like *50 Ways to Save the Planet.* They list organizations to contact and specific things to do.

The disadvantaged and the emotionally or physically disabled: There is a vital need for people willing to be involved with various populations. Some of these are the hungry, the home-less, the illiterate, those in hospitals or hospice centers, home-bound people, the blind, the deaf, people in halfway homes, the handicapped, and battered women. Suicide prevention, crisis clinics, and programs for families at risk for child abuse need people to help.

General, special, and miscellaneous: Some places that can be contacted are: UNICEF, The United Way, the American Cancer Society, AIDS Foundation, animal rights groups, art museums, historical societies, the Veterans Administration, volunteer fire departments, and public television stations. People to help with fund-raising are a necessary part of most organizations. There are walkathons, candlelight vigils, and adopt-an-animal programs that all need support. "Habitat" is a volunteer orga-nization which builds homes for needy families. Animals are being used therapeutically to give the ill and the handicapped the touch and affection they cannot get otherwise. (Contact your local Humane Society for information.)

The following resources will help you find specific places in your community where you can become involved. Your local public library should have various directories and catalogues.

- Your local Chamber of Commerce
- Crisis intervention organizations listed in your phone book
- The National Center for Volunteers
  1111 North 19th Street #500
  Arlington, VA 22209
  703-276-0542
- The National Directory of Service Organizations
- The Catalog of Service Opportunities

You can meet your own needs at the same time as you meet other people's needs. Expressing yourself in a way that contributes to others is in everyone's interest. How you become involved will evolve naturally out of the entire context and process of your life.

These exercises will help you clarify and construct your plan of action.

9. Choose three or four areas either from those listed above or others that have not been covered that you feel would be interesting for you to participate in, (for example, going back to school, renovating antique cars, working with animals, getting involved politically, helping with the environment, or working with the blind).

_____

_____

_____

_____

10. By following these exercises you should have a clearer idea of your loves and abilities, your dreams, your needs, your skills, and the characteristics you admire. Briefly summarize these below.

Your loves and natural abilities:

_____

_____

Your dreams:

_____

_____

Your needs:

_____

_____

Your areas of competency and expertise:

_____

_____

_____

Characteristics you admire and want to have:

_____

_____

_____

You will be combining all of these things to create several new dreams. Here are some examples of how some people followed through on attaining their dreams:

- Pam and David sold their home, moved closer to the ocean, and pursued their love of the arts which they had neglected previously. They found that they could live on their savings, retirement, and part-time work. Pam worked half-time in a shop and David became the neighborhood handyman to supplement their incomes. The rest of the time Pam could paint and David was free to compose music.
- Maggie at sixty-two joined the Peace Corps and went to Western Africa. She learned a new language, the customs of a new country, met dynamic, caring, and committed people and was able to travel to places she never would have been able to on her own. Leaving her "easy chair" gave her a chance to grow and contribute.
- Scott had managed restaurants most of his life and had not felt challenged by it, even though it paid well. He had some personality- and preference-testing done and found that he would probably enjoy creating computer programs. He went back to school and took classes in computer science and eventually found a position and career that met his needs.
- Isabel, who had always loved quilting and stitchery, initiated making a peace quilt at her church. The project

drew so much interest that the group ended up opening a shop offering crafts made by seniors, which included all kinds of handmade items.

- Tyrone finally began to deal with his alcoholism which he had denied for over forty years. He and his wife, Sally, became involved in Alcoholics Anonymous and Al-Anon. By working on their own issues, they became a model for those around them.

- Roberta, in her seventies, decided to volunteer at a small thrift shop for the Salvation Army. She met new people, helped children find clothing, and especially enjoyed being able to tell her family and friends about items they received that she thought they would want.

- Herb had worked all his life and had been active politically and socially. He decided that the way he needed to contribute was by drastically reducing his obligations and commitments and just learning how to be at peace. He began to take some trips, read the books he had always wanted to read, and just walk in nature. He made new friends, who were also more relaxed, and created an extended family made up of people he selected and who selected him.

The following stories show in more detail how two people used this process to enhance their own lives and the lives of those around them:

After visiting his mother at the board and care facility she had been in for the past few months, it occurred to Jim, who had always wanted to be a journalist, that an in-house newspaper could make a big difference to many of the residents. He thought that having choices, being heard, and having some control over their lives would give the people motivation to go on living in a more fulfilling way. Through a newspaper, they would be able to communicate with each other. They would have a place to share their thoughts, their needs, their accomplishments, and anything else they wanted to write.

All that was needed were paper, pens, and a few people who were well enough to write down some thoughts. His wife remarked that it couldn't be that much harder than setting up a bingo game. Some of the residents could do the typing, printing, collating, and distributing and perhaps some of the staff or relatives could help them. Although some residents could not participate, many more of them could. Letters to relatives or friends could be sent out to solicit their help. The most valuable resource, however, would be the people themselves once they were helped in getting started. All this project needed was someone to organize it and Jim decided that he would be the one to do it. His children were grown and there was plenty of time after work and on weekends to do something significant to him and to others.

Ruth, neglected as a child, had received support and comfort while she was growing up, from teachers who had taken her under their wing. She had decided then that she would be a teacher when she grew up, but had never had the opportunity to pursue a higher education and realize her dream. Teaching to Ruth meant feeling valuable, sharing knowledge, and helping and inspiring others. Now, divorced, with adult children, Ruth felt a great need to reach out to others, to participate, and to feel useful. Ruth revived her former dream and decided to find a way to teach. She did not need financial compensation, as she was earning an adequate income.

Ruth lived near a junior high school, and she felt that she would enjoy spending about four hours a week tutoring children who were having trouble with basic math. Ruth went down to the school and let the principal and the counselors know that she was available to help, and they sent a notice around to the classrooms. To her amazement, in the next two weeks she was given the names of fourteen children who badly needed assistance in math! In a few weeks, Ruth was helping children several hours a week, some of whom offered to pay her for tutoring. She found a place of special importance in some of the families she was working with. Her work helped her be a valuable member of the community and she became known and valued in her neighborhood.

EXERCISE

Write down three different ways you can contribute and participate in the world, in a way that would also be exciting for you. Create dreams that draw you forward, that you feel you can do and that you feel are significant.

Dream 1:_____

_____

_____

_____

Dream 2:_____

_____

_____

_____

Dream 3:_____

_____

_____

_____

Where will you be in one year, five years, ten years if you follow through on one of your dreams?

One year:_____

_____

_____

Five years:_____

_____

_____

Ten years:_____

_____

_____

WHAT DO YOU NEED TO ATTAIN YOUR DREAM?

- You will need to overcome your doubts and fears so that you can minimize their control over you. Use them as guides or checks on impulsivity but do not let them undermine your courage. Self-doubt is the quicksand that keeps us from succeeding. As William Blake wrote, "If the sun and moon should doubt, they'd immediately go out."

- You will need to continue working on increasing your sense of self-worth, avoid comparing yourself to others, and refrain from having perfectionistic expectations of yourself. The purpose of reaching for a dream is to find your own voice and to feel good about yourself and your place in the world—not to add more burdens to your life.

- You will probably need a support person or several support people to help you move forward. These can be family members, mentors, counselors, friends, classes, groups, other people who are involved in the field you are interested in, or people who have similar goals and want to work on them with you.

- You will need to break up your plan into small, workable steps so that you can get where you want to go without becoming discouraged.

- You will probably need to do some things that you do not enjoy doing in order to attain your vision. It will be up to you to balance what you have to do with what you want to do in a way that works for you in the context you are in.

- You will probably want to read more and investigate many areas before you go forward in actualizing your new dreams. The possibilities are unlimited, and the purpose of this chapter has only been to introduce you to a few.

In the space below, draw up a plan that you are able to commit to.

MY PLAN FOR MY FUTURE

Reading:_____

_____

_____

_____

Support:_____

_____

_____

_____

Steps to take:_____

_____

_____

_____

Notes:_____

_____

_____

_____

Author Jerome D. Lamb, in *The Way We Are,* wrote this statement, which has helped put life and dreams into perspective for me:

Slowly I learn bits of what there is to see, and then forget
and learn again. And learn too that mortality is the stuff of life;

learn how soon the young get old, how short a while forever is. . . . What we're meant to do, I hope, is fill some small and temporary slot, to give off a little light for a little while and then lie down. I'm comfortable with that, with the notion of being a small voice yapping away at the edge of a large prairie in the northern half of a small planet. One of many voices, neither the wisest nor the best, but mine, and fairly close to as good as I can make it.

While you have been working at making peace with your adult children you have also been going through a process for discovering your own voice. Your intrinsic voice is the gentle, loving, powerful, and curious one you had as a child. You have begun to separate it from the voices of your parents, your society, and the ineffective patterns you have learned. You have begun using your own voice in trying to communicate with your adult children, to negotiate, and to grieve. I hope this book has also helped you to find a way to express your unique voice, in the world that we share as a common home, in a way that brings you satisfaction and meaning.

RECOMMENDED READING

The Search for Meaning, Victor Frankl
Wishcraft, Barbara Sher
What Color Is Your Parachute? Richard N. Bolles
The Three Boxes of Life, Richard N. Bolles
Oh, the Places You'll Go, Dr. Seuss
Waging Peace in the Nuclear Age: Ideas for Action, David Krieger and Frank Kelly, eds.
Save Our Planet: 750 Everyday Ways You Can Help Clean Up the Earth, Diane MacEachern
The Global Ecology Handbook, Walter H. Corson, ed.
Planethood, Benjamin B. Ferencz with Ken Keyes, Jr.

Recommended Reading

Ackerman, Robert J. *Perfect Daughters: Adult Daughters of Alcoholics.* Deerfield Beach, Florida: Health Communications, Inc., 1989.

Buscaglia, Leo. *Personhood.* New York: Fawcett Columbine, 1978.

Bass, Ellen, and Laura Davis. *The Courage to Heal: A Guide for Women Survivors of Child Sexual Abuse.* New York: Harper & Row, 1990.

Beattie, Melody. *Beyond Codependency: And Getting Better All the Time.* San Francisco: Harper & Row, 1989.

Beattie, Melody. *Codependent No More: How to Stop Controlling Others and Start Caring for Yourself.* New York, Harper & Row, 1987.

Berne, Eric. *Games People Play.* New York: Grove Press, 1964.

Black, Claudia. *It Will Never Happen to Me: Children of Alcoholics.* Denver: MAC Publishing, 1981.

Black, Claudia. *Repeat After Me.* Denver: MAC Publishing, 1985.

Bolles, Richard Nelson. *The Three Boxes of Life.* Berkeley: Ten Speed Press, 1981.

Bolles, Richard Nelson. *What Color Is Your Parachute? A Practical Manual for Job-Hunters & Career Changers.* Berkeley: Ten Speed Press, 1970–1990.

Bradshaw, John. *The Family: A Revolutionary Way of Self-Discovery.* Deerfield Beach, FL: Health Communications, Inc., 1988.

Bradshaw, John. *Homecoming.* Deerfield Beach, FL: Health Communications, Inc., 1990.

Bruckner-Gordon, Fredda, Barbara Gangi, and Gerry Wallman. *Making Therapy Work.* New York, Harper & Row, 1987.

Capacchione, Lucia. *The Creative Journal: The Art of Finding Yourself.* Ohio: Swallow Press Books, 1979–1985.

Carnes, Patrick. *Contrary to Love: Helping the Sexual Addict.* Minnesota: Comp-Care Publishers, 1989.

Clark, Don. *The New Loving Someone Gay.* Berkeley: Celestial Arts, 1990.

Colgrove, Melba, Harold Bloomfield, and Peter McWilliams. *How to Survive the Loss of a Love.* New York: Bantam Books, 1976.

Corson, Walter H., ed. *The Global Ecology Handbook.* Boston: Beacon Press, 1990.

Davis, Bruce. *The Magical Child Within You*. Berkeley: Celestial Arts, 1985–1987.

Davis, Laura. *The Courage to Heal Workbook: For Women and Men Survivors of Child Sexual Abuse*. New York: Harper & Row, 1990.

Davis, Martha, Mathew McKay, and Elizabeth Tobbins Eshelman. *The Relaxation and Stress Reduction Workbook*. Oakland: New Harbinger Publications, 1982.

Deits, Bob. *Life After Loss*. Tucson, Arizona: Fisher Books, 1988.

Dr. Seuss. *Oh, the Places You'll Go!* New York: Random House, 1990.

Ehrenberg and Ehrenberg. *The Psychotherapy Maze: A Consumer's Guide to Getting In and Out of Therapy*. New York: Simon & Schuster, 1986.

Erickson, Erik. *Childhood and Society*. New York: Norton, 1985.

Faber, Adele, and Elaine Mazlish. *Liberated Parents Liberated Children*. New York: Avon Books, 1975.

Ferencz, Benjamin, and Ken Keyes, Jr. *Planethood: The Key to Your Survival and Prosperity*. Coos Bay: Vision Books, 1989.

Frankl, Viktor. *The Search for Meaning*. New York: Pocket Books, 1959.

Gil, Eliana. *Outgrowing the Pain: A Book for and about Adults Abused as Children*. San Francisco: Launch Press, 1983.

Ginott, Haim G. *Between Parent & Child*. New York: Avon Books, 1969.

Gordon, Thomas. *P.E.T. In Action*. New York: Bantam Books, 1988.

Gordon, Thomas. *P.E.T.: Parent Effectiveness Training*. New York: Peter Wyden Inc., 1970.

Greenwood, Sadja. *Menopause Naturally: Preparing for the Second Half of Life*. San Francisco: Volcano Press, 1985.

Groening, Matt. *Childhood Is Hell*. New York: Pantheon Books, 1983.

Janssen, Martha. *Silent Scream: I Am a Victim of Incest*. Philadelphia: Fortress Press, 1983.

James, Muriel, and Jongward, D. *Born to Win*. Reading, Mass: Addison-Wesley, 1971.

Jampolsky, Gerald G. *Love Is Letting Go of Fear*. New York: Bantam Books, 1982.

Keyes, Ken, Jr. *A Conscious Person's Guide to Relationships*. Living Love Publications, 1979.

Kiersey, David, and Marily Bates. *Please Understand Me: Character and Temperament Types*. Del Mar, CA: Prometheus Nemesis Book Co., 1984.

Krieger, David, and Frank Kelly, eds. *Waging Peace in the Nuclear Age: Ideas for Action*. Santa Barbara, CA: Capra Press, 1988.

Kritsberg, Wayne. *The Adult Children of Alcoholics Syndrome: A Step-by-Step Guide to Discovery and Recovery*. New York: Bantam Books, 1988.

Lerner, Harriet. *The Dance of Anger: A Woman's Guide to Changing the Patterns of Intimate Relationships*. New York: Harper & Row, 1986.

Lindbergh, Anne Morrow. *Gift from the Sea*. New York: Vantage Books, 1955.

MacEachern, Diane. *Save Our Planet: 750 Everyday Ways You Can Help Clean Up the Earth*. New York: Dell, 1990.

McKay, Mathew, and Patrick Fanning. *Self-Esteem*. Oakland: New Harbinger Publications, 1987.

McKay, Mathew, and Patrick Fanning. *Self-Esteem*. Oakland: New Harbinger Publications, 1987.

McKay, Mathew, Martha Davis, and Patrick Fanning. *Messages: The Communication Skills Book*. Oakland: New Harbinger Publications, 1983.

Middleton-Moz, Jane, and Lorie Dwinell. *After the Tears: Reclaiming the Personal Losses of Childhood*. Deerfield Beach, FL: Health Communications, Inc., 1986.

Miller, Alice. *For Your Own Good: Hidden Cruelty in Child-Rearing and the Roots of Violence*. New York: Farrar, Straus & Giroux, 1984.

Miller, Alice. *Thou Shalt Not Be Aware: Society's Betrayal of the Child*. New York: New American Library, 1986.

Perls, Frederick S. *Gestalt Therapy Verbatim*. New York: Bantam Books, 1969.

Rogers, Carl R. *On Becoming a Person*. Boston: Houghton Mifflin, 1961.

Sanford, Linda Tschirhart, and Mary Ellen Donovan. *Women & Self-Esteem: Understanding and Improving the Way We Think and Feel About Ourselves*. New York: Penguin Books, 1986.

Satir, Virginia. *Making Contact*. Berkeley, CA: Celestial Arts, 1976.

Satir, Virginia. *Peoplemaking*. Palo Alto, CA: Science and Behavior Books, 1972.

Sher, Barbara, with Annie Gottlieb. *Wishcraft*. New York: Ballantine, 1979.

Silverstein, Shel. *The Missing Piece Meets the Big O*. New York: Harper & Row, 1981.

Smith, Ann W. *Grandchildren of Alcoholics: Another Generation of Co-dependency*. Deerfield Beach, FL: Health Communications, Inc. 1988.

Sonkin, Daniel Jay, and Michael Durphy. *Learning to Live without Violence: A Handbook for Men*. San Francisco: Volcano Press, 1985.

Steiner, Claude M. *A Warm Fuzzy Tale*. Rolling Hills, CA: Jalmar Press, 1977.

Steiner, Claude M. *Scripts People Live*. New York: Grove Press, 1974.

Tetelbaum, J. *The Courage to Grieve: Creative Living, Recovery and Growth Through Grief*. New York: Harper & Row, 1980.

Viorst, Judith. *Necessary Losses*. New York: Simon & Schuster.

White, Louise. *The Obsidian Mirror: An Adult Healing From Incest*. Seattle: Seal Press, 1988.

Woititz, Janet Geringer. *Adult Children of Alcoholics*. Deerfield Beach, FL: Health Communications, Inc. 1983.

Wright, Bob, and Deborah Wright. *Dare to Confront: How to Intervene When Someone You Care About Has an Alcohol or Drug Problem*. New York: MasterMedia Limited, 1990.

Index